THE FORGOTTEN SQUADRON

THE FORGOTTEN SQUADRON

The 449th Fighter Squadron in World War II

Flying P-38s over China with the Flying Tigers, 14th Air Force

Daniel Jackson

Schiffer Military History
Atglen, PA

Book design by Robert Biondi.

Library of Congress Catalog Number: 2010925098.

Printed in Hong Kong.
ISBN. 978-0-7643-3537-2

Published by Schiffer Publishing Ltd.
4880 Lower Valley Road
Atglen, PA 19310
Phone: (610) 593-1777
FAX: (610) 593-2002
E-mail: Info@schifferbooks.com.
Visit our web site at: www.schifferbooks.com
Please write for a free catalog.
This book may be purchased from the publisher.
Please include $5.00 postage.
Try your bookstore first.

In Europe, Schiffer books are distributed by:
Bushwood Books
6 Marksbury Ave.
Kew Gardens, Surrey TW9 4JF
England
Phone: 44 (0)20 8392-8585
FAX: 44 (0)20 8392-9876
E-mail: info@bushwoodbooks.co.uk
www.bushwoodbooks.co.uk

CONTENTS

ACKNOWLEDGEMENTS

When I first embarked on this project in May 2007, I thought I might write a short paper on a squadron about which there was very little information published. I had no idea the magnitude of the response I would receive from veterans, friends, mentors, and professional authors and now feel indebted to thank them for their help. First of all, I would like to thank God for his hand in this. Lieutenant Colonel Plating from the Air Force Academy History Department mentored me through this process and helped transform this book from a simple unit history into a more-significant case study on the air war in China and is probably the single most important person in helping me with this project. Lieutenant Colonel Brosius read through and provided valuable comments and Lieutenant Colonel Watanabe graciously read through several drafts and gave me excellent feedback. Marie Barrett provided moral support and patiently read through several drafts. Hiroshi Ichimura and Nick Millman lent their expertise on the Japanese Army Air Force and Steve Blake, John Stanaway, and Carl Molesworth volunteered their knowledge and research on the 449th. Mr. Blake's patient advice and volumes of information were particularly helpful. Jeff Greene aided me considerably in my trips out to China. Dr. Wang and Haning Hughes, as well as Lieutenant Colonel Barrett provided invaluable assistance with Chinese and French translation respectively. Lieutenant Colonel Timothy Jung helped me understand some of the issues relating to aeronautics. Major Jesse Long, Lieutenant James Tippets, and cadets David Corpman and Antony Mascaro were a great help and a lot of fun on my most recent trip to China.

More important than anyone, however, were the pilots and crews from the 449th whose story this is and who gave me first-hand information you cannot find on any bookshelf: Bob Burris, Jim Borge, Jack Bowman and his son David, George Brabec and his son Bob, Bruce Carnachan, Joe Chiara, Mrs. Madeline Church, wife of Dan Church, Victor Copeland, Jack Darnell, Jerry Doughty, Lewden Osborn, nephew of Lewden Enslen, Harold Franklin, Joe Fodor, Forrest Green, Jim Heitkotter, Jim Hyde, Don McCloud, Stephen Williams, son of David Williams, and especially Richard Maddox, who provided invaluable assistance despite his wife's failing health.

I also need to thank the veterans from other units whose stories were important in giving this book context and dimension. From the 21st and 35th Photo Reconnaissance Squadrons were Sterling Barrow, Arthur Griggs, Allen Larsen, Robert Neely, Ed Penick, and Frank Pinchak; from the 19th Liaison Squadron was Leonard Logar; from the 22nd Bomb Squadron were Ernest Koury and Chapman Hale; from the 25th Fighter Squadron were Clifford Long, Edward Mark, William Mitchell, Cecil Simmons, Samuel Soulis, and Ernest Weisemiller; from the 26th Fighter Squadron were Grant Forsythe and Jerry Ravenscroft; from the 27th Troop Carrier Squadron were Bruce Batchelor, Bob Binzer, Jerry Disharoon, Bob Jones, Paul Rittenhouse and Melvin Waymire; from the 76th Fighter Squadron was Glen Beneda, and from the 75th Fighter Squadron and 118th Tactical Reconnaissance Squadron were Luther Kissick, Everson Pearsall, and John Conn. I appreciate all your help and may God bless you all for your service to this country. Throughout the journey of writing this book I feel I have grown in knowledge, in my ability as a writer, and in my appreciation for the men and women that fought and died for the United States of America. Without them none of this would be possible.

Chapter One

The Forgotten Squadron

Xiangyun is a small town in China's remote Yunnan Province, 140 miles west of Kunming, the provincial capital. It is unremarkable except that just outside the town is a twelve-foot-tall stone monument dedicated to a young American named Robert Mooney. The monument is located on the apex of a modest hill, in a small clearing amongst pine trees and dry grass. It is a quiet, peaceful place. Five stone steps lead up to the monument's two-and-a-half-foot-tall rectangular base. On the front is a likeness of Mooney carved into stone, his epitaph recounted in Chinese and English on the left and right sides respectively. The Chinese villagers erected the monument to remind themselves of something *they* consider important, for only very rarely do foreign visitors come to pay their respects.

Lieutenant Robert Mooney was a pilot in the 16th Fighter Squadron based at the nearby airfield at Yunnanyi. On 26 December 1942, Mooney's squadron scrambled in response to a Japanese air raid. In the violent action that ensued he shot down one of the enemy fighters before attacking another head-on over the town of Xiangyun. Guns blazing, the two aircraft closed at high speed. Bullets struck home and the Japanese fighter went down in flames, but Mooney's P-40 Warhawk was severely damaged. Smoke belched from the engine and he knew that he had mere moments to take to his parachute and escape alive. But herein lies the reason why Robert Mooney is remembered in Xiangyun today: Looking down, he saw the town below him and realized that to bailout would mean letting his fighter crash in the midst of it, killing perhaps ten, or fifty, or maybe one hundred Chinese civilians – nobody will ever know how few or how many. He then made a fateful decision to stay with his plane until it cleared the outskirts of the town, by which time he was too low and his parachute jump proved fatal.

In an age where human life in China was exceptionally cheap, where a Chinese lieutenant had to request permission from his commander to shoot a horse, but could shoot one of his men of his own volition, Robert Mooney had put the lives of impoverished Chinese civilians above his own. He could have bailed out and lived. His fighter could have crashed in the town and killed a thousand civilians and the Chinese would have praised him as a hero. They would have thanked him for

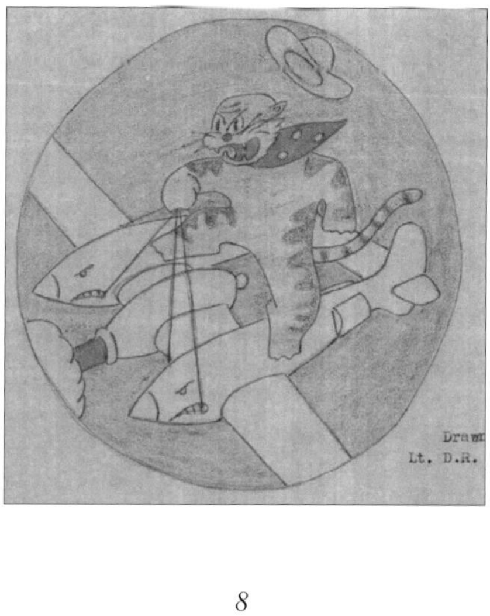

Left: Insignia design drawn by Disney but never implemented. Sean Collins Center: "Lightning Tiger" insignia drawn by Lt D.R. Forsythe. Air Force Historical Research Agency Right: Leather patch from Jerry Doughty's A2 flying jacket. Jerry Doughty

coming to China to fight the Japanese, held a great banquet in his honor, and taken the casualties in stride. Instead Mooney gave his life for their survival. It was for this reason that the Chinese remembered him and built a monument dedicated to his sacrifice.

At one time, such monuments littered the Chinese countryside – each honoring brave American airmen that gave their lives in China's defense. In the town of Huangmei, twenty miles north of Jiujiang in the Hubei Province, a large white stone marker once stood in remembrance of Captain Lewden Enslen, an unassuming man from Springfield, Missouri. He was a husband and a father. He was a man who planned on a career in journalism before the war overtook his ambition. He was a P-38 pilot in the 449th Fighter Squadron. At the time of his death he was the much-respected and well-liked squadron commander. At the time of his death, he was only twenty-three years old. His neighbors thought he would return home a hero, but instead he died a slow and agonizing death after falling victim to a Japanese ambush. Few in the United States besides his family and friends in Missouri mourned him and yet over four thousand Chinese attended his funeral in Huangmei. To them he *was* a hero.

Between 1966 and 1969, the Red Guards tore the monuments down in accordance with Mao Zedong's Cultural Revolution. The new China cleansed itself of anything having to do with the West, but the townspeople in Xiangyun buried the pieces of the Mooney monument and for that reason it exists today, rebuilt in 1992. Unknown is how many other monuments or markers remain hidden away, or how many are lost forever. Regardless, it is interesting to note that the Chinese hold so dear the memories of American dead that are largely unknown in the United States. The grander efforts at Normandy and throughout Europe eclipsed what happened in China, but most Americans did not choose where they fought and the sacrifice of a young pilot in the air war over China was no less noble than that of an infantryman landing on Omaha Beach. Yet the greatest symbol of cooperation between China and the United States is all but unknown in the West, save for the half-known legend of the "Flying Tigers." To further complicate matters, many members of the American Volunteer Group (AVG), volunteer airmen who fought the Japanese as civilian mercenaries in Burma and China, believe only *they* earned the right to be called "Flying Tigers," that the men of the United States Army Air Forces, who did not necessarily volunteer, who in fact were usually *ordered* to go China, did not deserve the moniker. But it was the Chinese who originally affixed the title "Flying Tigers" to the AVG, and it was this label that they also attached to every American flying in China, whether he flew a transport, a bomber, or a fighter, whether he was a civilian volunteer or a member of the Army Air Forces (AAF).

Thus shrouded in confusion and obscurity, the China-Burma-India (CBI) Theater remains a forgotten chapter of World War II. Nevertheless, despite the fact that the war in China – unique in that it was predominantly an air war from the American perspective – received less men, material, and press than any other fighting front, it served a vital function in the greater conflict against Japan. Without the American air force, the disorganized armies of Chiang Kaishek would have been loath to resist the Japanese, whose occupation would have been disputed only by destitute guerrillas. Were it not for American planes, pilots, and personnel working with the Chinese, Japan would have been free to materially exploit China and turn the full force of its military against the United States in the Pacific.

Stylized "Lightning Tiger" insignia design drawn by Lt Jim Heitkotter. James Heitkotter

Here, the story of the air war in China is recounted through the exploits of the 449th Fighter Squadron – a forgotten squadron within that forgotten theater. Many veterans now consider the history of their units forgotten, but members of the 449th considered themselves forgotten *during* the war – forgotten not

The Robert Mooney Monument in the town of Xiangyun, Yunnan Province, China. Author's Photo

only by the public, but also by their own chain of command. Whereas the AVG and its successor, the 23rd Fighter Group, periodically received acclamation, the 449th merited little attention from the American military establishment in China or from the American public in the United States. This lack of attention was not for any lack of action on the part of the 449th, for it vigorously and effectively conducted a wide variety of missions against Japanese aircraft, shipping, transportation, and troops in China and Southeast Asia from July 1943 until the end of the war. Though America entered the war in December 1941, this critical two-year-period saw the pursuit of America's loftiest goals – and the realization of its greatest fears – in China.

According to pilot Dick Conway, however, the 449th was not just forgotten, it was hardly even recognized.[1] Promotions and decorations were rare, as with many units in China, especially when compared to those serving in Europe, the Mediterranean, or the Pacific.[2] Often the squadron's P-38s were scattered across the country in small detachments, making it "a rare occasion when we had twelve planes in the air at once."[3] Robert "Buck" Burris, an armorer with the squadron, thought of the 449th as a forgotten squadron "because we were kind of an illegitimate child over there. I'm not saying we got persecuted in any way, we just ... didn't get recognized."[4] Father Joseph Cosgrove, a Catholic missionary who became the squadron's chaplain, stated that the men "performed their assigned tasks efficiently and quietly and expected and received little or no thanks."[5]

Though not the recipient of much publicity, the 449th made itself into a unit feared by the Japanese and was highly successful as the only P-38 fighter squadron in China. Armorer Dick Maddox declared, "The 449th Fighter Squadron had a World War II war time record to give us every reason to be more than just a little bit proud."[6] That record included more than seventy-three enemy aircraft confirmed shot down, while losing only nineteen of their own personnel in action or accidents. According to Conway, the 449th also "knocked out most of the bridges along the Burma road in Japanese held areas and down to Mandalay. ... We were used in close support of troops, fighter sweeps for targets of opportunity, high altitude interception, dive bombing, skip bombing, you name it."[7] This wide variety of missions against a variety of targets gave the 449th a unique experience. The squadron at times functioned not only as a fighter squadron, but also as a bomber squadron, an attack squadron, and even a transport squadron on occasion. It served all across China, spreading its wings from Taiwan to the Salween Front. Thus, in the following pages, a case study of the 449th and the units with which it interacted – and consequently, a study of the experiences of the gifted and hardworking pilots and ground crews – tells the story of the air war in China. As Dick Maddox wrote:

> To each 449th Fighter Squadron member every day was a turning point in the war, but also each day held a special memory for us. It was a day of a successful mission, or the day we lost a close friend; crew chiefs and mechanics changed an engine or kept one perfectly tuned, aircraft armorers maintained the machine guns and 20mm cannon, loaded ammunition to each pilot's specs., prepared and loaded bombs as required. Ground support personnel performed administrative, medical, and other assignments as needed.[8]

The effort of every individual formed the effort of the squadron, the effort of the squadron contributed to the effort of the American air force in China, and the effort of the air force in China contributed to the eventual downfall of Japan. Dick Conway stated, "We were not a showy squadron but a solid one. Plane for plane we contributed to the misery of the Japanese as much as any other squadron in China."[9]

The War in China

Despite the importance of the period through which the 449th Fighter Squadron served, by the time it arrived in the summer of 1943, China's war against Japan had been raging for six long years. The conflict was the result of Japan's rash imperial ambitions in Asia and America's involvement was a consequence of democratic idealism and friction over foreign trade. Ever since Commodore Matthew Perry opened Japan to the West in 1854, the country had modernized in earnest. A revolution in 1868 rid it of the last vestige of the feudal Tokugawa regime, and its elite-dominated government and military strove to emulate Europe in building an overseas empire. It snatched Korea and Taiwan from Chinese influence in the 1894 Sino-Japanese War and solidified its control over Korea after dealing a devastating defeat to Russia in 1905.

China, on the other hand, was in decline. The increasingly ineffective Qing dynasty gave all manner of territorial and trade concessions to foreign powers in the wake of continual military and political defeats. A revolution in 1911 led to the abdication of the emperor and engendered hope in the United States that China would become a thriving Eastern democracy. The fragile republic soon fragmented, however, and fell to the designs of competing warlords. Hopelessly cast adrift, China lay vulnerable to the whims and machinations of the rest of the world.

China had long been the ultimate goal of Japanese imperial ambition, but with the onset of the Great Depression, Japan determined that exploiting China was the *only* feasible response to its trade being stymied by Western colonialism in Southeast Asia and by other nations' protectionist tariffs. In 1931, the Guandong Army staged several incidents of Chinese terrorism to justify their occupation of Manchuria.[10] Japanese mechanized forces easily swept across the rolling hills of the lowland Manchurian plain, but concern over Chiang Kaishek, leader of China's Nationalist Party, using the incident to unite the disparate factions in China led to an attack on Shanghai in January 1932.[11] Chinese troops turned the fighting in Shanghai into a bloody stalemate and the incident earned Japan condemnation from the West, especially the United States. To Japan, however, this condemnation was hypocritical, as it perceived the United States' racist immigration policies and high protective tariffs as the very things pushing it to expand into mainland Asia.[12]

Chiang tried to appease the Japanese. He knew that fighting them would put a pause to the consolidation of his power over China and instead focused on exterminating the Communists, his most bitter political foes. The more Japan encroached into China, however, the more it filled the Chinese people with a resolve to halt its advance. On 7 July 1937, fighting broke out between Chinese and Japanese troops at the Marco Polo Bridge near Beiping and this time the Chinese were determined to resist. Yet despite the fact that Japan was preparing to undertake a significant campaign, some Japanese military officers urged caution. Ishihara Kanji, chief of the Operations Division of the General Staff in Tokyo, argued that Japan should not become involved in China because it would "be sucked into the quagmire of China just as Napoleon was in Spain"[13] and that operations in China would distract from Japan's defense against the Soviet Union. Prime Minister Konoe, however, yielded to the demands of zealous militants and declared that Japan's action in China was a crusade to halt communism and European imperialism, and to unite Asians.[14]

At the outset of the conflict, China enjoyed a superiority in manpower, but of its 176 divisions, only thirty-three were trained by German advisors and equipped with modern weapons. Japan's seventeen well-equipped, highly-mobile divisions advanced along the wide, flat alluvial plains of the Yellow River valley and conquered China's five northeast provinces by October 1937.[15] In August, Chiang had opened a second front by attacking Japanese marines stationed in Shanghai. He calculated that his German-trained divisions would be able to create a stalemate as they had in 1932, but the Japanese drove them back.

After the fall of Shanghai, the Nationalist government knew it was only a matter of time until the fall of the capital at Nanjing. Consequently, it planned to move eight hundred miles west to Chongqing in the Red Basin of the Sichuan province. Most of the basin lies 1,200 feet above sea level, surrounded by mountains reaching from three thousand to as high as fifteen thousand feet. Throughout Chinese history, the province proved a nearly impenetrable obstacle, holding off the Mongol hordes for decades in the thirteenth century.[16] The only access to the basin from the east was through the precipitous gorges cut through limestone by the Yangzi River. The Yangzi's current through the steep canyons averaged four to six knots, making it dangerous to navigate. For thousands of years, small junks pulled by up to one hundred coolies from paths cut into the canyon walls were the only vessels capable of navigating the gorges successfully.[17] Chongqing was an ideal location from which to continue resistance against Japan.

Nanjing fell on 13 December 1937, and the Nationalist government retreated westward, trading space for time, determined to fight a prolonged war of resistance. Japan continued its drive along the Yangzi River, taking Hankou before driving south to Changsha. However, in October 1939, Chinese Marshall Xue Yue skillfully used the terrain around Changsha to draw in the Japanese before cutting their supply lines and destroying them piecemeal. A counterattack stopped the Japanese advance, but failed to make significant progress. The war in China ground to a stalemate.[18]

In response, Japan changed its strategy to an indirect approach: to undermine the Nationalist government materially and politically. The Japanese advanced down the coast to Hainan Island, isolating China's interior and leaving the Burma Road as the only link to the outside world. The road linked the British seaport of Rangoon, Burma, to Kunming in southwest China – zigzagging its way through the deep valleys and towering mountains that separate the two countries. In 1940, Japan also created a Chinese puppet government under Wang Jingwei, formerly a member of the Nationalist government. Most Chinese, however, viewed Wang as a traitor, and the puppet government failed to gain legitimacy at the expense of the Nationalists in Chongqing.[19]

Throughout much of this time, China received extensive aid from the Soviet Union, including entire combat groups of Soviet planes and pilots. The Japanese came into direct conflict with the Soviets along the Mongolian border in the Nomonhan Incident of 1939, (which ended in disaster for the Japanese), but they ensured the halt of Soviet support for China with the Soviet-Japanese Neutrality Pact in April 1941. Thereafter it was American support for China that they perceived as a growing danger. The United States had repeatedly expressed its displeasure over violations of China's territorial integrity, but American interests in China, though potentially important, were not worth going to war.[20] President Roosevelt did advance credits and loans to China, and in 1941, imposed an embargo on shipments of petroleum and scrap metal to Japan. Determined to strangle China by expanding into Southeast Asia, the Japanese calculated that an attack on Pearl Harbor would convince the profit- and consumption-minded Americans to withdraw their support from China. They grossly miscalculated. The attack on Pearl Harbor brought Japan and the United States into direct conflict and ensured America's continued support for China.[21]

Prior to Pearl Harbor, President Roosevelt had been concerned over the prospect of simultaneous wars with Germany and Japan. A strengthened China was essential because American strategy advocated a holding action against Japan until the defeat of Germany. Thus in August 1941, Roosevelt approved the formation of the AVG: one hundred modern fighters and pilots for service in China. The first contingent of the group arrived for training in Burma in August, and the group was in place for the defense of Burma and key cities in China by the time the Japanese attacked Pearl Harbor in December.

The commander of the AVG was Claire Lee Chennault, a former captain in the United States Army Air Corps. Madame Chiang Kaishek, then Secretary-General of the Chinese Aeronautical Affairs Commission, hired Chennault as an advisor for the Chinese Air Force (CAF) following his retirement in April 1937. He arrived in June and found the CAF in a deplorable state. Madame Chiang allowed him considerable latitude in putting the CAF on a combat footing, but he accomplished little before the outbreak of war. As the Nationalists retreated, he attempted to implement his ideas on defensive pursuit aviation developed during his time in the Air Corps, engineering several successful intercepts of Japanese bombers by Chinese and Russian fighters.

In early 1939, Japan began an intensive bombing campaign on key Chinese cities to encourage the Nationalists to surrender. In thirty-nine raids on Chongqing of up to one hundred bombers each, the Japanese dropped two thousand tons of bombs, making Chongqing the most-bombed city in the world until the Battle of Britain. The CAF continued to intercept the raiders, claiming a total of seventy bombers destroyed, but in August 1940, the Japanese unleashed their new A6M Type Zero Carrier Fighter. The "Zero" outclassed any airplane the Chinese possessed.[22] The CAF withdrew its remaining aircraft from Chongqing to preserve a core of experienced pilots.

Between 1938 and 1939, despite the fact that the CAF virtually ceased to exist, Chennault spearheaded a pilot training program and a campaign to build an air raid warning net and over one hundred airfields at key points throughout China. Hundreds of thousands of Chinese laborers built runways out of crushed rock by hand, manual labor being China's most abundant resource. Several of these fields became major American bases later in the war, while many were seldom used. All of them, however, featured in Chennault's strategy.

Throughout his time in China, Chennault kept extensive notes on Japanese equipment and tactics. In addition to observing from the ground, he convinced Madame Chiang to buy him a Curtiss Hawk 75 fighter, allowing him to observe air combat first-hand. According to Chennault, "It was in the Hawk Special that I got my first taste of Jap flak and fighter tactics, and that I learned some of the lessons that later saved many an American pilot's life over China."[23] By the time pilots and crews of the AVG began arriving for training in Burma in mid-1941, his preparation paid off. Not only did the AVG find a vast network of airfields and a sophisticated air raid warning net at its disposal, but it was also inundated with "lectures from my notebooks, filled during the previous four years of combat." Chennault "taught them all I knew about the Japanese."[24] With these resources, the AVG successfully defended Free China from Japanese bombers and attempted to oppose the invasion of Burma. Fighter planes, no matter how skilled the pilots, however, could not stymie the overwhelming Japanese advance. Burma fell in May 1942. Japan finally severed China's last ground line of communications, leaving an air route over the Himalayas from India (known as the "Hump") as the only source of outside aid.

On 4 July 1942, the AVG was absorbed into the new China Air Task Force, part of the U.S. 10th Air Force based in India, and Chennault was reinstated in the Army Air Forces (AAF) as a brigadier general. With only four squadrons of P-40s and one under-strength squadron of B-25s, he deftly defended the skies over Free China and made tentative offensive stabs against Japanese outposts in China, Indochina, and Burma.

In the meantime, American leadership debated the exact role of China in the overall Allied strategy. Roosevelt envisioned China as a future world power and stabilizing force in Asia and therefore placed high importance on aggressive programs to free China from the yoke of Japanese oppression.[25] Original plans for China involved reopening the Burma Road and making an amphibious landing on the China coast to link up with a reformed and retrained Chinese army. China would then become a base from which to launch an assault upon Japan. American commitments across the globe quickly made this plan impractical.[26] General Joseph Stilwell, commander of American resources in the CBI Theater, advocated reequipping and reforming sixty divisions of the Nationalist Army for operations in Burma and China with an emphasis on reopening the Burma Road.[27] Stilwell's plan could have little effect on actual operations in China until after the liberation of Burma, however, considering China's limited resources – Japan having captured most of its agriculture and modern infrastructure.[28] Army Chief of Staff General George Marshall did not wish to devote many resources to China, but feared the implications of China falling to the Japanese. According to Marshall, if China succumbed, its vast resources would become available to support the Japanese war machine, and if the United States invaded Japan, the Japanese government could retreat to China to continue the war.[29] Thus, Marshall advocated sending just enough support to encourage resistance and keep China in the war.

Chennault advocated a far more radical strategy: build up the American air force in China, supplied entirely by airlift over the Hump, and use it to destroy the Japanese air force, disrupt Japanese shipping, and eventually attack Japan itself. Chennault's plan promised a high return for a relatively modest investment and was favored by Chiang, who saw a centrally-controlled air force as a way of keeping power out of the hands of his warlord rivals.[30] Roosevelt eventually sided with Chennault because his plan presented the most expedient method of showing support for the Nationalist government.

Operations in China never reached the lofty goals of the American leaders. China did not become a base from which to launch the invasion of Japan, Chinese troops never swept the Japanese out of mainland Asia, and American bombers never delivered a knockout blow to Japan from Chinese airbases. In reality, China became exactly what Ishihara Kanji thought it might, a quagmire. Throughout World War II, China absorbed an increasing amount of Japanese troops and material that could have been used to devastating effect against Americans in the Pacific. The small American air presence in China forced Japan to devote resources out of proportion to the American commitment and drew it deeper and deeper into a conflict from which it could find no exit. With Japan distracted in mainland Asia, the American island-hopping campaign in the Pacific advanced to the doorstep of Japan without encountering overwhelming opposition.

Squadron X

Lieutenant General Henry "Hap" Arnold, Chief of the AAF, traveled to China in February 1943 to survey the situation for the Joint Chiefs of Staff. When he arrived, Chiang Kaishek revealed to him his frustration over the seeming lack of support from the 10th Air Force in India and the meager resources made available to China compared to America's other allies. Britain, for example, received $285.5 million in lend-lease aid from the United States in 1941 and 1942. China, on the other hand, received only $2.7 million.[31] Chiang demanded that Chennault be given five hundred planes for his own inde-

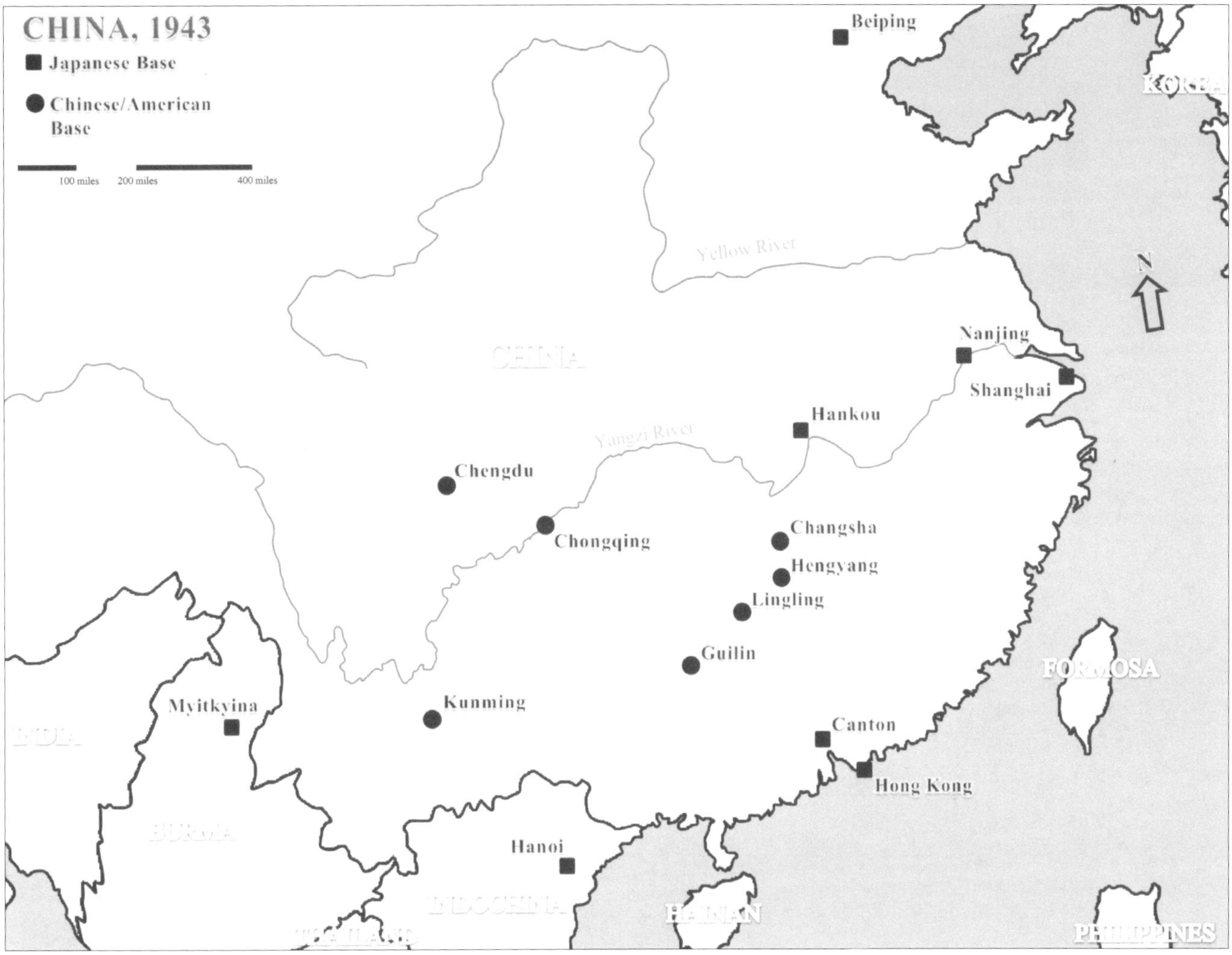

pendent air force and that tonnage over the Hump be increased to ten thousand tons per month. Arnold did not favor giving Chennault an independent command, as he saw the war in China inextricably linked with that in Burma and India and recognized that logistical difficulties were the limiting factor in expanding the war in China, not a lack of Allied support. To Arnold it seemed that Chiang was not interested in the global situation, but rather intended to use the Allies to fight the war in China for him.[32] Nevertheless, he agreed to limited expansion of American air power and spent much the rest of his time in the Far East coordinating logistical support to make possible the fulfillment of this promise.

Chiang repeated his demands in a letter to President Roosevelt who, despite Arnold's reservations, decided to give Chennault an independent air force as a show of support for China. On 10 March 1943, he created the 14th Air Force with Major General Claire Lee Chennault commanding. In fulfillment of his promise, Arnold sent the 308th Bombardment Group, equipped with long-range B-24 heavy bombers, to China in March. The 308th was to fly its own bombs and fuel over the Himalayas so that its operations would not add pressure to the already overtaxed airlift effort.[33] Arnold hoped the self-sufficient 308th would pave the way for the B-29 very-long-range bombers he planned to deploy to the theater in a little over a year.[34] Additional reinforcements waited for the end of the war in North Africa, to which the Joint Chiefs had attached a higher priority than China.[35]

In June 1942, as Rommel advanced on Alexandria, the Joint Chiefs had transferred most of the aircraft destined for the CBI Theater to operations in North Africa, leaving General Stilwell in the awkward position of having to tell Chiang that America had to renege on its commitments until more resources became available. It was appropriate then, that when the war in North Africa ended in the spring of 1943, the AAF transferred units not needed for the invasion of Italy to the CBI. Included among these was the 449th Fighter Squadron.

The 449th was originally formed from elements of Northwest African Training Command and three fighter groups stationed in North Africa during the summer of 1943: the 1st, 14th, and 82nd. The 9 June 1943 radiogram from the War Department called for fifty-eight enlisted personnel, twenty-eight officers and twenty-five P-38 aircraft for a unit dubbed "Squadron X." Twenty of the enlisted men came from the three squadrons of the 82nd Fighter Group: seven from the 95th, seven from the 96th, and six from the 97th. Major E. Dansie, first sergeant for the 96th Fighter Squadron, called crew chief Jim Hyde into his office one day and told him they were "forming a squadron in China ... would you like to go?" Hyde responded, "Yes I would."

Dansie asked, "Well have you got anybody that you'd like to take with you?" Hyde picked six other men he was friends with and joined the squadron in Casablanca. Unfortunately, Hyde "lost a friend out of the deal because after the war he wanted to know why I didn't pick him!"[36] From Casablanca, the enlisted men flew by C-47 to India in advance of the P-38s.[37]

The commander of Squadron X was Major Robert Kirtley, commander of the 95th Fighter Squadron during the North Africa campaign. He was a sandy-haired man of small stature, but lethal intensity. One of his pilots remarked, "What he can't do with a P-38 just isn't done anywhere." To his men, he was "the type of man you would fly through hell upside down with."[38] His first kill took place before he even arrived in the theater. While flying across the Bay of Biscay on the way to North Africa, four Ju-88s attacked his formation and shot down two aircraft. Kirtley and his wingman turned after the attackers and shot down two of them in return.[39] With a total of four confirmed aerial victories and two probables, Kirtley's experience made him an ideal commander for the new squadron. He immediately busied himself with the details of moving the squadron and

Right: Tom Harmon with his P-38G-10 (42-13415) Little Butch II, named, ironically, after his future wife Elyse Knox. The cartoon character painted on the nose wears Harmon's football jersey from his college days. History. SanDiego.edu

Below: Robert "Bruce" Schultz posing with the "beautiful" nose art applied to P-38G-10 #301 (42-13437) Golden Eagle. Michael Bates

its supplies some seven thousand miles to China. Because the enlisted men had preceded the rest of the squadron into India, the pilots would have to function as their own ground crews. Additionally, any pilot whose plane broke would have to find his own way to China or return to Africa.[40]

The squadron took delivery of its twenty-five Lockheed P-38G Lightnings in Casablanca, Morocco, and Telergma, Algeria. There, the pilots got to know one another and began painting nose art on their assigned aircraft. Lieutenant Tom "T-Bone" Harmon, a former Heisman Trophy winning Michigan football player, had a bulldog wearing his college football jersey painted on the nose of his airplane with the name *Little Butch II* painted underneath (ironically, "Little Butch" was Harmon's nickname for his future wife, actress Elyse Knox). Robert "Bruce" Schultz from Sandusky, Ohio, had flown his P-38 to North Africa from the Lockheed reassembly plant in Langford Lodge, Northern Ireland, and agonized over what to name his mount. Finally, he decided on naming it after a boat he had sailed on Lake Erie as a child: *Golden Eagle*. Unfortunately, Schultz did not find as good a painter as had done Harmon's artwork. According to Harmon, "His painter must have been a guy with surrealist ideas. It was the worst painting I have ever seen. In one of the eagle's claws was a bottle, and in the other a swastika, indicating, I suppose, that he was out of lick the demon rum as well as the Nazis." The other pilots made fun of him for it, but Schultz thought his nose art was beautiful.[41]

Lieutenants Ryan "Moonbeam" Moon and Lewden Enslen also joined the squadron at Telergma. Moon was a redheaded hothead from Oklahoma City.[42] Enslen, on the other hand, had been "a small fellow, a lightweight, really, fixing to make a journalist of himself and not particularly distinguished ... Just another college boy," according to a fellow resident of Springfield, Missouri.[43] However, in 1941 he joined the Air Corps, marrying his hometown sweetheart the day he earned his wings. After a short tour flying air defense for San Francisco, he went overseas and met Bruce Schultz while ferrying P-38s to North Africa. He flew ten combat missions, dive-bombing and escorting bombers to targets on Sicily and Pantelleria with the 49th Fighter Squadron, before volunteering for Squadron X in June 1943. The war made him grow up fast. Bruce Schultz recalled, "He had a fine, dry sense of humor which he never lost, and between us we took great pleasure in pulling pranks on Harmon and Moon."[44]

Left: Lieutenant Lewden Enslen. Lewden Osborn

Right: Captain Sam Palmer (right) was thrust into the role of commander after Kirtley's reassignment to the 1st Fighter Group. Here he shakes the hand of Colonel "Casey" Vincent, commander of the 14th Air Force's Forward Echelon, in November 1943. Steve Blake

To move Squadron X to China, Kirtley's plan was to fly the P-38s from Telergma to Benghazi, Libya; Cairo, Egypt; Tel Aviv, Palestine; Habbaniya, Iraq; Abadan, Iran; Bahrain; Sharja; Jiwani and Karachi in India (modern Pakistan); and then on to Agra, home of the Taj Mahal, to meet the ground crews. All

P-38s from Enslen's squadron over Oakland, California, in 1942. Lewden Osborn

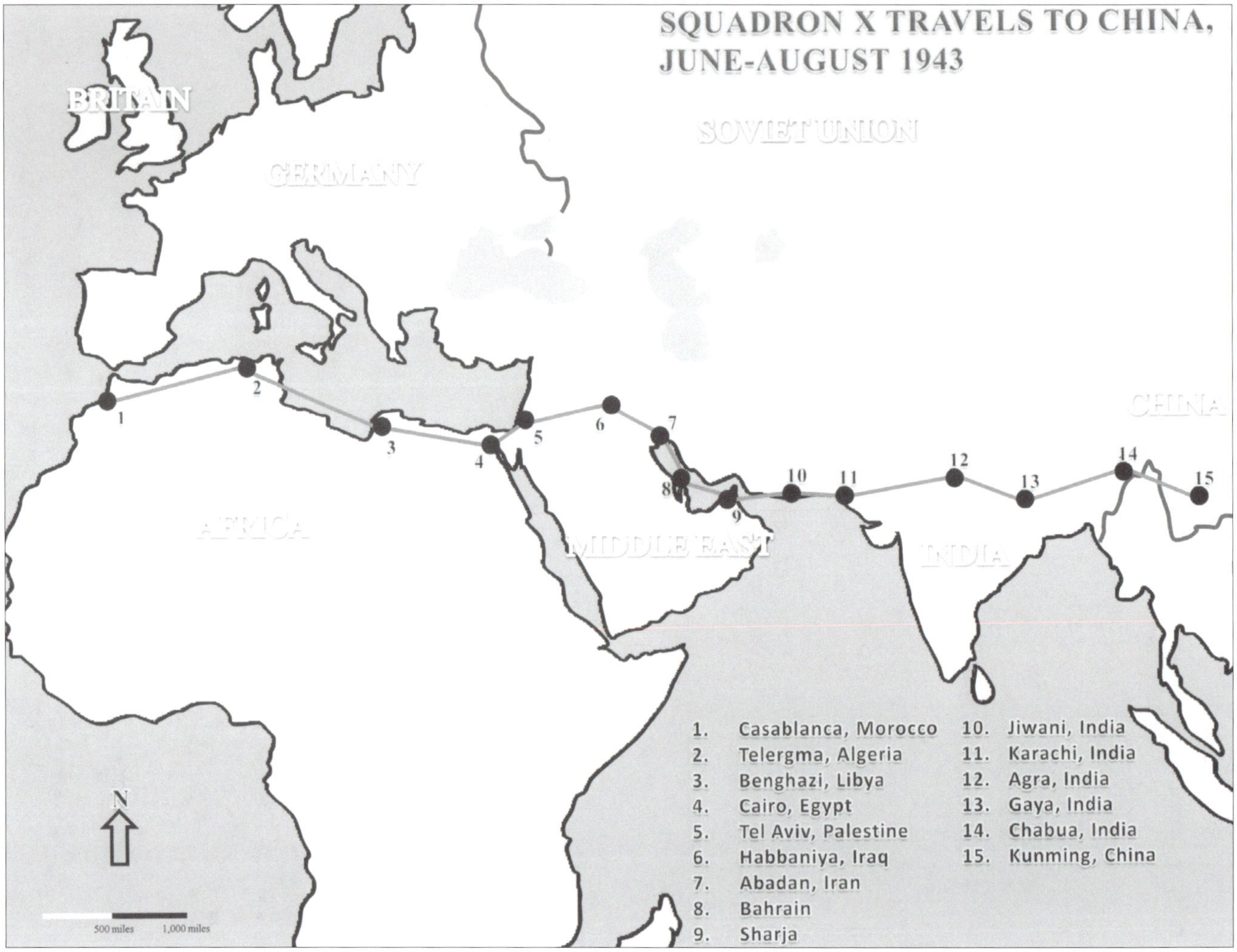

the men were volunteers and enthusiastic to make the longest Army pursuit flight on record and to be the first to take P-38 fighters into combat against the Japanese in China.[45] The day before the squadron was to depart, however, Northwest African Command reassigned Major Kirtley to the 1st Fighter Group as executive officer. Captain Sam Palmer, senior ranking pilot in Squadron X, took his place as acting commander.

The squadron finally departed Algeria on 6 July 1943. Captain Palmer walked across the dark, dusty airfield to his airplane and climbed the foldout ladder onto the wing. He opened the canopy, settled into the cockpit and strapped himself in. He connected the headset and throat mike and checked the gauges and switches, set the clock and altimeter, locked the brakes, and started the engines. Palmer gave the ground crew the signal to pull the chocks from in front of the wheels and taxied to the end of the runway. At exactly 0430 in the morning, he and his flight took off, kicking up a cloud of dust. Palmer led the first flight, while Moon brought up the rear. Tom Harmon remembered it as "a beautiful sight as the flights followed each other. It reminded me a little of the movies, for there was almost something unreal about it. Planes taking off at dawn for an objective and spraying up a fine silt of African dust as they took to the air."[46] One plane turned back because of mechanical problems, but followed the rest of the squadron the next day with Lieutenant Moon.

When the squadron arrived in Cairo on 8 July, they learned of a C-46 also departing for the CBI in two days time. Captain Palmer elected to follow the transport, equipped with more and better navigation equipment, rather than proceed alone. Lieutenant David Williams remembered that the C-46 flew "approximately 40 miles an hour slower than normal cruise for the P-38s. We hung in and slowly eased behind the C-46." The navigation plane soon proved its worth. On 16 July, while flying from Bahrain to Sharja, the fighter pilots became disoriented in hazy weather. One of them asked the transport to level off, to which the pilot replied: "Hey you fighter jocks, how about checking your needle and ball and attitude gyro and see what condition you are in." According to Williams, "When they had the aircraft leveled out again and back in formation , you could look into the cockpits and see the fighter pilots leaning on one side or the other of their respective cockpits wondering and hoping the instruments were right as the seat of their pants were not."

The bulk of the squadron made it to Agra by 19 July without incident, though two P-38s were lost en route. Lieutenant Ivan "Rocky" Rockwell destroyed his aircraft in Iraq when his engine cut out on takeoff, forcing him to make an emergency landing with the gear up. Lieutenant Lee Gregg's aircraft was severely damaged in an accident at the depot in Karachi, in which the airplane jumped its chocks and went through the side of a shed during run-up. Lieutenant John Opsvig lost his canopy landing at Benghazi, but he made the remainder of the trip without it.

Once the P-38s reached Agra, the ground crews split into groups (maintenance, armament, and communications) and busily set to preparing the planes for the long flight over the Hump. Jim Hyde remembered staying in Agra for about a month, taking advantage of the Indian accommodations, which were far better than those in North Africa. In Africa, the men primarily ate C-rations; in Agra, they could go to restaurants. Hyde remembered one time when the enlisted men went to dinner at an English place called Piccadilly Circus. All sixty of them sat at one table (or maybe half a dozen tables strung together) and the bill came to a total of ninety-eight dollars. "So they brought the bill and they handed it to Orvil Splitt. He looked at it and passed it on to the next guy. The next guy looked and it went all around the table. It came back to a guy named Rose and Rose looked at it and he handed it back to Splitt but Orvil said 'Oh no, I've seen it.' We got up and walked away and left Rose with the bill and two years later he was still trying to collect some of it."[47]

Outside the luxurious British accommodations, however, the Americans encountered a mass of impoverished humanity. The native Indian people literally filled the streets, along with horses, donkeys, cows, and carts. Human waste flowed in ditches alongside roads and human and animal feces littered the streets. Beggars swarmed like flies around the Americans to the point where some bought riding crops with which to beat them off. The heat and humidity was oppressive.[48] Finally, in mid-July, after about a month in Agra, Jim Hyde and Buck Burris flew by air transport to Kunming, China, where they prepared for the arrival of the rest of the squadron.

Over a period of several days, the P-38s proceeded in flights to Chabua, India, an airfield east of the Brahmaputra River in the lowland tea-growing province of Assam. From there, they flew to Kunming over a spur of the Himalayas which juts south into Burma and prominently divides India from China. The first five aircraft arrived on 23 July 1943, winging over the jagged granite peaks to the Yunnan Plateau. The plateau lay on the southwestern frontier of China, a highland with an average altitude of six to seven thousand feet, bordered by hot, humid lowlands on three sides. During the summer rainy season, a deep, brilliant green covers the rugged, mountainous land, with rice terraces reaching to the tops of many hills and mountains.[49]

The P-38s descended over the West Mountains toward the six-thousand-foot-long gravel runway on the north side of Lake Dianchi, a twenty-mile-long fresh water lake oriented north-south at the base of the valley. The Lightnings made "the fan" approach, a landing pattern used by most fighter units in World War II to both reconnoiter the field and showoff. With the fan, the flight leader signaled for his flight to form into right or left echelon by dipping his wing. He would fly toward the runway at five hundred feet and then start a slight dive

The air depot at Karachi centered around a massive dirigible hanger. Note the partially-assembled P-38s in the foreground. National Archives

to arrive over the approach end with minimal altitude, flight stacked level or upward. At the end of the runway, the flight leader cut his throttle and chandelled upward, trading airspeed for altitude in a continuous 360-degree turn that lined him up for final approach. Each plane in the formation peeled-off, one at a time, to land.[50]

Tom Harmon's flight was the last to fly the Hump, but not without incident. Poor weather held the flight up for several days at Chabua. For fighter aircraft with little instrumentation to fly over peaks reaching eighteen thousand feet with winds gusting from one hundred to one hundred fifty miles per hour, the weather had to be near perfect.[51] Harmon's flight took to the air on 5 August. Colonel Bruce Holloway, commander of the 23rd Fighter Group, flew the lead P-38. Harmon flew on Holloway's wing as the flight climbed to thirty-two thousand feet, trying to find a way around the towering cumulus clouds.

Robert "Buck" Burris shares the burden of a few local Chinese workers. Buck Burris and Jim Hyde, armorer and crew chief, respectively, were the first two 449th Fighter Squadron personnel in China. Robert Burris

LITTLE
TOOTSIE

LITTLE
TOOTSIE

Above: P-38G-10 #320 (42-12948) Sweet Adeline's Can Opener flown from North Africa to China and converted to a two-seater later in the war. American Aviation Historical Society via Steve Blake

Right: Colonel Bruce K. Holloway, commander of the 23rd Fighter Group from January to September 1943, escorted a flight of P-38s from Chabua over the Hump to Kunming. Holloway became Vice Chief of Staff of the United States Air Force in 1966. National Archives

Holloway led them dodging around cloud formations until they inadvertently flew into a pocket; the only way out was the way through which they had come. Harmon remembered Holloway calling for a 180-degree turn to the left, but "I guess not everyone had heard him, because airplanes were going all over." Lieutenant Bob Barrett plunged into the clouds to avoid hitting other airplanes and went into a spin. Harmon remembered Barrett calling Lieutenant Moon on the radio and telling him that he had been in a spin, was out of it now, and wanted to know the flight's position. Moon radioed back: "We are at 30,000 feet heading 220 degrees, fly this heading for forty minutes and then pick up 235 degrees and you will come out in the valley." Barrett replied that he understood and would see them back at the field. According to Harmon, however, "That was the last we saw or heard from Bob Barrett. It was about two months later that a search party found his plane on the side of a mountain. He had apparently tried to let down through the overcast, and smacked right into something solid up there."[52] Bob Barrett was one of the squadron's most experienced pilots, with two confirmed kills flying with the 95th Fighter Squadron in North Africa. On 11 April 1943, in a fighter sweep off Sicily, the 95th caught twenty Ju-52 transports and their escorts at low altitude. They claimed twenty-seven aircraft destroyed, including two German transports shot down by Barrett.[53] The unpredictable Chinese weather proved a more challenging adversary than the Germans, however, and he died amongst the snow-capped peaks between the Salween River and Kunming.

Colonel Holloway brought the rest of the flight back to Chabua, where they waited for a break in the weather. Harmon's second attempt at crossing the Hump was much more successful than the first. He and his squadron mates landed safely at Kunming. The squadron made it to China with twenty-two P-38s, twenty-eight officers, and fifty-eight enlisted men. The trip had not been without incident, but was finally done. Squadron X was in China and ready for action.[54]

Chapter Two

Joining the Fight in China

The first elements of Squadron X arrived in China on 23 July 1943, the same day the Japanese Army Air Force (JAAF) launched its greatest offensive to wipe out the 14th Air Force. The Japanese believed the United States was building its air strength in southwest China to destroy Japanese air assets and cut lines of communications with the ultimate goal of bombing the Home Islands. Lieutenant General Moritaka Nakazono, commander of the 3rd Air Division, was determined to destroy the Americans before they gained enough strength to deal a decisive blow to the Japanese (the Air Division Headquarters, *Hikoshidan Shireibu*, was responsible for coordinating flying operations and airfield management in the China Theater).[1] To accomplish this, Nakazono designed a three-phase offensive. Phase One would last from the end of July to mid-August and consist of attacks on Chennault's airfields north of Guilin. Phase Two would last from mid-to-late-August and consist of attacks on the capital city of Chongqing and traffic on the Yangzi River. Phase Three would last through the month of September and consist of raids launched from south China and Indochina on the 14th Air Force in Yunnan Province.[2] To counter a force of approximately two hundred Japanese aircraft, which "came swarming out of [Guangzhou] and [Hankou] like angry wasps," Chennault had only four squadrons of P-40s. The 16th Fighter Squadron, however, was split between Kunming and Yunnanyi to protect the Hump, leaving only the 74th, 75th and 76th Fighter Squadrons with fifty P-40s between them to oppose the Japanese air offensive in the east.[3]

Chennault knew he needed more airplanes to defeat the Japanese. In April, he had asked Arnold to increase his strength to 150 fighters, thirty-two medium bombers, and eight photoreconnaissance planes, in addition to the 308th Bombardment Group already on its way from the United States. Arnold informed him that no units were immediately available, but that he would begin a gradual buildup.[4] Also of paramount importance to Chennault was his need for modern interceptors. The P-40 had served him well, but was very limited in its air-to-air capabilities. The Warhawk was already obsolescent by the time it first engaged Japanese fighters over China in 1941. It was only able to counter the maneuverable and quick-climbing Ki-43 Army Type One Fighter, known by its Allied codename, "Oscar," because Chennault taught his airmen to take advantage of the P-40's superior diving speed and firepower in hit-and-run attacks. Such attacks, however, required the Americans to engage from an advantageous position, which was only possible because of the air raid warning net.

Chennault beat the Japanese time and again because of his clever tactics and resourceful innovations. One of these innovations was the air raid warning net that he began assembling when he first arrived in China. As he saw it, the "biggest problem of modern fighters was intelligence. Without a continuous stream of accurate information keeping the fighters posted on exactly where the high-speed bombers were, attempts at interception were like hunting needles in a limitless haystack." When Chennault was commander of the 19th Pursuit Squadron at Ford Island, Hawaii, in the 1920s, he developed a crude air raid warning system that consisted of two enlisted men with binoculars scanning the horizon from the top of a water tower.[5] As his career progressed, and he began teaching pursuit tactics at the Air Corps Tactical School at Maxwell Field, Alabama, he realized that a formalized ground intelligence net would allow a small force of defending fighters to concentrate advantageously against attacking bombers. He put his ideas to the test during the 1933 Fort Knox Exercises and codified them in his 1935 treatise, *The Role of Defensive Pursuit*. Chennault wrote that a warning net required trained personnel and a great deal of communications equipment, though existing telegraph and telephone systems could be employed. Additionally, the net had to cover the entire area being defended so that enemy aircraft could be detected even when they attacked from the flanks or rear.[6] In late July 1937, Chennault set up an improvised warning net around Nanjing to protect the Chinese capital. Using the net, Chinese and Russian planes made several successful intercepts, but the weight of Japanese numbers and the superior quality of their equipment and training eventually swept them from the sky.[7]

When Chennault and the remnants of the CAF arrived at Kunming in 1940, he immediately began work on a new warning net. Free from attack by Japanese ground forces in remote Yunnan, the net around Kunming fanned out 270-degrees, with observers stationed initially at one hundred, two hundred, and three hundred kilometer intervals extending throughout Free China and into Japanese-occupied territory. Eventually, Chennault divided China into geographic sections with observers assigned to each area. He set up training schools lasting anywhere from two to twelve months for Chinese observers and linked their telephone and radio equipment into a central command post, where American fighter controllers tracked the progress of incoming raids.[8]

Chennault's defensive plan consisted of three simple phases of operation: detection and reporting, interception by pursuit, and destruction of the enemy.[9] To preserve precious gasoline flown over the Hump, defending fighters remained on the ground instead of patrolling the sky. When the warning net detected an incoming raid, fighter controllers tracked it until it came within twenty or thirty minutes of reaching its target. The intended target was typically easy to predict based on the enemy's course and twenty minutes was just enough time for the P-40s to takeoff and climb to twenty thousand feet. After scrambling the fighters, controllers gave them a heading to intercept the Japanese planes, placing them between the enemy formation and the American airbase. Normally one set of transmitters was located in an underground bomb shelter while a second was located in an aboveground revetment so controllers could visually guide the fighters to interception.[10]

Tactically, the P-40 was faster than the escorting Oscars in level flight and dives, was much more durable, and possessed heavier firepower. As was typical of Japanese fighters, however, the Oscar was much more maneuverable and could easily defeat the P-40 in a dogfight. In the 1937 air battles over East China, Chennault found his "Hawk Special acquired some bullet holes much too close for comfort as I learned very, very early in the game that trying to turn with Jap fighters was non-habit forming."[11] Instead, he taught his pilots to dive from above in hit-and-run attacks on the Japanese instead of engaging them in dogfights. Fighter ace John Alison, who served in the 75th Fighter Squadron from the summer of 1942 until May of 1943, remembered: "There was no stigma if you didn't stay and fight." In fact, Chennault reinforced his distinctly guerrilla tactics with an easy-to-remember ditty: "It's better to fight and run away, and live to fight another day." The Japanese Bushido mentality espoused the opposite: "They were not supposed to leave a fight and if they were wounded or damaged in a battle, they were to pick a likely target and dive into it. We saw that happen several times."[12]

With the warning net, Chennault could engage the Japanese at a time and place of his choosing. Though strategically defensive, his P-40s blurred the line between attacker and defender when they pounced upon Japanese formations. The AVG's first combat over Kunming on 20 December 1941 bagged nine out of ten unescorted bombers. The Japanese did not return until July 1942. The AVG was so effective in its defensive operations that even the threat of interception held the Japanese at bay. In June 1942, Chennault kept a squadron of P-40s flying at low altitude over Chongqing daily. After one week, he was confident the Japanese received word that the city was well defended and moved the squadron elsewhere, leaving only a handful of defending fighters and an airfield "full of well-painted bamboo P-40 dummies."[13] The Strategic Bombing Survey, a post-war study on the effectiveness of airpower during World War II, claimed that the warning net was essential to Chennault's success in China. Despite its humble beginnings, the net achieved such efficiency that it was rumored Chinese observers reported Japanese bombers when they began warming up their engines.[14]

Personnel on the ground also benefitted from the net. Americans came to know air raids as "Jing Bao," which means "warning" or "alarm" in Chinese. At friendly airfields, air raids were announced as one-ball, two-ball, or three-ball alerts. Chinese raised a tethered balloon on the Jing Bao pole for each alert notification. One ball indicated that Japanese aircraft were in the air. Two balls indicated the Japanese were heading towards that specific field. Three balls meant the enemy had arrived. Pilot Jerry Doughty commented that "when you saw the three of them, you better do something fast!"[15]

The warning net was also useful to friendly aircraft lost over China's vast expanse. Few modern maps and navigation aids existed in China, thus it was easy to become lost. Once lost, aircraft could circle a point and ask fighter controllers to radio their position based on observations made by the net. When Lockheed Lightnings first arrived in China in their unarmed reconnaissance form, however, the Chinese had a hard time identifying them. According to the *CBI Roundup*, a wartime newspaper circulated to troops in the CBI Theater:

> When the first photo recon P-38 Lightnings arrived in China, late in 1942, they created quite a bit of excitement. The first ones were flown by the late Maj. Frank Schiel, former AVG, Maj. Dale Schwartz and the late Maj. John W. Robinson. The Chinese had never before seen such an airplane and it was quite a chore for them to identify it properly. But one aged Chinese figured it out. He sent out the word: "When you see a friendly airplane that looks like two P-40's tied together... that's a P-38 Lightning." The description stands to this day.[16]

Of course, part of the problem with a plane that looked like "two P-40's tied together" is that it used almost as much gasoline as two P-40s. Chennault had been clamoring for high-altitude, modern interceptors, but P-38s were at the bottom of his list.[17] J. Forrest Green, a pilot with the 449th late in the war, stated that, "Gen. C was not too pleased with the unit at first because he felt that two engines were an unnecessary [and unaffordable] drain on supply."[18] Indeed, pilot Billie Beardsley affirmed, "There is a very good reason why there wasn't another P-38 squadron in China. The 14th AF couldn't keep us supplied in gas."[19] The Chinese minister for foreign affairs, T.V. Soong, wrote a letter to General Arnold on 11 June 1943, in which he asserted that, "the twin-engine P-38 consuming more gasoline should be kept in India instead of being sent to China," and that "the logistics in the China Theatre is so difficult and relatively so few planes could be maintained there, that none except the best ought to be sent there."[20] What Chennault really wanted were P-51 Mustangs. The Mustang was fuel efficient, fast, nimble, and effective at high altitudes. In 1943, the P-51 was brand new and Chennault had everyone he knew in Washington working on getting it assigned to China.

General Arnold, however, quickly tired of Chennault's repeated requests for "equipment of the latest type, regardless of the importance of the command in relation to others, regardless of the schedules worked out by the Joint or Combined Chiefs of Staff, regardless of production, and regardless of the effect upon other theaters," a condition Arnold referred to as "theateritis."[21] The fact of the matter was that in July 1943, the AAF possessed 1,421 P-38s and only 327 P-51s.[22] Additionally, P-51s were slated for the air war in Europe, which was a much higher priority than China. As Arnold saw it, not only were P-38s modern interceptors with a high-altitude capability, they were also conveniently available after the war in North Africa ended. Thus, Arnold sent P-38s to China, though he later conceded in an 18 October 1943 letter to Roosevelt: "The fact that General Chennault has requested an exchange of P-51's for his present P-38's, which burn more gasoline, is a definite indication of the narrow margin on which he is operating."[23]

Chennault's attitude about receiving P-38s instead of P-51s made a definite impression on the men of the 449th. According to Jim Hyde, "It was common scuttlebutt in our outfit General Chennault didn't want us to start with. ... He kept us stationed as far from Kunming – where his offices were – and as close to the Japanese as he could. We were always the furthest outpost in China."[24]

Chennault may not have wanted the 449th, as it was officially designated on 31 July 1943, but he sent it into combat immediately. On 16 September 1943, the *CBI Roundup* reported:

> The P-40 now has a stable mate to battle the enemy Zero in China's blood-drenched skies after being the sole

Below and opposite top: Chinese aircraft spotters become familiar with the P-38 Lightning. Confusion abounded among Chinese spotters when the P-38 first appeared in China until it was described to them as "two P-40s tied together." National Archives

Opposite bottom: General Chennault chats with a group of P-51 pilots in November 1944. Chennault, being a fighter pilot himself, especially liked interacting with the fighter pilots in his command. National Archives

> fighter plane of Maj. Gen. Claire L. Chennault's 14th Air Force command. The sleek P-38 Lightning, which has given an excellent account in other theaters of war, is the newcomer to join the tried-and-true P-40. On his recent 53rd birthday, Chennault revealed the P-38's had arrived to augment his squadrons, accompanied by airmen who piloted them in North Africa. The pilots were in action one day after they arrived against Jap raiders near a forward base and have participated in subsequent action. Official disclosure of the arrival of the Lightnings in China is bad news for the enemy. The two-engined, two-tailed, 400-mile-per-hour P-38 is one of America's most versatile planes and its presence in China is interpreted to mean the stepping up of aerial activity against the enemy. Chennault said the Japs are using a new type of Zero fighter[25] which is speedier, climbs higher, dives faster and is more strongly built and heavily armed than previous types. "But they still blow up easily when hit," he added.[26]

The Lightning was heavily armed and armored in addition to being fast and agile. Armament included four fifty-caliber machine guns and a twenty-millimeter cannon all situated in the nose. Most fighters had guns mounted in the wings, which converged at a certain distance from the plane (usually three hundred yards) to concentrate firepower. This meant that if a target was not at the set distance from a fighter, firepower from the wing guns would not be optimally concentrated. Because the P-38 carried its armament in the nose, the weapons did not need to be set to converge, and thus optimum firepower could be delivered at a multitude of different ranges. The sheer firepower concentrated in such a small area could easily pulverize a target.[27] The P-38 provided its pilot with a stable gun platform at all speeds and attitudes except when in a high-speed dive, when buffeting would make it difficult to control.[28] The Lighting could also carry over two thousand pounds (later models could carry over four thousand pounds) of bombs, rockets, or fuel under the wings.

As far as performance was concerned, the P-38 could outclimb any aircraft in the AAF's inventory, though it was slower than the P-47 at all altitudes and the P-40 and early-model P-51s below fifteen thousand feet. At low altitudes, the Lightning had a wider turning radius than other American fighters, but it could match most of them above twelve thousand feet, and equal or better them above fifteen thousand feet. The Lightning's slow roll rate, however, gave it a significant disadvantage in a turning fight. The P-38 was simple to fly once a pilot got used to it, but the number of instruments and controls overwhelmed the inexperienced.[29] Forrest Green initially wanted to fly the P-51 Mustang, partly because his mother worked for North American Aviation in Grand Prairie, Texas. He explained that after single-engine fighter training "The P-38 was a lot more airplane and it was an adjustment. For the first 25 hours I felt it was flying me instead of me flying it, but once that transition was made I did not want the P-51 anymore."[30]

As each flight of P-38s landed at Kunming, General Chennault required the pilots to report to him personally so that he could inform and indoctrinate them in his ways. Chennault was not conducting a typical air campaign like those in North Africa or Europe. On the contrary, his operations were more like aerial guerilla warfare than anything else. The basic principle Chennault employed was to pit his force's strengths against the enemy's weaknesses. Besides the air warning net, which supplied a tremendous advantage, the 14th Air Force benefited from interior lines of communication, which allowed Chennault to move squadrons from base to base to keep the Japanese unsure of the time, target, and nature of his next move. Additionally, the proximity of his bases at Guilin, Lingling, and Hengyang allowed fighters from one to provide defense for the others. The Americans had one more advantage: Chennault's uncanny ability to outguess the Japanese. Time and again this talent gave the American air force in China the edge it needed to achieve victory.

Harmon related, "It was with deep respect and some awe that Schultz and I and all the other boys went through the door of headquarters." When the pilots entered Chennault's office, he asked them to sit down and began to educate them on the nature of aerial combat in China.[31] He told them that they must use teamwork to defeat the Japanese and to utilize the strong points of their equipment against the weak points of the enemy's. This meant using their speed and firepower in hit-and-run attacks rather than turning and dogfighting with the maneuverable Japanese fighters. He talked to them about the challenges associated with fighting in China, namely the rugged terrain, poor weather, and meager supplies.[32]

The men "made a great effort to keep our minds tight on what he was saying," but were distracted by the general's attractive secretary in the same room. According to Harmon:

> As if magnetized, the glances of about twenty fighter pilots were going in her direction while the General was explaining the method which the men of his group had found best in fighting the Japs. The pilots of our group were making every effort to grasp what he said and look at Miss Davis at the same time.

After this went on for some time, Chennault broke down and laughed. He had been aware of it all along! Harmon "began to understand why his men called him 'Pappy' Chennault."[33] Chennault temporarily attached the 449th Fighter Squadron to the veteran 23rd Fighter Group for operations and placed Major Edmund Goss of the 75th Fighter Squadron in charge as an advisor. Major Goss was an experienced fighter pilot with six confirmed aerial victories in P-40s.[34]

Starting on 23 July 1943, the Japanese 3rd Air Division made a series of well-coordinated attacks on Hengyang, Lingling, and Guilin, often feinting toward one base to confuse the warning net before diverting to another. Billie Beardsley was in the first flight of P-38s to cross the Hump on 23 July. Chennault immediately sent three of those P-38s with Captain Elmer Richardson, a pilot from the 75th Fighter Squadron, to Guilin. Guilin lies on the west side of the Li River in the northeast corner of the Guangxi Province, distinctively surrounded by dark, jagged, limestone peaks covered in deep green foliage and sweet-smelling osmanthus trees. Many pilots thought the mountains looked like inverted ice cream cones. In fact, the limestone formed from sediment deposits when an inland sea or ocean covered the area, resulting in some of the most beautiful scenery in the world after the waters subsided. During the summer rainy season, the heat and humidity are oppressive and heavy mist or fog often enshrouds the lush, green mountains. Guilin featured prominently in Chennault's string of bases through central China, and the railroad passing through from Hankou to Nanning made it an important communications hub and target for the Japanese.[35]

The day after their arrival, fighters from the 25th, 33rd, and 85th Sentais escorted Ki-21 Type 97 Heavy Bombers, Allied codename "Sally," to Lingling, losing one Ki-21 and one Ki-43 to P-40s of the 76th Fighter Squadron. The basic fighting unit of the JAAF was the flying regiment (*sentai*) which was typically composed of three squadrons (*chutai*). Each sentai included between forty-two and forty-nine aircraft and four hundred men, including 320 repair and maintenance personnel.[36] One hour after the bombing raid, future ace Captain Yukiyoshi Wakamatsu led eight fighters from the 2nd Chutai of the 85th Sentai from Guangzhou to Guilin.[37] The 85th had recently moved from Manchuria with new Ki-44 Type Two Single Seat Fighters, codename "Tojo." P-40s from the 74th Fighter Squadron and two P-38s scrambled to intercept.

The distinctive limestone mountains of the Guilin area in China. Ed Penick

Morning mist drifts across the Li River near Guilin. Author's Photo

Major Goss assigned Lieutenant Walter Smith, a pilot from the 74th Fighter Squadron with P-38 experience, to lead the other Lightning. Lieutenant Lewden Enslen accompanied him and was credited with the unit's first victory. Unfortunately, the 449th also lost its first P-38. After Smith took off, he turned south toward the direction from which the Japanese were coming. According to P-40 pilot Bill Hawkins, "He got shot down right off the end of the runway. I saw his P-38 go in – SPLAT. I didn't see him bail out, but apparently he did." Hawkins turned to provide support to other American fighters taking off and then flew to where Smith had gone down. There he found two Japanese fighters and dove to attack, shooting down one of them.[38] In the battle over Guilin, the Americans claimed seven Japanese fighters destroyed. The Japanese admitted losing two: Sergeant Fumio Yonezu and Corporal Fukuichi Okada of the 85th Sentai were both shot down, an inglorious debut for the Tojo in China.[39] Smith survived, but was in bad shape, with burns to his hands and face. Beardsley complained that Smith was flying "his" P-38 and lamented, "My P-38 was the first P-38 fighter shot down in China. I was very bitter."[40]

On 25 July,[41] Enslen was back in action, claiming one Japanese fighter destroyed and two probables over Hengyang. That morning, nine B-25s bombed the airfield at Hankou, and Major General Rokuro Imanishi ordered Ki-43s of the 25th and 33rd Sentais to pursue them. Nine Oscars followed the bombers to Hengyang, where they met fifteen P-40s and two P-38s, claiming to have shot down three of the former and one of the latter while losing Lieutenant Shiro Murakami of the 25th Sentai. In fact, neither of the Lightnings were shot down, and Sergeant Major Shigeru Tanaka of the 33rd Sentai, who claimed to have destroyed one, was killed on the ground the following day during another bombing raid on Hankou.[42]

Four days later, Chennault sent eighteen B-24s, with several P-40s and P-38s for escort, to Hong Kong, the source of many of the attacks on his eastern bases. Colonel Holloway led the fighter escort. According to Holloway, as the formation arrived over Hong Kong, "somebody yelled 'Zeros!' I started weaving violently but never did see any." Two P-40s made a head-on pass on the enemy fighters. One got on the tail of a P-38, but a P-40 came to its rescue. Another Lightning dove onto an enemy fighter's tail, but overshot. Lieutenant Earl Helms claimed a Japanese fighter destroyed, (though the JAAF admitted to losing none), but he got lost on the return trip. Holloway talked to Helms for some time on the radio, trying to ascertain his position, but Helms finally ran out of gas and made a belly-landing in a rice paddy near Lingling.[43] Poor weather prevented the Americans or Japanese from making any more raids until

Chinese soldiers and laborers pull a P-38 (possible Helms') out of a muddy rice paddy near Lingling. Michael Bates

449th pilots in front of Earl Helms' P-38, Lethal E-Luce-Eve, at Lingling. In the front row, from left to right, are Beardsley, Harmon, Schultz, and Arpin. Standing in the back are Williams, Helms, Gregg, Dowis, and Rea. 14th Air Force Association

The flight line at Lingling. Note how some of the squadron's P-38Gs did not yet have identification numbers on the tail boom. Michael Bates

mid-August, which was fortunate because by the end of July, the 14th Air Force's defensive strength was down to thirty-three P-40s and six P-38s.[44]

While the lead echelon was in combat against the Japanese, Captain Palmer, officially commander as of 6 August, began assembling the rest of the squadron at Kunming. Jim Hyde remembered: "After we got to China our squadron was filled in with people from other spots in India and China. Like most outfits, they were people nobody else wanted. They were hard drinking but the hardest working guys I've ever known. It was not that uncommon for us to work a twenty-four hour shift."[45] The squadron was spread out in detachments at Guilin, Hengyang, and Kunming until 14 August, when the unit moved to Lingling, "a rather small town" approximately halfway between Guilin and Hengyang. According to Bruce Schultz, "a lot of maps I have seen do not show its location even though it was one of our most important air bases."[46] Chennault kept two or three P-38s for air defense at Kunming for the rest of the war.

The Japanese had engaged P-38s over the South Pacific and did not wish to engage them over China as well. Lieutenant Commander Mitsugu Kofukuda, commander of the Japanese 6th Naval Air Corps near Bougainville, reported that high-speed formation dives by P-38s in the Pacific scattered Japanese formations and "inflicted unexpectedly heavy losses."[47] Thus, once the weather broke in August, Japanese fighters avoided Lingling and attacked Hengyang and Guilin instead. For pilots new to air combat in China, the tension in the alert shack was unbearable. Tom Harmon related:

> Everyone would jump when the first plot would go on the board. If we had had our way, we would have been up in the air right away doing nothing but waste a lot of precious gasoline. Major Goss, however, with his experience in that theater, would sit still and calmly follow the course of the enemy planes. He wasn't going to have us up in the air for nothing, not he, for he knew that gasoline is more precious than gold in China, and what we had we had to make count. When the Japs did get close enough, Major Goss would say, "Okay, they are coming in. Let's get 'em." The men would run to their ships and take off. The procedure was standard, and went on every day.[48]

On 20 August, Japanese fighters attacked Guilin with Ki-44 Tojos of the 85th Sentai and Ki-43 Oscars of the 33rd Sentai. This time the Japanese pilots used the Ki-44's higher ceiling and faster airspeed to their advantage. Flying higher than the maximum ceiling of the Warhawks, the Tojos dove down in hit-and-run attacks similar to what the American pilots were accustomed to using. The new Japanese machine proved far superior to the P-40. The Americans lost three fighters and the Japanese lost none.[49] The 449th attempted to intercept the raiders, but arrived after the battle was over.[50]

The next day, thirty bombers and twenty-five Oscars from the 33rd Sentai attacked Hengyang. Typically the Japanese would launch from Hankou to the north and fly to Guangzhou in the south (or vice versa), bombing Lingling, Hengyang, and Guilin in between. Ed Penick, a pilot with the 21st Photo Reconnaissance Squadron, scrambled to get his plane airborne and out of the way of falling bombs and subsequently witnessed the air battle that took place. Twelve P-40s scrambled to engage the enemy while nine P-38s raced from Lingling to reach the battle before it was over.

As the P-40s clawed for altitude, the Oscars dove from out of the sun. When the 449th arrived, they found the fight already in progress. The P-38s were well above the altitude of the Japanese formation, which in turn used its altitude advantage to make diving attacks on the P-40s. Each squadron was assigned a color for radio identification; the 449th was "Black." Ed Penick remembered hearing the ground controller instruct the P-38s to engage the enemy by saying "Black come on to the party."[51] The enemy fighters broke off to the north but the Lightnings had no trouble catching them. The Oscars were flying at thirty thousand feet when the P-38s caught up. They split into four elements; Ed Goss and Bruce Schultz charged into the leaders, Willard Bolton took his wingman to the left, and Sam Palmer and his wingman went right. The fourth element stayed high

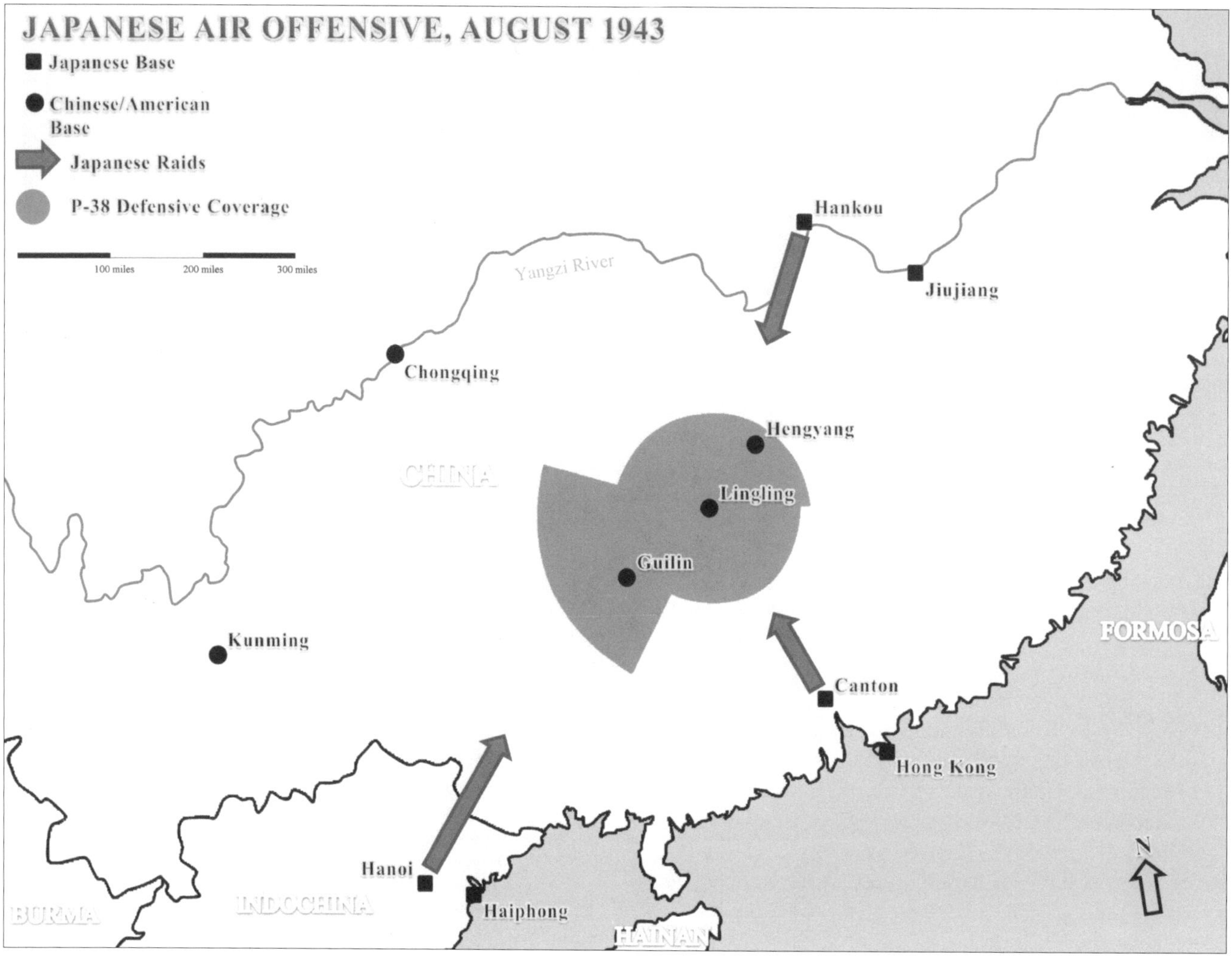

as top cover. As Goss approached an Oscar from behind, the Japanese executed the "Prince of Wales" maneuver, where the lead Oscar continued straight and level as bait while his wingmen looped around to get onto the tail of his pursuer.[52]

Goss let loose a hail of bullets and sent the lead Oscar smoking toward the ground while Schultz shot at the Oscars trying to get on Goss' tail. Bolton charged into the left flank and sent one Oscar down before the Lightnings broke off, low on fuel. The remaining Oscars dove away and headed back to Wuchang.[54]

The fight lasted fifteen minutes. Major Goss, Lieutenant Schultz, Lieutenant Edward Burbank, and Lieutenant Bolton all claimed their victims as probably destroyed, though observations from the warning net later upgraded Bolton's claim to a confirmed kill. The Lightnings were also successful in driving the enemy to a lower altitude where P-40s claimed another four fighters shot down. In reality, the 33rd Sentai lost four aircraft: Lieutenant Kiyotake Takahashi, Sergeant Major Hiroshi Yamashita, Sergeant Teruo Tsuji and Corporal Shiro Fukuda were all killed in action.[54] Penick remembered seeing "Jap planes falling from the sky like autumn leaves."[55]

After the 21 August fight over Hengyang, the 449th's records noted something interesting: "Enemy fighters were falling into tailspins when they attempted to turn with the Lightnings at 26,000 feet."[56] Indeed, Schultz told Harmon "he thought he had noticed that when a Zero tried to turn with a P-38 at that altitude, the ship spun out of the turn."[57] A 10 May 1944 AAF intelligence summary seems to support this observation. That month, the AAF pitted a captured Ki-43-IF against a late-model P-38 in the southwest Pacific area. The intelligence summary noted that a P-38 could evade an Oscar at altitudes above twenty thousand feet by initiating a fifty-degree climbing turn. At those altitudes, the Oscar quickly lost airspeed and was unable to stay with the P-38, often stalling. By the time the 449th arrived in China, however, the Japanese were replacing the model I Oscars with more capable model II Oscars, and the new Tojo boasted better altitude performance and rate of climb than any Oscar. At altitudes of ten thousand feet or below, where the 449th fought most of its engagements, the intelligence summary stated that "the P-38 outclimbed and outran the OSCAR," but "On diving on the OSCAR's tail, both in right and left turns, the OSCAR was on the P-38's tail in 1 1/2 x 360° turns."[58] Thus newer model Oscars and Tojos, and older models at lower altitudes, were much more maneuverable than the P-38. Consequently, the observation noted in the unit records would cause pilots to lose their lives – or at least their aircraft – in future engagements. General Chennault was infuriated that his pilots would ignore his instructions not to turn with enemy fighters and was

Ed Penick (right), photoreconnaissance pilot who witnessed the air battle over Hengyang on 21 August 1943, with fellow pilot Robert Neely. Robert Neely

Bruce Schultz and Jack Dewey, technical representative from the Allison Engine Company, in front of the Golden Eagle at Lingling. 14th Air Force Association

frustrated by the losses they suffered because of it. Chennault wrote in his autobiography:

> They arrived from North Africa with a fondness for dogfighting and without spare parts. These pilots refused to believe a P-38 couldn't turn with an Oscar, Zero, or Tojo. As a result the 449th became the only American fighter squadron in China against which the Japs approached an even break.[59]

It did not take long for the 449th to adjust its tactics. After several months in China Harmon commented that Schultz's observation must have been wrong, because P-38s could not challenge Japanese fighters in a turning fight. "The differences in tactics in fighting against different types of planes is amazing. In the European Theater, the P-38 pilots always made a tight turn as their first maneuver against the Germans. But the maneuver that might save your life against the Germans would mean quick death or at least plenty of trouble against the Japs."[60]

Dick Conway wrote, "As far as our pilots trying to turn with the Zero's, Oscar's etc. some might have tried it once but our tactics were built around speed not maneuverability."[61]

Chennault was not the type of man to take his disappointment over receiving P-38s instead of P-51s out on his men, but he did not take kindly to people ignoring his orders. He had told the pilots not to turn with the Japanese. A possibly erroneous observation made in the confusion of battle led the 449th to ignore this advice until they learned the hard way. From then on, the men were battling General Chennault's opinion in addition to Japanese fighters.

Upsetting Japanese Plans

Despite the 449th's successful intercept on 21 August, the Japanese clearly held the initiative in their campaign to eradicate the 14th Air Force. Obsolete Warhawks could not compete with high performance Japanese fighters and there were too few Lightnings to adequately defend every airbase. In an attempt to seize back the initiative, Chennault ordered Colonel Clinton D. "Casey" Vincent, commander of the 14th Air Force's Forward Echelon, to plan a series of bombing missions against Japanese airfields.[62]

Ironically, just as Japanese raids began affecting the 14th Air Force, General Nakazono ordered Phase Two of his campaign to commence. This meant that as of 22 August, the 3rd Air Division would halt its attacks on Chennault's eastern fields and instead focus on bombing Chongqing and interdicting Chinese river traffic. Nakazono was not entirely pleased with the results of Phase One, but nevertheless considered it a success. Despite poor weather, Japanese fighters claimed fifty-two enemy aircraft destroyed, including one P-38.[63]

On 21 August, Vincent launched the first of his bombing missions; fourteen B-24s from the 308th Bomb Group attacked

Chennault presents Brigadier General "Casey" Vincent with an Oak Leaf Cluster to his Air Medal. Vincent commanded the 14th Air Force Forward Echelon, which became the 68th Composite Wing in December 1943. He became one of the youngest general officers in the United States military since the Civil War when he was promoted to Brigadier General at age 29. National Archives

Hankou. The air raid on Hengyang, however, robbed the bombers of their fighter escort. Major Bruce Beat, commander of the 374th Bomb Squadron, circled Hengyang and noted evidence of the Japanese raid.[64] The B-24s flew alone to the target and were attacked by more than sixty Japanese fighters after dropping their bombs. Two bombers were shot down, including Major Beat's, and ten more were seriously damaged. The 374th and 375th squadrons of the 308th were badly mauled, but the group's other two squadrons, the 373rd and the 425th, immediately began preparing for the next raid. On 24 August, another fourteen B-24s were to bomb Hankou, with ten P-38s for top cover at thirty thousand feet and P-40s for close support. The 373rd's seven bombers, however, encountered bad weather on their way to the rendezvous and turned back, leaving only seven B-24s from the 425th to carry out the mission.

En route, several bombardiers mistook the airfield at Wuchang for that at Hankou and bombed it. Most of the crews recognized the error in time to save their bombs for the real target. The P-38s preceded the bombers over Hankou and circled at twenty-seven thousand feet. The B-24s bombed successfully, but then an estimated forty enemy fighters from the 33rd and 25th Sentais attacked. Some P-38 pilots heard the commotion over the radio but were unable to contact their flight leader and therefore did not intervene. General Chennault was understandably upset and commented: "Enemy fighters snatched the cheese without springing the trap. Four out of seven Liberators went down in flames while the P-38s buzzed along at 30,000 feet oblivious to the fight raging below."[65] Major Watanabe, commander of the 33rd Sentai, died when defensive fire from the B-24s hit his Oscar during the forty-five minute running battle. P-40s shot down Sergeant Yukiji Nogawa from the 33rd and Warrant Officer Hasumi Kono from the 25th.[66] The Japanese sacrifice was tempered by its achievement; even the three bombers not shot down were severely damaged.[66]

The 449th had a chance to redeem itself two days later. This time the Japanese did not attack the bombers and they successfully bombed Guangzhou and Hong Kong. Casey Vincent led the fighters and recorded in his diary: "I shot down my sixth Japanese plane today! I took seven P-40's and ten P-38's and met fourteen B-24's over Wuzhou for the mission against Hong Kong. About eight Zeros tried to get at the bombers after they left the target area, but we kept them off."[67] This time the P-38s flew two to three thousand feet above the bombers and when they saw 85th Sentai Ki-44s coming in from behind, Captain Palmer and Lieutenants Helms, Enslen, and Enssler all shot at one. Palmer received credit for its destruction, though the Japanese claimed two American planes destroyed (erroneously) for no losses.[68]

The 308th flew one last mission in August, this time to Gia Lam Airdrome near Hanoi. By staging out of the airfield at Nanning, near the French Indochina border, twenty-two P-40s from the 16th and 75th Fighter Squadrons and two P-38s were able to escort sixteen B-24s all the way to Hanoi. The plan was for nine of the heavy bombers to bomb the nearby army barracks while the other seven dropped fragmentation bombs on the airdrome. The fighters were then to bomb flood control dams in the Red River Valley in an attempt to flood the field. The nine

American military cemetery in Kunming where George Enssler was buried in 1943. George Brabec

bombers slated for the barracks could not bomb because of a large thunderstorm, but the other seven dropped their bombs directly on target.[69] Next, the fighters dove to attack. Tom Harmon carried a one-thousand-pound bomb under his wing and made a skip-bombing run on a dam. He released too high and the bomb hurtled after Roy Brown's P-40. Brown "nearly broke my neck trying to dodge the monster which finally, after its 2 to 4 second delay fuse expired, obliterated a Jap gun position and put dents in my plane and scared me to death."[70] Despite the close call, no planes were lost over the target. On the way back to China, however, eight P-40s became lost and ran out of fuel. Seven of the pilots bailed out or ditched, but one died in a crash landing.[71]

Utilizing fighters in ground attack or bombing roles was not unusual in China. Chennault believed in employing his squadrons to the maximum extent possible, thus, all his P-40s were capable of carrying bombs and his pilots were experienced in ground attack. He could not afford to send an entire group of heavy bombers with hundreds of bombs to destroy one bridge for example, the method commonly used in Europe. Instead, he would send one flight of fighters at low altitude to do the same job. In fact, throughout the war, fighters in the CBI Theater dropped 18,680 tons of bombs, only seventy-eight tons less than the amount dropped by heavy bombers. By comparison, fighters in Europe dropped only thirteen percent the tonnage of bombs dropped by heavy bombers.[72]

In other theaters, the P-38 had already distinguished itself as a great dive-bomber because of its heavy bomb load and counter-rotating propellers, which minimized the turning tendencies suffered by single-engine fighters and improved accuracy. Chennault intended to make it a great skip-bomber too. During the latter part of August, the 449th began training for bombing missions. Every morning the squadron would practice skip-bombing and dive-bombing, knowing that speed and surprise were their only protection against heavy ground fire. The P-38 in particular did not make much noise coming in low and fast; its long exhaust pipes directed engine noise upward, away from the ground.[73] Enemy troops would not hear the distinctive high-pitched whine of a P-38 on the deck until it was right on top of them. According to Harmon, "We had the speed, and if we achieved surprise we could raise a little general hell with the Jap ships."[74] Unit records noted that on a 27 August practice mission, pilots hit a ten-foot by eight-foot target with fifty-percent accuracy.

On 30 August, four P-38s set out to test their skip-bombing skills on enemy river traffic on the Yangzi. They found no enemy vessels, but Lieutenant Ryan Moon destroyed two locomotives in a series of strafing runs. The following day, Colonel Vincent sent the squadron to strafe Yueyang and Songzi. The strafing was successful, but ground fire hit Lieutenant George Enssler's P-38. He crash-landed, but later died from his injuries. Jim Hyde remembered: "Shortly after [Enssler died] ... he was buried in a Chinese cemetery outside of Kunming. I was ... the commander of the firing squad that did burial honor guard for him."[75] Enssler's death was the first incident in what the 449th perceived as a string of rotten luck. From the successful intercept on 21 August, morale only seemed to drop. Regardless, the ground attack missions continued unabated into September. On the 1st, five P-38s attacked a Japanese barracks twenty miles north of Nanchang. Then, they attacked four locomotives, destroying two of them, and sank a tugboat and a barge. They attacked and destroyed another train near Yueyang. On 3 and 4 September P-38s scrambled in response to reported Japanese raids but the enemy did not arrive.

Though the men of the 449th did not know it, 9 September 1943 was a turning point for the war in China. Phase Two of General Nakazono's plan had not been as successful as hoped. Vincent's bombing missions left the Japanese off balance and only able to launch one raid against Chongqing. Nakazono decided his best option was to initiate Phase Three to eliminate the 14th Air Force in Yunnan. 9 September was the day it was to start. In order to complete the shift to bases in southern China and Indochina, Nakazono intended to fly from Jiayi, Taiwan, to his command post in Guangzhou that afternoon. He and his staff boarded three MC transports (converted Mitsubishi Ki-21 Sallys) and took off early in the afternoon. On board the transport with Nakazono were several members of his staff, including Lieutenant Colonel Taro Miyazawa, Major Masumi Takada, and Captain Ogata. The second transport held Colonel Yoshii, Nakazono's chief of staff, and the third aircraft carried war correspondents from the Japanese press.[76]

Four P-38s of the 449th had already completed a successful dive-bombing mission against Japanese shipping that morning and another four were off at 1405 hours for a dive-bombing mission to the Huangpu docks near Guangzhou. The P-38s evaded enemy fighters and successfully bombed the docks, but as they were coming off the target, Lieutenant Billie Beardsley spotted a Japanese transport southeast of the city. Beardsley and his wingman, Lieutenant Kendall Dowis, set off after the enemy plane.

General Moritaka Nakazono, commander of the Japanese 3rd Air Division in 1943 and mastermind of the summer air offensive. Richard Maddox

The 1st Hikodan (equivalent to an AAF wing) issued a warning for aircraft to remain clear of Guangzhou for an hour because of enemy action, but Nakazono's transport did not receive the message.[77] According to eyewitnesses on the ground, at 1530 hours, two P-38s came alongside Nakazono's transport while a third dove from behind and fired, sending the transport crashing down six miles southeast of Guangzhou onto an island in the Pearl River. Billie Beardsley was credited with its destruction. Japanese medical personnel examined the bodies pulled from the wreckage and determined that Nakazono had been killed by gunfire prior to the crash.[78] Dick Lee, a crew chief with the 16th Fighter Squadron, sent a letter to Beardsley after the war, which read:

> I have a Japanese friend who is an aviation historian who is specializing in Chinese aviation history. He told me about the Japanese General over all the Japanese Army Air Units in China. This General, whose name was Nakazono, was moving his HQ from Hankow [sic] to [Guangzhou] in preparation for an all out aerial offensive against the U.S. air bases in the southern part of China. On the 9th of September 1943, he and his staff were moving to [Guangzhou] when they were intercepted. The plane in which the staff was riding escaped but the General's plane was shot down, crashing on an island in the Pearl River near [Guangzhou]. Witnesses on the ground confirmed that the aircraft had been shot down by a P-38. My friend asked if I could help find the pilot who shot the General down. I have researched the records and found that you shot down a transport on that day and at 15:30 in the afternoon near [Guangzhou]. Since yours was the only claim in that area on that day for a transport, you are the one that changed the Japanese plans.[79]

General Nakazono's timely demise occurred less than five months after the 18 April shoot down of Admiral Yamamoto by Rex Barber over Bougainville. The Japanese feared that the Americans knew all their plans, though according to Dick Maddox, "It wasn't until the Portland, OR convention [more than forty years later] that we learned the transport crashed and killed General Nakazono."[80] Consequently, Phase Three was a flop. The Japanese attacked Yunnan province only once, an

Wallace Weber in the cockpit of his P-38. Weber claimed a probable victory over a Tojo on a mission to Huangpu, 10 September 1943. Jerry Doughty

A reconnaissance photo of Japanese ships steaming into Hong Kong harbor. Robert Neely

attack on Kunming parried by twenty-four P-40s and P-38s on the 27th, and attacked Chennault's other bases only a handful of times. They were not successful in inflicting any meaningful damage on the American air force. During the entire offensive, the Japanese estimated they destroyed 124 American aircraft, but in reality, the 14th Air Force lost only forty-five in aerial combat and only twenty-eight destroyed on the ground during the entirety of 1943.[81]

For the 449th, business continued as usual with a number of dive- and skip-bombing missions and scrambles during the remainder of September. On the 10th, P-38s flew another mission to Huangpu. This time, four Lightnings dive-bombed the target while two more acted as top cover. Lieutenant Lee Gregg was one of the latter and was credited with one A6M "Zeke," while Lieutenant Wallace Weber, his wingman, was credited with a probable victory over a Tojo. Ki-44s from the 85th Sentai led by Captain Wakamatsu pursued the P-38s but claimed none destroyed or damaged.[82] On the 12th, Lewden Enslen, promoted to captain at the beginning of the month, led a flight to hit shipping near Hong Kong. Attacking at low level, the P-38s sent a bomb into a five hundred foot steamer. The bomb came out the other side and destroyed an adjacent vessel. They hit another five-hundred-foot ship before Enslen led them out of the target area to the southwest. As they approached Sanzao Island near Macau, however, he spotted a Japanese destroyer and decided to attack it. Lee Gregg approached the warship only ten feet above the water before bouncing up to sweep the deck with machine gun and cannon fire.[83] With the crew thus distracted, the rest of the P-38s raked the vessel until an explosion rocked the destroyer amidships. The Lightnings left it burning.[84] Meanwhile, Japanese anti-aircraft fire had hit Lieutenant Rockwell's aircraft, knocking out one of his engines. He flew for some time on the other engine before that also gave out. He attempted to bail out, but the canopy collapsed on him and he died when his P-38 crashed and exploded.[85] His loss was another that was keenly felt.

Though Chennault did not know of Nakazono's death, he did notice a fundamental shift in operations. By the end of the summer of 1943, the 14th Air Force was on the offensive, with most aerial engagements taking place over the enemy's airfields instead of Chennault's.[86] The JAAF's greatest effort to destroy the 14th Air Force had failed. Chennault would soon be free to demonstrate the full offensive capability of his small force.

CHAPTER THREE

The Yangzi River Mission

During World War II, merchant shipping became the lifeblood of Japan's expanding empire. Japan possessed little in the way of natural resources and depended on material imported from its conquered territories. Oil from the East Indies, rubber and tin from Malaya, iron ore from Hainan, tungsten from China, and bauxite from Indochina, all traveled by merchant ships along the coast of China to Japan. In turn, Japan shipped troops and war material abroad. Thus every ship sunk, whether it carried troops or raw materials, was a blow to Japan's war effort. Aircraft based at Shanghai, Taiwan, Hong Kong, Hainan, and Indochina protected ships hugging the coast of China in an attempt to neutralize the American submarine threat. As early as September 1942, however, General Stilwell directed Chennault to make destruction of Japanese shipping his third priority, focusing first on air defense and strikes against Japanese airbases.[1] By August 1943, Chennault finally had the resources to conduct all three missions, and directed his B-24s and B-25s against ports and shipping along the coast from Shanghai to Haiphong.[2] This effectively put Japan's merchant shipping in a vice, trapped between American submarines in the east and the 14th Air Force in the west.

China's interior waterways were also an important means of transportation. Because China lacked modern roads and Japanese-held railroads were often incomplete or of inadequate capacity, the Japanese depended heavily on China's navigable rivers. The Yangzi, which flows from the Tibetan Plateau over three thousand miles to meet the Pacific Ocean just north of Shanghai, was the most important river in China. Though its precipitous gorges made an impressive defensive barrier against a thrust on Chongqing, the river was navigable to five thousand ton merchant ships to the Japanese-occupied ports at Anqing, Jiujiang, and Hankou (ten to fifteen thousand ton ships during the summer, when the river's depth at Hankou could increase from six feet to fifty).[3] In addition to merchant ships, the Yangzi hosted steamers, launches, barges, junks, and sampans, all capable of carrying raw materials to China's coastal ports for shipment to Japan or troops and weaponry into the interior of China. Chinese guerilla outposts along the river provided the 14th Air Force with intelligence on shipping which allowed it to concentrate its few aircraft against the most inviting targets.[4] As the JAAF shifted to a defensive posture in the fall of 1943, Chennault increasingly turned his fighters and medium bombers to interdicting river traffic.

Poor weather during much of September and October, however, kept the 449th grounded. According to Tom Harmon, "When the weather in China gets bad it doesn't fool. It really means it, and is likely to mean it for days on end. When the weather is bad in China, even the birds don't fly."[5] In lieu of missions, the squadron underwent several administrative changes. On 17 September, Forward Echelon Headquarters assigned Captain Palmer to a staff job. Captain Lewden Enslen assumed command in his place. Harmon noted, "The whole squadron breathed a sigh of relief," because, "we knew him and respected his ability."[6] On 2 October, official word came down that the 449th would be permanently assigned to the 51st Fighter Group. The 51st had been in combat in India since the beginning of the war and its 16th Fighter Squadron had been on detached service in China since 1942. In September 1943, the 80th Fighter Group arrived in India from the United States, freeing the 51st to move to China.[7] The 449th was the only twin-engine squadron in the group; the others were equipped with P-40s, and later, P-51s.

On 1 October, the weather cleared enough for one mission: a bomber escort to Haiphong. Liberators from the 308th bombed the power plant, warehouses, and docks, but two formations of Ki-43s from the 25th and 33rd Sentais intercepted them as they turned to leave the target area. The fighter escort of P-38s and P-40s charged into the first formation, breaking up a frontal assault and shooting down two of the attacking enemy. Lieutenant John Opsvig shot down one enemy fighter, while Lieutenant Henry Wood of the 75th Fighter Squadron went head-to-head with another. Major Henry Brady, a flight

Sampans on a river near Mengzi, China. Both Chinese and Japanese used sampans to carry supplies along China's waterways. George Brabec

American GIs on a Sampan in southern China. Jerry Ravenscroft

commander in one of the B-24s, saw the P-40 close with the Oscar. The Japanese fighter exploded, and the P-40 went down smoking. Altogether, three P-40s went down before the second formation of Oscars engaged the B-24s in a forty minute running battle. Wood successfully bailed-out of his fighter, but was captured by the Japanese. The other two P-40 pilots, both Chinese, went down with their ships.[8] Six days later, ten B-24s with P-40 and P-38 escort returned to Haiphong and destroyed a cement plant without loss.[9] The weather subsequently closed in across much of East China.

It was during this time that the 449th came to know and love its contract chaplain, Father Joseph Cosgrove. Father Cosgrove was an Irish Catholic from New England who had previously maintained a small mission south of Lingling. He was nearly fluent in Chinese, which became a major asset to the squadron. More importantly, he took as his personal responsibility the spiritual welfare of every man in the squadron, whether he was Catholic, Protestant, Jewish, or agnostic (Cosgrove did not believe there was such a thing as a true atheist). Accordingly, he treated everyone equally, and did not express condemnation for some of their unwholesome behavior. He believed that creating functional relationships with those around him was the best way to share Christ's love. Though not Catholic himself, Buck Burris remembered Father Cosgrove fondly and corresponded with him after the war. He commented that Cosgrove "was out to help everybody. He was just a good guy."[10]

One day, Ryan Moon insisted that Cosgrove fly piggy back with him in a P-38. The Lightning's cockpit was spacious enough that another man could just barely squeeze in behind the pilot so long as he did not wear a parachute. Cosgrove watched as Moon flew first with the flight surgeon, Major John Burns. Moon put the fighter through its paces, first performing two barrel rolls, which sent the watching priest's heart into his stomach. As Moon dove at high speed from thirteen thousand feet, Cosgrove's jaw dropped. He felt absolutely sick when Moon's subsequent buzz-job nearly took the top off the alert shack. The chaplain's apprehension was evident as his turn drew near. To his obvious relief, Captain Enslen offered to fly him in Moon's place.[11]

The poor weather throughout much of October made for an otherwise boring month. On the 17th, a lone transport plane descended out of the overcast and landed at Lingling, forced down because of the weather. Included among the passengers were CBS commentator Eric Sevareid and *New York Times* correspondent Brooks Atkinson. Atkinson, "a small man with wiry black hair, a thin moustache and a pipe, and a warm, likeable personality,"[12] was not initially happy at the diversion, but decided to make the best of the situation and write a story about the P-38 squadron "near our fighting air front in China." He was thrilled to meet Captain Enslen and Captain Moon, the "redheaded ... chief of operations," and spent much time with them over the following two days. Atkinson noted, "This outfit has swept into an isolated part of China, where they live in a muddy compound amid water-filled rice paddies. Even indoors it was cold, for there is no glass in the windows, no stoves in the rooms."[13] In a letter to his parents, Enslen affirmed that "It has become very brisk these days: we have ... no panes ... in our windows, so the wind blows through the room unrestrained." Consequently, "day and night, the warmest place to be is in bed; thus we have developed the habit of early to bed and late to rise – when possible. That's the only redemption for rainy, wet weather – it permits late sleeping."[14] It was not until the 25th that the Chinese installed glass in the windows and wood and charcoal stoves in the rooms, making it "very cozy."[15]

Lockheed technical representative Rex Martin took this photo of several of the officers playing cards at Lingling during a spell of bad weather. From left to right: Captain Carl N. Hutter, Lewden Enslen, Lee Gregg, Kendall Dowis, and Lieutenant King M. Wu. Lewden Osborn

Atkinson was impressed with the 449th and relished the opportunity "to discover how American pilots live in the isolated interior of China." For their part, the men did their best to convince him that the P-38 was "the best fighter in the world," informing him that while the maneuverable Japanese may have an advantage in a dogfight, "in diving from a position of top cover ... the P-38 is invincible." The night before Atkinson departed, he, Enslen, and Moon walked out from watching a movie and, looking up, saw stars in the sky. "It's clearing up," said Enslen, "maybe the Japs will come over tomorrow." "I hope so," Moon replied, "Just give us one good crack at those Japs." While the weather did not clear enough for a mission, Atkinson's transport was able to leave the next day. His accidental stopover left him feeling very positive about the war effort.[16]

The weather did not break again until 28 October, when the 449th flew another uneventful escort mission.[17] The next day, Captain Enslen and his men planned a mission to attack Japanese shipping near the port of Jiujiang. The area was familiar to the 449th and was known to have little flak and few fighters. Nine P-38s would take part in the mission: five dive-bombers, each carrying a single five-hundred-pound bomb, and four fighters to provide top cover. Five-hundred-pound demolition bombs were the weapon of choice against river traffic, as a direct hit was usually fatal, and even a near miss could sink or severely damage a large river craft.[18] Lieutenant Schultz led the top cover flight with Lieutenant Robins on his wing. Lieutenant Tom Taylor led the second element and Harmon flew tail-end Charlie. Captain Enslen led the dive-bombers; Robinson, Rea, Weber, and Dowis filled out his section.[19] Enslen had a reputation for being the best navigator in the squadron. Harmon noted that when he led a mission, "we always knew that we would have no trouble reaching our target and getting home."[20] By the time Enslen finished planning the mission, however, it was late in the afternoon and they would not have been able to return before dark. Instead, he rescheduled it for the next day.

On the morning of 30 October, Lieutenant Robinson blew-out his nose-wheel tire on takeoff, but nonetheless managed to struggle into the air. After dropping his bomb in the mountains, he turned back to base and made a belly-landing. The other eight aircraft continued north to Hengyang, where they topped-off their fuel tanks and talked with a couple P-40 pilots who reported encountering a patrol of two Japanese fighters over the river.[21]

As the Yangzi flows east from the Sichuan gorges through Jiujiang, it rolls gently across the lowland plain, reaching a mile wide at Hankou, bordered by occasional hills and mountains, numerous lakes, and fed by several tributaries. The P-38s flew north beyond the river and then turned around so they would hit Jiujiang on their way home.[22] The dive-bombers flew at six thousand feet and the top cover flew at eight thousand. They found only a lone steamer ten miles from Jiujiang, however, frantically leaving the seemingly deserted port. Most steamers ranged from fifty to two hundred feet in length and transported coal from China's interior to Shanghai. To the 449th, the ship was an inviting target. The dive-bombers approached the vessel from the east at 1110 hours, while the top cover weaved

New York Times correspondent Brooks Atkinson lights his pipe as he waits in the damp, cool China weather for transportation. 14th Air Force Association

overhead. Once over the target, Captain Enslen chopped his throttle, raised his nose to bleed off airspeed, and winged-over into a sixty- to eighty-degree dive.[23]

Enslen released his bomb at two thousand feet and was pulling out of his dive when Schultz's voice called out on the radio: "Six Zeros at three o'clock!" The top cover flight was in a slight turn to the left, heading west. Harmon scanned the sky off his right wing and sure enough saw the fighters in the distance, one thousand feet above him. He reached down to release his external fuel tanks and simultaneously rolled left to get a good look behind him. There he saw six more fighters coming around from behind Lushan, a nearly five-thousand-foot, monolithic mountain rising up just southeast of Jiujiang. He called, "Six more Zeros at nine o'clock."[24] The lone steamer, the deserted port, and the perfect positioning of the enemy fighters all pointed to a trap. Japanese spies, prevalent throughout much of China, probably transmitted details of the raid after it was delayed the previous day. The fighters belonged to the 25th Sentai, which was the principal Japanese fighter unit in China. In late September the 33rd was transferred to Burma, leaving the 85th and 25th Sentais, based at Guangzhou and Hankou respectively (though one chutai of the 85th was based at Hankou until February 1944), as the only JAAF fighter units in China.[25] Now the Oscars of the 25th barreled in to reap the harvest of their well-laid ambush.

Lewden Enslen and Stuart Rea were in a gentle left-hand turn to rendezvous with the top cover, regaining altitude after

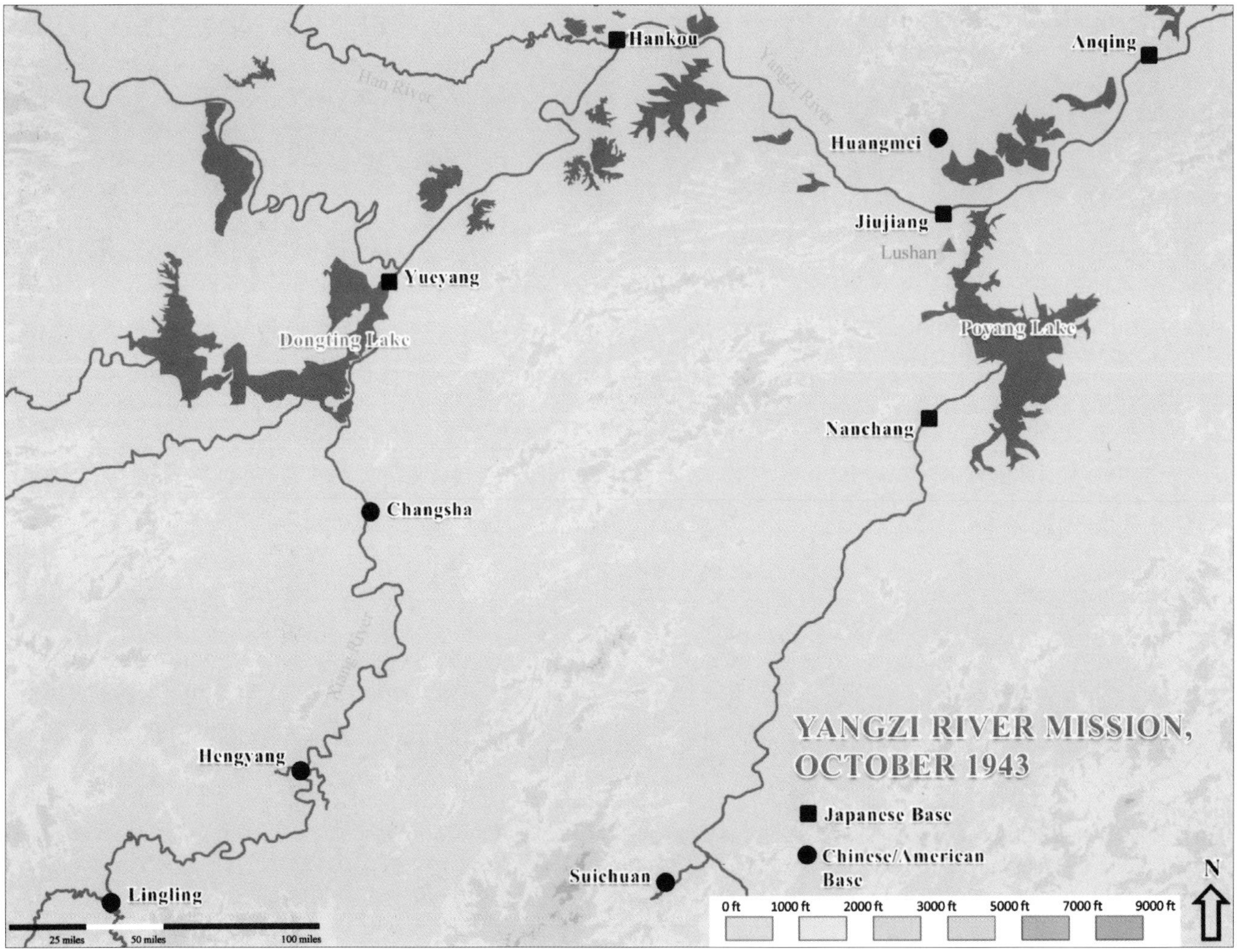

their bomb run, when two Oscars dove onto Enslen's tail and fired into his right engine. Rea was 150 yards behind, but "before I could shoot they had broken off and Captain Enslen's right engine exploded." Enslen's P-38 went into a spiraling dive to the right. Rea last saw his airplane at eighteen hundred feet "with the right engine enveloped in flames."[26] Schultz, Robins, and Taylor dove to assist. Alone, Harmon turned head-on into the fighters coming from the left and fired a short burst. The Japanese scattered in all directions rather than go head-to-head with the P-38. Three dove to the left and two dove to the right. The sixth fighter turned left and dove alone. Harmon was already lined up with the lone fighter and fired a short burst. The machine gun bullets slammed into the Oscar's engine and a cannon shell blew off the canopy. The smoking plane plummeted toward the ground.[27]

Meanwhile, Schultz, Robins, Taylor, and the dive-bombers desperately tried to fight their way out of a massive dogfight. Schultz glanced back and saw Robins on his right wing as he climbed into the Oscars. He got on the tail of one of the Japanese that shot down Enslen and fired a short burst. The pilot took immediate evasive action – right into his wingman. Both ships fell burning from the sky and Schultz claimed two victories for the price of one. Another fighter pulled onto Schultz's tail, but Robins shot it off, himself getting shot down in the process.[28] Schultz saw an Oscar dive by on the right and, looking back, noticed that Robins was missing. Looking left, he noticed Taylor and Harmon were also gone. He was alone in the wild mess of Oscars.[29]

According to Harmon:

> The air now sounded like a million buzzing bees, as the motors wound up and the ships started around each other. Added to the infernal noise came at irregular intervals the sharp brrrrrrrr-upp, brup, brrr-upp of the machine guns of all the ships. I didn't see our dive bombers come off the target, so I climbed back looking for another Zero.[30]

Harmon looked down and saw a Japanese fighter two hundred yards away, climbing over a small lake. He dove and gained speed rapidly before pulling into a steep climb behind it. He fired a short burst, which tore off part of the fighter's wing. Pressing the attack, he closed to fifty yards, where he could clearly discern the mottled green paint scheme, colored tail stripe, and big red "meatballs" on the wings.[31] He let loose another burst and the fighter "went up like a matchbox."[32]

As Harmon nosed-over from his ascent, he heard "a sharp ring against the armor plating behind me." Though his initial action in turning into the enemy fighters to break-up their attack was tactically sound, not to mention very brave, he made a grave error in pressing the attack without a wingman and in bleeding off his airspeed: "I made a beaut of a mistake. ... I was concentrating so hard on getting this Zero that I forgot I was climbing."[33] Rather than diving out of the fight, Harmon made himself into an easy target.[34] A second shot immediately followed the first and a third passed between his legs and hit the gas primer, blowing his legs off the rudder pedals, tearing his pants off at the knees, and lighting the gas line on fire. He attempted to put the fire out with his gloves while his P-38 headed straight for the ground. However, the flames only grew more intense, so he released his straps and jettisoned the canopy at five thousand feet. Immediately the suction from the prop wash pulled him clear of his aircraft and he pulled the ripcord:

> The first sight that met my eyes after I had come to was a P-38 going by, hell-bent for election towards home with two Zeros on his tail throwing enough lead at him to sink a battleship. It was Schultz. I was sure I recognized that Golden Eagle. ... Schultz made off for home praying like a man with the devil on his tail.[35]

Schultz saw Harmon's parachute drifting down a thousand feet above the ground as he dove to the north, away from the marauding Oscars. He heaved his Lightning to the right and the Oscars overshot, without a chance to fire at him or the parachute.[36] Suddenly Harmon noticed two more Japanese fighters circling him. He had heard tale of Japanese aircraft strafing American pilots as they drifted helplessly to earth and thus played dead, hanging limp in his harness and "setting the world's record for 'Hail Mary's.'" The ploy seemed to work, as neither Japanese plane fired a shot and Harmon landed safely in Poyang Lake southeast of Jiujiang.[37] Schultz turned back around to the south, but could not find where Harmon had landed.[38]

The 449th claimed six Japanese fighters shot down, two by Harmon, two by Schultz, one by Robins, and one by Rea, while losing four P-38s. The 25th Sentai, however, claimed eight Lightnings for the loss of only one Oscar, and noted that P-38s were even easier to destroy than P-40s![39] In reality, the Japanese shot down Harmon, Robins, Taylor, and Enslen. Lieutenant Mamoru Inomata, the pilot of the downed Oscar, was killed in action.

The disparity on both sides causes one to wonder over the integrity of victory claims. However, several factors complicated the process of making accurate claims in China, the dogfight over Jiujiang being an atypical exaggeration of these. John Alison, fighter ace from the 75th Squadron, asserted that victories were confirmed "Somewhat haphazardly." He went on to say that fighters in China often did not carry gun cameras, "... and so you had to take people's word for some of the victories."[40] Even when they did carry cameras, the film was not always helpful, especially with early-model P-38s, where vibration problems made the cameras almost useless.

Ki-43-II Oscar of the 25th Sentai which served as the mainstay of Japanese fighter strength in central China throughout much of the war. Yusuho Izawa via Steve Blake

Additionally, in a dogfight like that over Jiujiang, confusion abounds. Often, several pilots unwittingly shoot at the same target, and damaged fighters trailing smoke and flames split-s, or dive away from the fight, looking all the world like they are going down. It does not help that records on both sides are incomplete: the Japanese destroyed many of theirs at the end of the war, now relying on personal memoirs and fragmented official documents, and Chennault was known as one of the worst administrators in the AAF. Not mentioned in Japanese records, for example, are how many fighters were damaged, and, similarly, how many they wrote-off as scrap or spare parts when they returned. As an example, though the 14th Air Force lost only seventy-two aircraft to enemy action in all of 1943, between May and August of that year, ninety-eight P-40s were rendered unserviceable: destroyed by enemy action, lost in accidents, or just worn-out.[41] This sort of undocumented attrition eventually led to the downfall of the JAAF, when, in 1944 and 1945, it could no longer keep its units supplied with enough replacement parts or new aircraft.

John Alison also mentioned that, while there were instances of over-claims, there were examples of under-claims as well, such as when Chinese spotters found airplanes that nobody declared to have shot down. He maintained that, when you take all the factors into account, victory claims balance out and serve as a useful estimation of the performance of a fighter unit.[42]

Tom Harmon after having returned from his thirty-two day ordeal. Standing, from left to right, are Doctor Burns, the flight surgeon, Lieutenant Murphy, Harmon, Chaplain Cosgrove, and Captain Ryan Moon. Kneeling are lieutenants Robertson, Machado, and Lynn. Michael Bates

Thirty-two days after the confusing air battle over Jiujiang, the men were playing softball when Tom Harmon stepped off a C-47 at Lingling, legs, wrists, and face badly burned, but alive nonetheless. He was outfitted in the cotton winter clothing of a Chinese soldier, which, along with his severe burns, made him barely recognizable. When he had landed in the lake, he had ducked underneath his parachute as the Oscars made three passes overhead. After the Oscars departed, a Chinese sampan set out to pull him from the water. A Japanese soldier charged the vessel as it left the shore, but a Chinese guerrilla on a nearby hillside calmly stood up, took aim, and dispatched the Japanese. The sampan crew pulled Harmon out of the water, and, noting the watchful Japanese nearby, had him exchange clothing with one of them. The Chinese then played a sort of shell game, transferring Harmon from sampan to sampan eight or nine times until he finally reached shore. He was then carried from farmhouse to farmhouse in advance of the vengeful Japanese, until finally at dusk, Chinese guerrillas loaded him in a sedan chair and carried him into the mountains.[43]

For ten days, the Chinese carried Harmon to safety in advance of aggressive Japanese pursuit. During this time, no medical aid was available for his burns save for applications of cold tea. On 3 December, Harmon's rescuers delivered him to Hengyang, where he boarded a plane for Lingling.[44] Captain Moon, Major Burns, and Father Cosgrove were the first on hand to welcome him back and the chaplain gave a thanksgiving Mass on his behalf that afternoon.[45] Robins, despite suffering a broken back, also eventually made it back to the squadron, but Tom Taylor and Lewden Enslen were not so lucky. Taylor, the epitome of "a fightin' Texan,"[46] according to Tom Harmon, was listed as missing in action. Schultz heard rumors that he crash-landed and "shot it out with the Japs on the ground, he was that kind of boy."[47] Enslen's P-38 crashed just south of

Enslen's poor condition following his crash-landing is immediately apparent in this photo he requested during his brief period of consciousness in Huangmei. Lewden Osborn

Bottom left: Enslen and his wife, Alleen at Yosemite National Park before he departed for China. Lewden Osborn

Bottom right: Mrs. Alleen Enslen and her daughter Patty Ann in September 1943. Patty Ann never had the opportunity to meet her father. Lewden Osborn

Huangmei, a small town approximately twenty miles north of Jiujiang. Eleven Chinese farmers rushed to pull him from his airplane and evacuate him by boat across a nearby lake in advance of a Japanese armored car sent to capture him. The crash had left Enslen unconscious and severely injured. He regained consciousness the next day and told the Chinese his name. The local doctors did everything they could for him, but with only primitive medical aid, he lapsed into unconsciousness and died ten days later.[48]

Lewden Enslen left behind his wife and a daughter he had never met, Patty Ann. When he learned of his daughter's birth in the first mail he received in China, he wrote his wife that he was "the happiest, proudest man in the Army."[49] Schultz recalled that within five minutes, "we were all smoking cigars which he had saved for the occasion. He was tremendously proud."[50] Enslen had written his wife that, "We three will have marvelous adventures touring the country in our little blue car when I get back. Sooner or later, you know, I am sure to come home. And the longer I stay over here, the nearer it brings that certainty."[51] One of his neighbors in Springfield predicted that Enslen would "come home a captain, maybe a major, a hero with medals and stories and memories."[52] Unfortunately, this was not to be. Not only did he not return alive, but the Chinese could not return his body to friendly territory. General Chennault explained in a letter to Mrs. Enslen, "He was forced down in an area where his return involved an excessively long and extremely dangerous trip."[53]

The magistrate of the Huangmei District, Tian Jiangchang, took responsibly for the burial of his remains. On the morning of 12 November, the Chinese dressed him in new clothes and placed him in a vermilion coffin. Over four thousand troops and civilians attended the funeral to pay their respects to a man they considered a hero. They built a brick wall around the grave and eventually placed a marker in front that read: "American pilot En-Sa-Len, Leader of 8th Corps [sic] 14th Air Force. This gravestone erected in his memory by Mayor Tian Jiangchang, of the village of Huangmei."[54] Chennault explained to Mrs. Enslen that while some of the details of the ceremony may have appeared strange, "They are merely indicative of the highest respect and the method by which the Chinese pay high honors."[55] After the war, Enslen's body was moved to the American military cemetery in Shanghai before the American Graves Registration Service finally transferred it to Springfield National Cemetery, Missouri, in October 1947.[56]

Father Cosgrove wrote to Mrs. Enslen that, "The death of Captain Enslen came as a severe shock to us all." While he believed that Enslen "was prepared to meet his God and Creator," he still felt as if he had "lost my own brother."[57] Bruce Schultz felt a great deal of guilt. He explained, "Lewden was the only one lost in his flight while I was the only one not shot down in mine. ... I couldn't get down to help ... there were too many ... how come they didn't get me will always be a mystery as they loaded me with holes but none in a vital spot."[58]

Meanwhile, when Harmon finally returned, he wanted to stay with the squadron during his recovery, but Major Burns thought it best for him to go to the hospital at 14th Air Force Headquarters in Kunming. Upon later returning to the squadron,

Enslen's grave in Huangmei. Over four thousand Chinese attended his funeral. His body was moved to Springfield, Missouri, in 1947. Lewden Osborn

Harmon was called into the commander's office and given his orders to return to the United States. He returned to America in early 1944. He did not fly any missions after the one in which the Japanese shot him down.

According to "Tex" Hill, the famous fighter ace and leader of the 23rd Fighter Group:

> When [Harmon] returned to the States, the pilot was interviewed by the press – and, to the shock and horror of his companions back in the theater, he revealed the name of a village along the escape route he had used in China. Sure enough, Japanese intelligence picked up the story and sent troops into the village, where they butchered every man, woman, and child.[59]

It is hard to say whether this accusation is true, but it was a widely circulated rumor in the CBI Theater. Newsmen certainly did interview Harmon when he arrived in the United States, but newspaper and magazine articles claimed he would not give any details of his escape, because "It would just mean reprisals by the Japanese and maybe a rope around some other pilot's neck."[60] This is not to say that the Japanese did not deduce his likely escape route from other information. For example, after the air battle on 30 October, American newspapers reported Tom Harmon missing in action near Jiujiang. Likewise, when he arrived in the United States the media reported his survival. From these reports, the Japanese knew the approximate date Harmon was shot down, and they knew the location, so it seems reasonable that they could have deduced his escape route. The move was not unheard of by the Japanese. After the Doolittle Raid, Japanese troops killed an estimated two hundred thousand Chinese civilians in villages through which the raiders passed.[61] Buck Burris thought the rumor was particularly unfortunate as he regarded Harmon with great respect. Father Cosgrove thought the rumor could be attributed to the fact that "Harmon was a figurehead in the public's eye," because of his prewar football fame, "and the public is paradoxically always ready to tear to pieces one of its own idols."[62] Whether or not Harmon was directly responsible for such a massacre, the rumors cast a shadow on his time in China.

Despite the heavy losses suffered by the 449th, the dive-bombers managed to sink the Japanese steamer. In fact, river interdiction was generally effective and, by the end of 1943, resulted in the Japanese restricting large river vessels to movement only by night.[63] The 30 October mission, however, demonstrated that even though the JAAF was no longer engaged in a concerted effort to destroy the 14th Air Force, it was a potent foe not to be discounted. Clearly, the 449th would have to exercise caution in the months to come.

Taiwan

The 449th was hit hard by the loss of Captain Enslen. If the squadron had thought it was plagued by back luck before, the 30 October mission brought morale to a new low. Captain Ryan Moon, the squadron operations officer, temporarily took command. While the trying events of October 1943 transpired, however, two old hands returned to the war in China. According to the 15 October 1943 issue of the *CBI Roundup*:

> After more than a year's absence from the CBI aerial front, two famed fighter pilots of the legendary American Volunteer Group this week returned to the 14th Air Force.
>
> They are Lt. Col. David L. (Tex) Hill, who shot down 12 enemy planes as a member of the AVG and four more wearing the uniform of an Army pilot, and Lt. Col. George B. McMillan, who got four bombers as an AVGer.
>
> Hill and McMillan returned to find the 14th Air Force a booming, offensive organization in stark contrast to the valiant shoestring operators of the AVG.
>
> "It looks good," said McMillan, "to see planes go down the runway to do some striking from this end."
>
> McMillan first came to the Far East in September, 1941. He landed at Rangoon from which base he destroyed three enemy bombers. As the Jap tide swept up Burma, his squadron was transferred to China. There he shot down his fourth bomber. During February, 1942, he made a trip to Africa to ferry back new fighters and thereby missed some of the AVG's best scraps, which has always been a source of regret to him. In July, 1942, the Army Air Forces took over from the war-torn AVG. McMillan, then an operations officer, remained with other AVG members to pass on their battle-proven knowledge to the new Army pilots.
>
> Hill remained as a squadron commander with the China Air Task Force until December, 1942. He helped activate the hard-hitting pursuit group which is still in operation in China with the 14th Air Force.
>
> The Texan (San Antonio) arrived in Rangoon in the early fall of 1941. "My first offensive fight," he recalls, "was in January against a Jap base in Thailand. There were three of us and we destroyed seven planes on the ground and knocked three confirmed from the air. The plane I destroyed was an I-97 fighter.
>
> "I had several good days with the AVG. Once while my squadron was stationed in Rangoon, a formation of Jap bombers escorted by plenty of fighters came over. Our first flight drew off the fighter cover and my flight was free to go after the bombers. There were seven of them and we made a perfect score. I managed to get one. Then I flew over the route their fighters normally returned and caught a straggler. I don't think he knew what hit him."
>
> Hill was born in Korea, the son of missionary parents. He graduated from the Navy Flying School in November, 1939. He served on the aircraft carriers *Saratoga*, *Yorktown* and *Ranger*. He was discharged in June, 1941, and sailed immediately to fight for the AVG, with whom he participated in more than 100 combat missions. He was subsequently commissioned a major in the Army Air Forces.
>
> Both Hill and McMillan were assigned to the AAF Proving Ground Command at Eglin Field, Fla., before returning to China.[64]

General Chennault assigned Tex to command the famed 23rd Fighter Group and George McMillan to a staff job with the 51st Fighter Group. On 9 November 1943, Chennault made him commander of the 449th. Captain Moon reverted to his role as operations officer.

Lieutenant Colonel "Mac" McMillan immediately captured the respect and admiration of the 449th. He was a tall, lean man and every inch a fighter pilot – "an old China hand who knew the country and hated the Japs."[65] With his striking features and thin, sharp mustache, he looked like a movie star. He was a 1938 graduate from the Citadel. At twenty-seven years old he was an experienced and seasoned pilot. He learned from Chennault how best to exploit Japanese weaknesses as a flight leader in the 3rd Pursuit Squadron, "Hells Angels," who defended Burma and China from Japanese bombers. He also brought a unique leadership style to the squadron, heavily influenced by his time under Chennault in the AVG and with Tex Hill at the AAF Proving Ground. Buck Burris remembered him as a straightforward man who always stood up for his men:

> His attitude was "Don't talk about it, hell, let's get it done." ... He was a good man. As long as you were straight with him, he would protect you until hell froze over. He was respected by the enlisted people; he was respected by the officers. All you had to do was be straight with him and you were okay. Just don't give him any funny stories; he didn't buy those. You could rob a bank and if you told him you did it, he'd probably try to get you out of it. But if you tried to lie to him, he didn't like that too well. I had the greatest respect for him.[66]

McMillan treated his men as capable adults and soldiers, always expecting their finest effort. His men worked hard so as not to let him down. Father Cosgrove remembered him as a man who led from the front; "first to roar down the runway and first to turn into enemy fighters when sighted. I never saw a pilot who so relished combat with the enemy." The priest kidded him that he must be Irish. "Irish be damned, Padre," McMillan replied. "I'm Scotch, and a Scotchman will lick a harp any

Above: Legendary Flying Tigers ace Tex Hill steps into the cockpit of his P-51B Bullfrog on his second tour of duty in China. Tex led the famous Thanksgiving Day Raid on Taiwan, 25 November 1943. National Archives

Below: George B. McMillan with the American Volunteer Group in 1941/42. Steve Blake

day." McMillan's experience and leadership breathed new life into the 449th The men felt confident with such a leader in charge. Chennault remembered McMillan as one of his most outstanding squadron commanders. Lt. David Williams stated, " I could not say more and mean more than to say ... I would ride his wing any day, any where." According to Jim Hyde, "He was a great guy."[67]

The "booming, offensive organization" Hill and McMillan returned to was still no larger than the Japanese air force in China and required accurate intelligence to pit its limited resources against the weak points of the enemy. While the air raid warning net was an important tool for defensive operations, it proved of little use in planning offensive missions. For this purpose, Chennault used aerial photoreconnaissance. He realized the utility of this method from the early days of the AVG, when he requested pilot Erik Shilling to convert one of the group's P-40 fighters into a photoreconnaissance machine. As the number of offensive missions increased throughout 1942-43, Chennault requested, and obtained, a detachment of two or three F-4 Lightning (a modified P-38 fighter) reconnaissance aircraft from the 9th Photo Reconnaissance Squadron in India. Fighter pilots from the 23rd Fighter Group flew the photo planes, including Frank Schiel, AVG veteran and commander of the 74th Fighter Squadron, who got lost in poor weather and died when his F-4 flew into the side of a mountain in December 1942.

With the creation of the 14th Air Force and the arrival of more bombers and fighters in the spring and summer of 1943, Chennault realized he needed more reconnaissance planes and with them, specially trained crews. Though a theater the size of China would normally require a photoreconnaissance group, the logistical problems made it impossible; Chennault requested one squadron. The 21st Photo Reconnaissance Squadron, nicknamed "China Falcons," trained in Colorado Springs, Colorado, and arrived in China during the summer of 1943. Ed Penick, a pilot with the 21st, had just arrived when he witnessed the 21 August air battle over Hengyang. To make this squadron capable of covering four million square miles of territory, Chennault divided it into four independent flights. Each flight possessed anywhere from one to five aircraft and two to seven pilots along with maintenance crews, photo interpreters, and camera repair specialists. Each flight would operate out of a different airfield and be responsible for a specific geographic area. Headquarters Flight was based at Kunming and was responsible for Burma and Indochina. "A" Flight flew from Chengdu, future base of the B-29 Superfortresses, and was responsible for northeastern China (including Manchuria). "B" Flight was based at Guilin and was responsible for Hong Kong and central China. "C" Flight was based farthest east, at Suichuan, and was responsible for eastern China and the outlying islands.[68]

The new F-5s (modified P-38Js) at Suichuan were particularly significant. Suichuan was 250 miles east of Guilin and provided the 14th Air Force with a field from which it could assail Japanese bases previously untouched by American planes. The most striking demonstration of Suichuan's potential occurred in early 1944, when Winfree Sordelett flew his F-5 on an epic eleven hour and forty minute photo mission from Suichuan to Nagasaki and Sasebo in southern Japan. Sordelett was so stiff from being crammed in the cockpit for such a long time that his crew had to lift him out when he returned from the mission. He was awarded the Distinguished Flying Cross for his achievement. Photoreconnaissance also aided shipping interdiction. Penick, commander of "C" Flight, remembered performing sea sweeps over the Straits of Taiwan during which he would mark the positions and headings of Japanese ships on a grid and use specially marked binoculars to estimate their speed. Naval intelligence personnel at Suichuan would radio this information to submarines in the Straits, which would track and sink the enemy vessels.

An F-5 reconnaissance Lightning over China in 1944. Note the camera bulges on the nose. Phil Schaff

In November 1943, Forward Echelon commander Casey Vincent ordered daily reconnaissance flights over the Japanese-held island of Taiwan. Japan used Taiwan as a base of supply and training not only for its units in China, but also for those in the Philippines and Southeast Asia. Prior to the fall of 1943, however, Taiwan was unscathed by Chennault's air force. P-40 Warhawks did not have sufficient range to make the long trip across the Taiwanese Straits, and Chennault did not have any bases far enough east to allow his B-25s to bomb the island. The new base at Suichuan, built by the hands of thousands of Chinese men, women, and children, and the arrival of sufficient numbers of long-range fighters, gave Chennault the tools he needed to finally strike.

Besides P-38s of the 449th, the 14th Air Force finally received long-range P-51 Mustangs. In fact, General Chennault sent Casey Vincent to Washington in October in part to plead for new P-51s. He returned to China on 3 November and was glad to see Tex Hill and Mac McMillan arrived in his absence.[69] He immediately sent Tex to India to lead a flight of P-51s over the Hump. John Alison "was in India with the 1st Air Commandos ready to fly a glider in behind the enemy lines," when his old friend Tex Hill "showed up at our forward base with a P-51 – a beautiful airplane." The P-51A used the same Allison engine as the P-40, but was aerodynamically a better airplane, forty-five miles per hour faster than the P-40 and with a 1,250-mile maximum range compared to the Warhawk's 750.[70] By mid-November, the 23rd Fighter Group's 76th Fighter Squadron at Guilin received sixteen old, second-hand P-51As, enough to make a significant mission possible.

Though November was another terrible month for weather, with low overcast preventing missions for the greater part of the month, reconnaissance flights to Taiwan during the first three weeks showed more than 150 Japanese planes on the northwest coast at Xinzhu Airdrome. According to Chennault, Xinzhu was "one of the largest bomber-modification and combat-training centers on [Taiwan]."[71] Unarmed, the F-5's only defense was its speed and altitude advantage. The F-5 flew above the island at thirty-five thousand feet, faster and higher than any Japanese fighter. Ed Penick remembered a particular mission to Taiwan during which a Japanese fighter scrambled to meet him. After photographing his objective, Penick dropped his external fuel tanks and sped for home. The enemy fighter could not climb high enough to reach his Lightning and was not fast enough to keep pace. Whenever the enemy pilot would lift his nose to fire, his fighter would slow down and Penick, cross-controlling to avoid being hit, would speed out of range. The Japanese fighter would drop his nose to catch up and then repeat the process. This happened for some time until the Japanese pilot finally gave up and returned home. Normally, the Japanese would not even bother responding to a lone photo recon aircraft.[72]

After reviewing the reconnaissance photos, Casey Vincent called a meeting with his staff at Guilin. Tex Hill remembered Vincent telling everyone: "You see before you a photograph of [Xinzhu] Airdrome on the island of [Taiwan]. There are eighty-eight bombers of the Imperial Japanese Navy lined up here, wingtip-to-wingtip. ... Tex, do you have any suggestions?" Tex could not help but answer: "Let's get 'em!" Vincent was eager to make a strike as soon as possible; he now had the capability and the weather seemed to be holding. He planned the mission for 25 November, Thanksgiving Day, and asked Tex to lead it. The surprise attack would consist of eight P-38s from the 449th, eight P-51s from the 76th, eight B-25s from the 11th Bomb Squadron, and six B-25s from the newly created Chinese-American Composite Wing (CACW). Vincent told Tex to maintain absolute secrecy: "Don't even tell the men where you're going until you're about to take off. This one can't leak out to the Japs." He also asked him to make a radio call on the return trip. If the mission was a failure, the code would be "New York," if a success, "San Antonio," per Tex Hill's suggestion.[73] Lieutenant Colonel McMillan, Captain Moon, and Lieutenants Schultz, Dowis, Yorston, and Rose were among the P-38 pilots on the mission. Despite McMillan's extensive experience fighting the Japanese, he humbly allowed Captain Palmer to return from Forward Echelon Headquarters to lead the squadron on the mission. In fact, rather than leading missions for his first several weeks as commander, he had been flying as Captain Moon's wingman to re-acclimate himself to combat in China.

Winfree Sordelett (right) with his F-5 reconnaissance Lightning at Suichuan. 14th Air Force Association

On 24 November, McMillan gathered the pilots together in the alert shack and told them to prepare for an overnight stay at an undisclosed airbase. He made sure to mention that they needed to bring their Mae West life jackets. According to Schultz, "We secretly flew to Suichuan at dusk. We told no one where we were going."[74] There they met the P-51s and B-25s and made last minute preparations for the next day's mission. At 0830 the following morning, Tex briefed the crews. The first plane took off at 0930 and the last at 1000. Captain Lee Manbeck had a problem with his P-51's hydraulic system and aborted.[75] The rest of the formation departed Suichuan to the

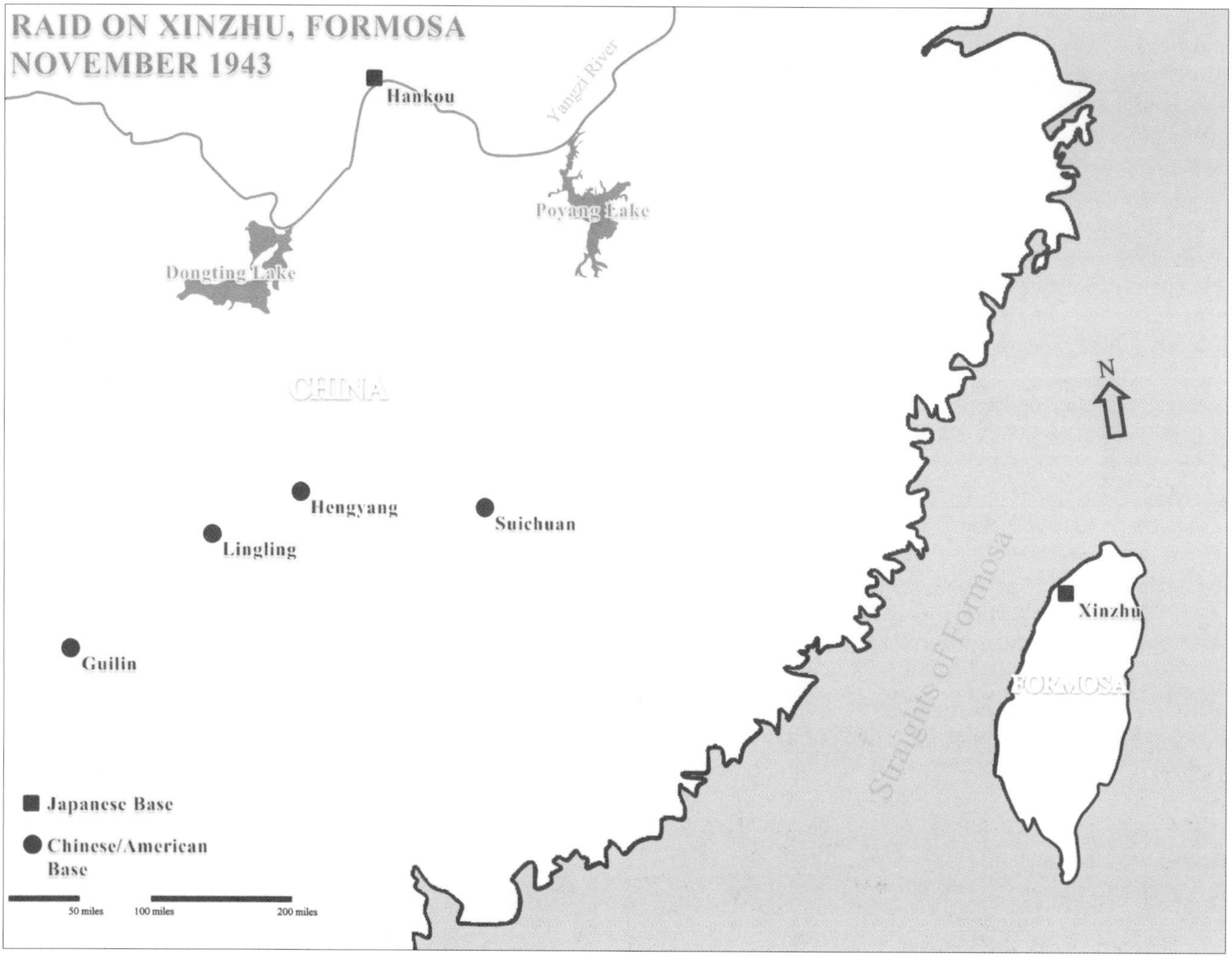

northeast, a feint toward Hankou to deceive any Japanese observers. After a period Hill judged to be sufficient, the formation turned to the southeast and, once over the Taiwanese Straits, descended to wave-top height. Twenty-nine American planes, a veritable armada by 14th Air Force standards, proceeded the 424 miles to Taiwan in complete radio silence. The B-25s led the way because they each carried a navigator.

As the coast of Taiwan came into view, the formation pulled up to one thousand feet. The P-38s charged ahead. Their job was to clear the way for the rest of the formation. The P-51s stayed with the bombers as close cover. Suddenly, a Japanese transport appeared to the south. Hill sent Captain Palmer to make sure the plane did not report the incoming Americans. The pilot probably thought the formation was friendly, however, because he took no evasive action as Palmer blasted him from the sky. The Lightnings crossed the coastline at 1200 hours, making the 449th Fighter Squadron the first American combat squadron over Taiwan. As they approached Xinzhu, a flight of Japanese bombers prepared to land, ground crews waiting with bombs and fuel. There were no Japanese fighters in the air yet, though Hill saw crews running to their planes. The P-38s roared into the enemy bombers and one by one sent them spinning into the ground.[76] Lieutenant Walter Rose pulled onto the tail of a Japanese dive-bomber and fired a few quick bursts, setting the engine on fire. As the pilot climbed out of the stricken plane to bail out, Rose could not decide whether or not to finish him off. Remembering Enslen and his other friends who had been killed, he stopped thinking and fired. The pilot slumped over, apparently dead.

Meanwhile, Bruce Schultz was heavily engaged:

> [I] caught a Jap in the landing pattern; he caught on fire and went straight in. I continued up and was head on with another plane that had a pronounced dihedral in the wings. I opened fire and I could see parts coming off his plane. He either had fallen across the stick or was trying to ram me. I continued to fire and large pieces flew off. I passed close underneath him and my windshield was covered with his oil. When I got back I claimed a Ju-87 Stuka.

After the mission Schultz was credited with shooting down a similar-looking Kawasaki Ki-32 Type 98 Light Bomber, codename "Mary," though he remained adamant that he shot down a Stuka. Other Lightnings claimed two Junkers transport planes. In fact, the American pilots made a common mistake in assuming a greater level of collaboration between the Axis powers than actually existed. For example, when eighty-five

Japanese bombers sank the British warships *Prince of Wales* and *Repulse* in December 1941, many startled British and Americans – convinced of the inferiority of Japanese pilots – insisted that German pilots must have led the mission.[77] In reality, besides sharing limited technical information, very little collaboration existed between Germany and Japan.

Bruce Schultz in the cockpit of Golden Eagle. Schultz claimed one transport and one dive-bomber shot down on 25 November 1943. Richard Maddox

Ed Penick with the F-5 Lightning he flew over Taiwan shortly after the 14th Air Force's Thanksgiving Day Raid. Ed Penick

After sweeping the sky clear of Japanese planes, the P-38s dove on the airfield in a strafing attack. The official tally was twelve destroyed in the air and ten destroyed on the ground, though an observer in the lead bomber counted fourteen parked planes on fire as his B-25 approached the target.[78] The 449th had certainly cleared the way for the rest of the formation – as the P-51s approached the field only two Zeros attempted to scramble. One of the Zeros pulled onto Rose's tail, but Tex Hill led his Mustangs into the fray and shot it down in short order. Lieutenant Dale Bell quickly shot down the other. The Japanese crews stared in shock as the B-25s flew line abreast one thousand feet over the field and dropped their fragmentation bombs. According to Hill:

> The enemy's world came apart in a hellish maelstrom of exploding gasoline and flying shrapnel. Planes disintegrated in all directions, as the bombers tore them up in a whirlwind of fury. The field became a sea of dark smoke, punctuated by flashes of detonating ordnance.

After the bombers passed, the fighters came around for a second strafing run. They expended the rest of their ammunition into the murky, smoke-filled field and then departed across the Straits to the northwest. Upon return to Suichuan, Tex Hill reported, "San Antonio – in a big way."[79]

The 14th Air Force claimed forty-six Japanese planes destroyed on the raid, though it was estimated that as many as fifty to sixty aircraft lay in ruins on Xinzhu. The Japanese Navy reported losing two A6M Zeros and two G3M Type 96 Land-based Attack Aircraft, codename "Nell," in the air, and twelve G3Ms on the ground. They also reported two Nells as severely damaged, eight moderately damaged, and eighteen as receiving minor damage.[80] The report did not state how many damaged aircraft the Japanese were able to make flyable nor how many JAAF aircraft the Americans destroyed or damaged on the raid. The cost was one bullet hole through the tail of a single P-38, minor damage from small arms fire to three of the B-25s, and minor damage to a P-51's wing that hit a tree whilst strafing.[81] The 449th claimed twelve destroyed in the air and ten on the ground. The squadron records mentioned the following: Captain Palmer destroyed an A6M Zeke and two unidentified aircraft types in the air; Lieutenant Colonel McMillan destroyed a bomber on the ground; Captain Moon destroyed two Ki-21 Sallys in the air and two more on the ground; Lieutenant Schultz shot down an unidentified type of transport and a Ki-32 Mary light bomber (claimed as a Stuka); Lieutenant Dowis destroyed one Sally in the air and three more on the ground; Lieutenant Yorston shot down two Sallys in the pattern; Lieutenant Rose shot down a D3A Type 99 Carrier Bomber, codename "Val," and a Nell, and damaged a Zero. Ed Penick confirmed the extent of the havoc wrought on Xinzhu on a reconnaissance mission over the island fifteen minutes after the raid. Penick first bombed a fuel dump with a five-hundred-pound bomb and then climbed to take photos. The photos confirmed the claims of aircraft destroyed on the ground, though smoke obscured much of the field.[82]

The 3 December 1943 issue of the *CBI Roundup* enthusiastically reported on the resounding victory:

A-27396 A

Striking at a part of the Japanese Empire for the first history-making time from China, Mitchell bombers and long-range fighters carried the air war to [Taiwan] Island in a smashing Thanksgiving Day raid directed against the large air base at [Xinzhu].

It was hardly a day of Thanksgiving for the enemy, for the raid cost them 46 planes confirmed, while all 14th Air Force and Chinese-American Composite Wing raiders returned safely from the island fortress, 100 miles off the China coast between the Philippines and Japan proper.

Lightning fighters led the Allied attack, which caught the Japanese with their pants down with only a few planes off the field. From the very outset, the opposition in the air was knocked out. Then, while enemy planes were frantically trying to get off the ground, Mitchell bombers followed by covering the airdrome and installations with fragmentation bombs in a low-level attack. Other American pursuits covered the B-25's over the target, shooting down two intercepting Zeros from behind the bomber formation before strafing the field on their own.

The final tally of the raid stood at 14 confirmed in the air by pursuits, one shot down by the B-25's and 31 destroyed on the ground. The bag included a Stuka dive-bomber and two Junkers-52 transports.

Teddy White, *Time & Life* correspondent and the only pressman to accompany the raiders, described the blow as a "complete surprise." "It was a peaceful, sunny afternoon," he said, "and Japanese transports and bombers were circling the field in slow traffic patterns. The P-38's struck the planes before any Jap was aware the raid was on. They plummeted into the sea, smoking, and the P-38's went on to blitz the parked airplanes on ramps and runways and to drive the terrified ground personnel all the way across the field. The B-25's followed hard at startling new low levels in a rigid echelon extending a mile and a half to the right. The fragmentation bombs cut a swath of destruction across the field, the runway, through the barracks and hangars, literally shattering all essential Japanese installations."

Unscathed except for a few minor bullet holes in three Mitchells from ground fire, the raiders returned to their home base too late to get their turkey dinner, but no one complained too vociferously after the satisfying success of the raid.

It was significant that the raid, which extended the sweep of operations closer to Tokyo, was carried out by medium bombers and not by longer-ranged B-24's. Crews reported that [Xinzhu] Airdrome, which is in the northeastern corner of [Taiwan], was covered with smoke from many blazing planes and buildings as the raid ended. [Xinzhu] is only 560 miles from the southernmost of the Japanese home islands.

Col. Clinton (Casey) Vincent, commander of the 14th Air Force Forward Echelon, planned and directed the raid.

Lt. Col. David (Tex) Hill, former AVG ace who recently returned to China, arrived just in time to swell his decisions to 18 by confirming one bomber in the air and another on the ground. Capt. Sam Palmer, leading another fighter outfit, knocked down three enemy planes.

The 14th Air Force Mitchells were led by Lt. Col. Joseph B. Welles, while Lt. Col. Irving Branch commanded the Mitchells of the mixed Chinese-American Wing.

The Japanese are known to be using [Taiwan] as a training and staging ground for aircraft sent to China, Southeast Asia and the Southwest Pacific, as well as a troop supply concentration base on the vital sea route.[83]

The raiders returned to Guilin and Lingling the next day, leaving little equipment or personnel to feel the effect of intensive

Opposite
Top: A photo taken from the nose of one of the B-25s before its bombing run on Xinzhu Field clearly demonstrates several G3M Nell bombers burning after having been strafed by 449th P-38s. Michael Bates

Bottom: Another photo of Xinzhu Field prior to the B-25s making their run. National Archives

A reconnaissance photo of Xinzhu Airdrome on 25 November 1943. The destruction wrought by the American raid is evidenced by the billowing plumes of smoke emanating from the field and aircraft parking areas. Ed Penick

retaliatory bombing by the Japanese.[84] This approach was typical of Chennault. To concentrate for raids without presenting the Japanese an opportunity to land a knockout counterpunch, he used his extensive system of airbases throughout China in a proverbial shell game to keep the Japanese guessing as to the size and location of his forces. Typically, the night before a major raid, Chennault's airplanes would fly to a forward airbase. Chinese coolies would refuel the planes from five-gallon cans, and the next morning the task force would execute the raid, refuel again at the forward base, and then return to a secure base in China's interior.[85]

The Taiwan raid was a great success in the annals of the 14th Air Force and the 449th remembered it as its most successful mission. If George McMillan's arrival had begun a steady improvement in morale, then the Thanksgiving Day Raid increased it by a thousand percent. Casey Vincent commented that, "We took a big risk, but it turned out well. Sent them in low – right on the water – and achieved 100 percent surprise."[86] The Americans struck a great blow to the Japanese, who responded by incessantly bombing Suichuan (to little lasting effect) and pulling fighter units from the Pacific to strengthen Taiwan's defenses. The raid highlighted the growing strength of the 14th Air Force and resolved the Japanese to destroy it. Perhaps even more important to the 449th, the raid's great success made Chennault think about the value of keeping the P-38s in China. At a staff meeting in India, Colonel Philip Cochran, commander of the 1st Air Commandos, approached Chennault with an offer to trade his P-51s for the general's P-38s. Cochran knew Chennault did not like the higher fuel consumption of the P-38 and, "We wanted the P-38, because we thought it was a better platform for air-to-ground action that we were planning." So Cochran "tried to con him out of his P-38s." Chennault listened, and replied, "That's very interesting," but according to Cochran, "He didn't buy it at all."[87]

Rice Raid

In November 1943, the Japanese 11th Army launched a "rice raid" into the Changde area southwest of Dongting Lake, an enormous body of water (approximately thirty-two miles long from north to south) south of Hankou, surrounded by a complex of lowland lakes, streams, and swamps fed by two of the Yangzi's tributaries. Periodically, the Japanese would make forays into this rice-rich region where the sub-tropical climate and plentiful rainfall allowed for two rice crops annually. The primary purpose of these raids was to seize the rice crop for Japanese Army units in China before withdrawing to Hankou.

When it became evident that the 11th Army was not merely engaging in training maneuvers, Chennault ordered Casey Vincent to support Chinese troops in the area by whatever means available. P-40s from Hengyang dropped food and ammunition in bamboo belly tanks to the besieged defenders of Changde. P-40s, P-51s, B-25s, and P-38s attacked Japanese troop formations, as well as waterborne supplies traveling across Dongting Lake. During the rice raid, 14th Air Force fighters flew 1,039 sorties, 280 of which targeted watercraft on the lake. The 14th claimed to have destroyed two tugs, five small steamers, and ninety smaller vessels, many of which were loaded with enemy troops.[88] On 3 December, the Japanese took Changde. Six days later, having accomplished their objectives, they began a withdrawal to Hankou.[89] Though the Japanese did not intend to hold Changde for long, to Chennault, their retreat "offered first concrete proof that the combination of well-directed American air support and Chinese ground forces could stop the Japanese."[90] Unfortunately, Chennault was wrong. Though the 14th Air Force was doing its best to punish the Japanese, the Chinese ground forces were merely advancing in the wake of the pre-planned Japanese withdrawal and had neither the equipment nor the motivation to meet the Japanese in pitched battle. The results of the rice raid gave Chennault false confidence in his ability to maintain his airbases against Japanese ambitions in East China.

During the withdrawal, Japanese troop concentrations and lines of communications were particularly vulnerable to air attack. To distract the 14th Air Force from the ground campaign, the 3rd Air Division launched a series of attacks on Hengyang and Lingling. The Japanese estimated American-Chinese air strength as approximately four hundred aircraft, greatly outnumbering the 3rd Air Division. In reality, the Americans possessed only 270 planes, and in turn estimated the Japanese air force as possessing 750 planes. It seems that with the arrival of the 11th Sentai from Manchuria in early December, the opposing air forces were more closely matched than either side suspected.[91]

Before dawn on 10 December, Japanese bombers carried out nuisance raids on Guilin, Hengyang, and Lingling to keep the American pilots in slit trenches instead of beds. At 0500, thirty-two Oscars and nine Tojos escorted Ki-48 Type 99 Twin-engine Light Bombers, codename "Lily," to Hengyang and bombed the field, claiming sixteen aircraft destroyed on the ground and three intercepting P-40s shot out of the sky for the loss of only two bombers. Later that day, Lieutenant Colonel McMillan scrambled after two enemy reconnaissance aircraft reconnoitering Lingling. Each Japanese air division was equipped with at least eighteen Ki-46 Type 100 Command Reconnaissance Planes, codename "Dinah," which, until the arrival of P-38s, could work unchallenged because of their exceptionally high ceiling.[92] McMillan put his aircraft into a maximum-performance climb to catch the enemy planes. High above Lingling, he shot down the first photo plane and made two passes on the second, damaging its left engine. He came around for a third pass but his guns jammed, allowing it to escape mostly intact.

At 1300, the warning net reported another attack on Hengyang. Ten P-38s rushed to assist, but the Japanese diverted to Lingling, which they bombed from two thousand feet, claiming eleven aircraft destroyed on the ground. The 449th missed the enemy again on 11 December, this time while escorting bombers to targets around Dongting Lake. Forty-nine Japanese fighters and bombers claimed eleven American planes destroyed on the ground at Lingling. Finally, on 12 December, the 449th had a crack at the enemy. Oscars and Tojos escorted a force of Lilys to bomb Hengyang. This time, eight P-38s met them in the air, attacking the escorting fighters and scattering the bombers before they reached the target. Lieutenant Lee Gregg and Lieutenant Colonel McMillan each claimed one Ki-44 destroyed. The 75th Fighter Squadron claimed another nine aircraft shot down, but lost Lieutenant John Beaty. Captain Eugene Lundy, commander of the 74th, claimed one Oscar, but was himself shot down and forced to bail out.[93]

The 12 December attack was the last diversionary raid made by the 3rd Air Division in December. Between 10 and 12 December, the Japanese claimed forty-one American aircraft destroyed, though prohibitive losses suffered in hit-and-run attacks on Japanese light bombers made further daylight raids unsustainable for the immediate future. In reality, the 14th Air Force lost only three P-40s, one B-25, and one B-24 – not quite the resounding victory perceived by the Japanese.[94]

With the conclusion of the rice raid on Changde, things quieted down considerably for the 449th. Operations consisted mostly of shipping strikes on the Yangzi River and local alerts. On 15 December, seventeen P-40s and two P-38s launched from Kunming in response to reports of an enemy raid. The Japanese did not make an appearance, but white vapor streaming from Lieutenant Aloysius Calvey's P-38 bore witness to a fuel leak. He came in for an emergency landing on one engine, but lost control on final approach. His P-38 burst into flames upon striking the ground.[95]

On the 19th, Lieutenant Colonel McMillan led ten P-38s on a shipping strike, but Casey Vincent radioed for him to report to Hengyang shortly after starting the mission. The rest of the formation proceeded without him. According to Tom Calder, after strafing two barges and several sampans, "we got lost due to high winds, haze, and the leader's compass was not operating right." They attempted to get a plot on their position through the air raid warning net, but to no avail. Navigation was particularly difficult in China. Instead of maps, many pilots had only a sheet of paper with a list of distances and headings between airfields. Out of fuel, one of Calder's engines quit and he left the formation to find a place to land. Unfortunately, "I could not find one. About that time the other engine stopped. I set the controls and bailed out." William Jones and Kendall Dowis also took to their parachutes. Local Chinese rescued them, returning them to the nearest airbase the day before Christmas.[96]

With the decreased operations tempo the pilots and ground crews had to find creative ways to keep themselves occupied. Though most 14th Air Force bases were located near Chinese towns, it was a rare thing for Americans to visit. Tom Harmon remembered visiting the town of Lingling only three times: "The first time, it was for a basketball game with the Chinese, the second I went to see Lee Gregg after he had had his appendix removed and the third time was to attend midnight mass with the orphans on Christmas Eve."[97] The orphans Harmon referred to were those at the Catholic Mission in Lingling. Many of the men visited the orphanage several times and decided to throw the orphans a Christmas Party in the squadron recreation hall. Ted Miazga, a sergeant with the ground crew, dressed up as Santa Claus and passed out candy and presents to the orphans while the other men serenaded them with Christmas carols. The children were so touched they promised to remember the men in their prayers, which they did at the Christmas Eve mass Tom Harmon attended.

The typical overland transport in China was no more advanced than a water buffalo pulling a wooden cart. Jerry Doughty

The Chinese were hard workers and appreciated the Americans who came to fight against the Japanese invaders. Here, Chinese farmers irrigate rice paddies. Jerry Doughty

There were plenty of orphans in Free China. According to Dick Maddox, "It was overrun completely [with refugees]." While some men of the 449th were indifferent to the Chinese people, Maddox was not:

> I was intrigued by the way the Chinese lived. I spent as much free time as I had to learn about their day to day lives. They were a very friendly nation ... They were very industrious, hard workers, and by our standards didn't have anything at all in the way of modern day to day existence. ... Yunnan Province was the most backward province of all of China. And in fact was probably considered as a place to just send their undesirables from the rest of the country. Kind of like Great Britain ... sent criminals to Australia.[98]

Buck Burris recalled that the Chinese, though very poor, "cared a great deal for the Americans and respected us."[99] Because the 14th Air Force was one of the only entities perceived as actively opposing the Japanese occupation of China, the Chinese took every opportunity to show their gratitude. In late December, the people of Lingling threw a magnificent Christmas party for the men of the 449th. Though the Chinese led modest lives, they went above and beyond to entertain their American guests. They seated each American at a large circular table with roughly ten Chinese officers, all of whom took great pleasure in intoxicating their guests to the maximum extent possible. In China, a toast is between two individuals, not the entire table, thus one at a time each Chinese officer would stand and say "Ganbei" (bottoms up), and he and the American would drain their glasses. Soon, the American had ten drinks while each Chinese had only one. According to Harmon, "The lights soon went out in the American section. The boys always remembered going to these parties – but few ever remembered coming home." The squadron commander would often receive more attention than anyone else and "would invariably be put away early in the evening."[100] It was fortunate the Japanese did not attack the next day, as there were few pilots in any condition to fly.

Also present at the Christmas festivities was the unit's new mascot, Lieutenant Dinkey. Dinkey was a Welsh terrier who had flown the hump with the 449th on a ferrying trip. Given the honorary title of 2nd Lieutenant, Dinkey stayed with the squadron for some time, and was a common companion for the pilots and ground crews.

New Year's was no less replete with parties than Christmas, though Jim Hyde and several of his friends thought of a more creative way to celebrate. He, Henry Ward, John Singer, and William Mitchell went into Lingling and bought a ten- to twelve-foot-long string of firecrackers. They rode the train back and accidentally got off one stop early, having to walk twelve miles back to base carrying their fifteen- or twenty-pound load. Hyde explained that Lingling was always threatened by paratroopers, so they brought the firecrackers to the barracks and laid them across the porch. "The barracks that we were staying in at the time ... had a long porch – the whole length of the building. The porch was maybe six feet wide and you could sit out on it and walk and stay out of the rain walking down that porch." Around midnight they lit the string at both ends and started hollering "Paratroopers! Paratroopers!" Suddenly, somebody "came roaring out of that thing with a Thompson submachine gun – he didn't hit anybody but it was a wonder he didn't! We were really dumb to have done something like that."[101]

Tech Sergeant William Jordan celebrated New Years in Kunming, where he was stationed with the 449th's small air defense detachment. Jordan's taste for alcohol exceeded his tolerance – something Buck Burris had warned him about multiple times. On New Years, it finally caught up with him. He was walking through Kunming somewhat inebriated and unaware he was being followed by a Japanese agent. The crowd was thick and he had let his guard down. As he pushed his way through, the agent stabbed him with a knife he had concealed in a staff or cane. Jordan staggered to the side of the road, bleeding furiously. There he propped himself up until Chinese authorities found him and rushed him to the 14th Air Force hospital. By the time he arrived, however, it was too late. As he lay there dying, he gasped to the doctor, "Tell Buck Burris he was right."[102]

Father Cosgrove was saddened by the loss of another comrade – one he considered a good friend. He remembered in particular Jordan's dry sense of humor and outstanding ath-

Left: Chennault was an avid ball-player and prolific pitcher, but too stubborn to leave the game when he got tired. National Archives Right: Chennault's face remains impassive as he contemplates losing the game. Robert Neely

letic ability. In one instance, Jordan had organized a basketball game with the local Chinese at Lingling. Things did not go as planned, however, as Tom Harmon related:

> The Chinese excel at this game. Perhaps on a large court playing under the standard regulations they might be beaten by a rangy American team, but on those mud outdoor courts they really gave us a lesson. They were small, fast and in top condition, and were some opponents. Chinese rules for basketball differ a little from ours, but basically it's the same game. They use a larger ball but have a smaller hoop on the basket, for one thing. The good-will of the American team was often put to the test in these games, for the boys couldn't help getting sore now and then when the Chinese had them wrapped in knots. Fists would start flying and international friendship would seem to be at stake for a minute or two.[103]

Fortunately, no lasting damage was dealt to Chinese-American relations, though Sergeant Jordan was embarrassed by his team's loss.

More popular and more common than the occasional basketball game was baseball. Tom Harmon declared, "Take an American boy and put him anywhere in the world, and before long you will find a baseball team."[104] Jim Hyde remembered winning $960 from General Chennault and his headquarters staff in one particular baseball game for which Chennault visited Lingling. Chennault was a good pitcher, and very competitive, but the 449th had Technical Sergeant Tony Scalzo. Chennault's team got off to an early lead, but as the game wore on, Chennault wore out. He was too competitive to leave the game, however, and eventually Scalzo caught up. Hyde "got $960.00 worth of bets – and we won!"[105]

Sports, cards, and other pastimes dominated much of January. Poor weather conditions only allowed for three missions against bridges and river targets. On 3 January 1944, two P-38s escorted twenty-eight B-24s to the Lampang railroad yards in Thailand. Heavy cloud cover prevented many of the bombers from finding the target, and five returned without dropping their bombs.[106] This slow pace of operations was not indicative as to what the new year had in store, however. Despite Chennault's hard-hitting offensive in the fall of 1943, the 14th Air Force would soon be on the defensive again. In fact, 1944 would show the 449th the toughest combat it had seen yet.

Chapter Four

Suichuan

At the beginning of the war, Japan estimated it would lose 1.8 million tons of shipping in the first two years of combat against the United States. By the end of 1943, however, the Allies had destroyed 3.8 million tons and reduced Japan's merchant fleet to seventy-seven-percent of its prewar capacity, despite desperate attempts by the Japanese to increase it. American submarines accounted for fifty-five-percent of shipping losses, while air interdiction accounted for twenty-four-percent. Because of this, Japanese Imperial Headquarters became increasingly concerned over its ability to supply its armies in Southeast Asia and began planning an operation to create an inland rail corridor through China from Korea to Southeast Asia. By January 1944, headquarters approved "Ichi-go" (Operation Number 1) to capture and/or complete the railroads between Beiping and Hankou, Hankou and Guangzhou, and Hengyang and Hanoi. This would allow Japanese shipping to operate safely between the home islands and Korea while a rail corridor would stretch from Korea to Saigon and from Saigon, through Thailand, to Burma.[1] Though the threat posed by the 14th Air Force and the possibility of air attacks on Japan from China were not the primary impetus for Ichi-go, the increasing strength and capabilities of the American air force – highlighted by the Thanksgiving Raid on Taiwan – convinced the Japanese to make the capture of Chennault's eastern airfields an important secondary objective. The Japanese also planned an advance from Burma into India to cut the rail line sustaining the Hump airlift.[2] If all went well, China would capitulate, allowing Japan to concentrate its forces against the American drive through the Pacific.

For Ichi-go, Japanese Imperial Headquarters devoted four hundred thousand men, twelve thousand vehicles, and seventy thousand horses to the China Expeditionary Force and greatly increased the strength of the 3rd Air Division, which it redesignated the 5th Air Army on 15 February 1944.[3] The 11th Sentai remained in China only until mid-February, but the 9th, equipped with Oscars and Tojos, arrived from Manchuria to replace it, and the 48th prepared to move from Manchuria in April. The 5th Air Army was to wrest air superiority from the Americans in advance of Ichi-go and protect shipping along the Yangzi River, which headquarters suspected would be subject to heavy interdiction.[4]

As early as 27 January, Chennault's intelligence reported Japanese buildups at both Hankou and north of the Yellow River bend, some four hundred miles south of Beiping and three hundred miles north of Hankou.[5] Under the cover of poor weather, the Japanese moved supplies into Shanghai and up the Yangzi River. Chennault redeployed his recently reorganized forces to counter the Japanese threat. In late-December 1943, Forward Echelon became the 68th Composite Wing, still commanded by Casey Vincent, with the 23rd Fighter Group, 449th Fighter Squadron, and CACW attached for operations. Chennault activated the 69th Composite Wing, commanded by Colonel John Kennedy, for coastal shipping strikes, protection of the Hump route, and operations in the west, with the other three squadrons of the 51st Fighter Group, three squadrons of the 341st Bomb Group (B-25s), and all four squadrons of the 308th Bomb Group (B-24s). In February 1944, Chennault stationed a flight of reconnaissance planes at fields north of Chongqing to monitor the Japanese buildup and shifted the CACW north for operations against Japanese forces along the Yellow River. He ordered the 449th to Suichuan where it would strengthen his foothold in East China and more easily strike Japanese shipping on the Yangzi River. A detachment of the 76th Fighter Squadron, equipped with P-51As, had been flying out of Suichuan for months, but the pace of operations left it with only four operational aircraft. When the 449th arrived, its pace of operations also increased. Curtis Perry, a ground crewman who transferred to the 449th from the 26th Fighter Squadron, declared: "It was pretty hot while I was with the 26th, but when I transferred to the 449th that's when things really started to burn."[6]

Also in early February, Captain Rex T. Barber joined the 449th. Barber shot down Admiral Isoruku Yamamoto on 18

April 1943 while flying with the 339th Fighter Squadron at Guadalcanal. He was not supposed to fly in combat after that mission, for fear that he would divulge sensitive information if the Japanese shot down and interrogated him. Instead, he was assigned as an instructor for replacement pilots in Karachi, India. However, when Chennault found out that an experienced and decorated P-38 pilot was cooling his heels in Karachi, he immediately arranged for his transfer to China. As far as Chennault was concerned, Barber would fly in combat again whether he was supposed to or not.

On 10 February, Barber accompanied Lieutenant Colonel McMillan, Lieutenant Mahon, and another pilot, escorting P-51s to Jiujiang. En route to the target, they encountered what they thought was a flight of three twin-engine Ki-45 Type Two Two-seat Fighters, codename "Nick." However, since there were no Ki-45s stationed in China, it is far more likely they encountered a flight of Ki-48 Lilys, a similar-looking aircraft designed by the same engineer.[7] The Lilys attempted to escape, but the P-38s caught up with and engaged them. McMillan and Mahon each received credit for one destroyed while Barber damaged the third. The P-38s lost contact with the P-51s, which proceeded to Jiujiang unescorted. There, Ki-43s from the 25th Sentai intercepted the flight and shot down Major Lee Manbeck. A Japanese anti-aircraft battery reported capturing the pilot, but he did not survive the war.[8]

On 12 February, as part of the 5th Air Army's effort to gain air superiority, eleven Ki-44s from the 85th Sentai departed for Suichuan. Shortly thereafter, fourteen Ki-43s from the 11th Sentai joined them after escorting Ki-48s to Nanyu. Fourteen P-38s and several P-40s and P-51s scrambled and met the raiders south of Suichuan at twenty thousand feet. The Japanese had an altitude advantage, but failed to exploit it. Captain Wakamatsu was flying top cover for the Ki-44s when he encountered a flight of P-40s. He shot down and killed William Butler of the 76th Fighter Squadron, but was himself severely damaged, and had to return to base immediately. Meanwhile, the P-38s roared into the Japanese formation, claiming six enemy planes destroyed. Captain John Stewart of the 76th Fighter Squadron also claimed one enemy fighter. Sergeant Teruyoshi Ito from the 25th witnessed a P-38 shoot down Corporal Futamata, and saw another Oscar severely damaged.[9]

After returning to base, Captain Wakamatsu waited for the rest the 85th Sentai, but only two returned. They reported one Ki-44 shot down, five missing, and two having crash-landed out of fuel. Apparently, the American fighters were so aggressive the Japanese could not disengage. Even the sentai commander, Major Tougo Saito, crash-landed after running out of fuel. Altogether, the 85th lost five pilots killed in action: Lieutenant Kiyoya Kon-i, Sergeants Tadashi Kikukawa, Haruzo Hayakawa, Keiishi Kimura, and Sergeant Major Kenji Takahashi.[10] However, in addition to Butler, the Japanese shot down Lieutenant Art Masterson's P-38. Masterson bailed out safely and returned to Suichuan two days later.

A 76th Fighter Squadron P-51A at Suichuan in 1944. A detachment of the 76th had been at Suichuan for some time and was down to four operational aircraft when the 449th arrived. Note the B-25 gunship in the background. Steve Blake

Lieutenant Art Masterson with Danny Church's P-38J-15 #312 (42-104335) My Achin' Ass at Chenggong in 1945. Joseph Fodor

The aftermath of a Japanese bombing raid on Suichuan. Ed Penick

The 449th claimed a total of six destroyed and six probables. Lieutenant Helms claimed two Tojos destroyed and one Oscar probably destroyed; Lieutenants Arpin, Conway, and Yorston each claimed one enemy fighter shot down; Lieutenant Gregg claimed one Tojo confirmed and an Oscar probable; and Captain Barber, and Lieutenants Campbell and Rose all claimed additional enemy fighters as probables. The Japanese believed they shot down five American aircraft instead of only two. Of note, one of the Japanese pilots present with the 11th Sentai was Captain Hironojo Shishimoto, one the few Japanese aces to survive the war. Shishimoto had been fighting the Americans since the beginning of the war and saw a lot of action in the South Pacific before the 11th moved to China. His section claimed four of the five Japanese victories. At the end of the war, his personal score stood at seven American planes destroyed.[11]

The Japanese took such a beating on 12 February that they avoided making daylight raids on Suichuan for the remainder of the month. They realized the warning net was too effective for them to achieve any measure of surprise, and therefore sent Lily bombers on night attacks. Japanese records claim the "highly trained" bomber crews "achieved excellent results."[12] On moonlit nights, bombers would often arrive over the field one at a time every fifteen to thirty minutes, dropping either delayed action bombs to crater the runway or anti-personnel fragmentation bombs. The frag bombs were about ten inches long and two inches in diameter and were filled with slit washers that scattered over an area fifty yards square. According to Ed Penick, they "sounded like a waterfall as they sliced through the trees."[13] In any case, no American personnel were killed in these attacks and runway damage was usually repaired the next morning by Chinese laborers.

The warning net usually gave adequate notice of the raids, but Suichuan did not posses any night fighters, so the men would hunker down in slit trenches until the bombers passed. Vernon Kramer and John Stewart of the 76th Fighter Squadron had tried intercepting the Lilys on the night of the 10th and had shot down one of them. At the time, Kramer's intercept was only the second successful night interception in China, but was the last one made by day fighters.[14] The Americans tried using the resources they had on hand, but night interception was extremely hazardous and so the raids persisted until the 426th Night Fighter Squadron arrived with its P-61s eight months later. In the mean time, the Japanese succeeded in keeping the Americans out of bed at night.

Though reluctant to attack Suichuan in daylight, the 5th Air Army often feinted toward the base to force defending fighters to scramble, thus exacerbating the already difficult supply situation. As the 14th Air Force's most remote outpost, Suichuan was at the end of an already stretched supply line. Gasoline and supplies flown in C-46 and C-47 cargo aircraft over the Hump to Kunming were loaded on Chinese carts, trucks, and sampans, which bore the slow and laborious task of transporting them to forward airfields. Often a month or two would pass before supplies from Kunming arrived at Suichuan. The lack of available fuel was especially frustrating to Rex

Barber, who saw the situation as detrimental to the 449th's combat effectiveness:

> We had only enough fuel to fly combat missions; we would wait until we had enough to refill all the aircraft, then fly a mission. There was no fuel for training, which was badly needed. George McMillan and I frequently talked, with great concern, about the lack of co-ordinated training and tactical co-operation.[15]

The fuel situation worsened throughout the spring of 1944. In fact, on 30 March, Casey Vincent restricted operations to a minimum and informed Chennault that the 68th Composite Wing would not have enough gasoline to last through the summer.[16]

According to Major General William Tunner, who took command of the Hump airlift in August 1944, "Every drop of fuel, every weapon, and every round of ammunition, and 100 per cent of such other diverse supplies as carbon paper and C-rations, *every* such item used by American forces in China was flown in by airlift."[17] Consequently, with a severe fuel shortage, the overtaxed Air Transport Command could ill-afford to carry extra American food and amenities. In one instance, Jim Hyde remembered paying four hundred American dollars for a gallon of ice cream. He and his friends had not had ice cream in a long time and found a Chinese man with a freezer and ice who would make it for them, provided they furnish him the ingredients and pay him four hundred dollars. Hyde and his friends scrounged up the ingredients. Hyde, however, "was the only one of us who had any money" out of the "six of us that went together. I was supposed to be paid eventually by the others and divide the cost but I never did get refunded." Of course, according to Jim Heitkotter, the reason Jim Hyde was the only one with money was because "he usually had everybody else's poker money." Hyde himself admitted that he was a rather lucky poker player, relating that one day he was standing in line to receive his pay when Ike Quick, another man on the ground crew, walked by counting the money he had just been issued. Quick looked at Hyde and asked, "Would you like me to give it to you now, or would you like to win it first?"[18]

In the days immediately prior to Ichi-go, however, poor weather, not lack of supply, was the primary hindrance to operations. Despite Chennault's fervent desire to attack the lines of communication that were pouring supplies into Hankou, most missions against shipping on the Yangzi turned back, or never launched in the first place, because of poor weather. In addition, many Japanese ships on the Yangzi traveled only at night, sheltering in well-defended river ports during the day. When the weather cleared up for a period of time, Japanese fighters would patrol the Yangzi in force, looking to disrupt any 14th Air Force interdiction activities.[19]

The 449th flew only two river sweeps in February 1944. On the 24th, nine P-38s left Suichuan for the stretch of river between Hankou and Jiujiang, where they bombed and strafed anything afloat. Schultz recounted that, "Rea hit a Japanese freighter and I put a thousand pounder right along side of it. This was at [Jiujiang] on the Yangzi, and I had never imagined that a ship could sink that fast."[20] As Lieutenant Campbell took aim at a river boat, a single Oscar from the 25th Sentai appeared out of the haze and shot out his radio, compass, and one of his engines. Campbell managed to break away and crash land, arriving back at Suichuan three days later. Twelve P-38s returned to the same area on 29 February. After two Lightnings made a bombing run on a couple of motor launches, a flight of eight Oscars made a slashing attack. Normally during such missions, one flight of P-38s would cover the other as it attacked river targets. After the attacking flight expended its bombs and three-fourths of its ammunition, the flights would switch. That day the P-38s in the cover flight jettisoned their bombs and turned to attack the Oscars, but they escaped into the haze.

Japanese Fighter activity over the Yangzi demonstrated the 5th Air Army's commitment to defend river shipping and convinced Vincent to pull the 449th from river sweeps to escort B-25s. The function of the B-25s was twofold: attack river shipping with guns and bombs and act as bait to draw Japanese fighters into combat with the Lightnings. Unfortunately, weather again prevented more than a handful of these missions and poor visibility on the missions that occurred meant the Americans were tactically handicapped and received little warning before the Japanese attacked.

On 4 March, Captain Schultz and Lieutenants Gregg, Nunn, and Desper escorted two B-25s up the Yangzi. The Mitchells flew low over the river, with the lead plane about a mile in front of the wingman until they found two 150-foot merchant ships. The lead bomber went in, guns blazing to discourage defensive fire, and dropped three five-hundred-pound bombs. The trailing bomber repeated the attack, but neither scored any hits. Meanwhile, the 3rd Chutai of the 25th Sentai received warning of the American sweep and moved to intercept with ten Ki-43s. As the B-25s came around for another pass (rare, unless the target appeared defenseless), Sergeant Tadashi Shono spotted the P-38s below. Captain Keisaku Motohashi, the formation leader, led the Oscars in a diving attack. The outnumbered Lightnings were flying at low altitude because poor visibility prevented them from flying high above the B-25s. Even so, they made a climbing charge into the enemy formation. Schultz went head-to-head with Captain Motohashi and Corporal Haruyuki Toda, Motohashi's wingman. The fighters fired at each other and the Oscars severely damaged Schultz's P-38, claiming it as destroyed. The Japanese lost one Ki-43.[21]

Schultz, Nunn, and Gregg each claimed one fighter apiece, but the Oscars damaged Shultz and Nunn's aircraft and shot down one B-25. Nevertheless, Bruce Schultz came back from the 4 March mission an ace.[22] Nunn's airplane limped into Hengyang but Shultz's was so badly damaged that the left engine caught fire as he was preparing to land at Suichuan. His wheels would not come down, so he decided to make a belly landing. He touched down at 180 miles per hour. The terrible racket of aluminum on gravel was overwhelming and the jolt upon hitting the ground slammed his face into the control panel, breaking his nose. By then, he had been in continuous combat for over eight months. He was tired and down to 128 pounds. The flight surgeon did not want him to fly until his health improved. He took part in only a handful of subsequent missions before he and Ryan Moon returned to the United States in June.[23] *Golden*

Captain Billie Beardsley and Tech Sergeant De Vito chalk-up another mission on the Golden Eagle, which served long after Bruce Schultz finished his tour in the spring of 1944. John Stanaway

Eagle was little the worse for the wear, however, as it was soon flying again. In fact, the plane kept flying long after Schultz's tour ended. According to Schultz, "although it was shot up several times including having to replace the right tail boom and being landed wheels up while on fire at approximately 180 mph, it survived the war."[24]

On 10 March, the 449th escorted B-25s on another river sweep but doubled the escort to eight. This time the two B-25s were gunships, outfitted with additional machine guns and a seventy-five-millimeter cannon in the nose in place of the bombardier compartment. Chennault was optimistic that the cannon-armed Mitchells would prove useful in river interdiction, but the modifications made them less maneuverable than standard glass-nosed Mitchells, thus making it more difficult for them to follow the winding river at low altitude. Additionally, the high approach needed by the gunships alerted enemy gunners and made defensive fire all the more dangerous. The seventy-five-millimeter cannon proved less accurate than five-hundred-pound bombs and was overkill for smaller targets.[25] Lieutenant Colonel McMillan led the escort at five thousand feet while the B-25s proceeded down the river, bombing and strafing two steamers, a launch, a barge, and five smaller vessels. As the Mitchells turned for home, fifteen Japanese fighters attacked from above. Tom Pugh and his wingman were about to follow McMillan in a sweeping turn to the left when he saw five Japanese fighters in front of him. The Lightnings were at a decided disadvantage; belly tanks still attached, low on gas, one thousand feet below their opponents, and throttled back to stay with the B-25s. According to Pugh:

> There is an old saying: "When in doubt bluff." I firewalled the throttles and props and pulled up into the lead Jap with all guns firing. My wing man, Lt. Dean, was following me. I could see his tracers on my right. At the same time I was trying to switch gas and get rid of my belly tank. When [I] pushed over and turned left, I could not have been doing more than 150 MPH. About this time, my left engine started coughing and putting out white smoke, indicating coolant burning. I feathered the engine and dove for the hills.[26]

The other American pilots made good their escape but became lost in the deteriorating weather. The warning net guided them back to Suichuan.

Japanese ace Lieutenant Moritsugu Kanai claimed Pugh as shot down,[27] but he managed to escape on one engine and land in a field near a remote Chinese village. A local Catholic priest helped Pugh determine his location and he radioed for a repair crew and gasoline. As it turned out, the only damage was a severed coolant line, which proved an easy fix. Taking off again, though, was not so easy. The longer Pugh looked at the field, the shorter it got, "I must have run the engines up and checked the mags a dozen times before I got up enough nerve to give the engines full power, release the brakes, gulp and hold my breath for takeoff." He dropped one-quarter flaps as he built up speed and staggered into the air at only seventy-five miles per hour. "One cough from one of the engines and I would have been a goner."[28] Pugh made it back to Suichuan without any further trouble.

On 18 March, Lieutenants Rose and Weber scrambled after a Japanese photo recon plane. The JAAF monitored the radio and knew interceptors were circling the field. They informed Captain Hiroshi Miura, piloting the Ki-46 from the 55th Independent Chutai, but before he could take action, Rose and Weber spotted him at twenty-nine thousand feet over Suichuan. Rose made the first pass, firing into the Dinah's left engine. Weber then closed from behind and fired, sending the Japanese plane spinning into the ground. The Japanese reported that Captain Miura failed to return from his mission. Later that day, the Americans attempted another river sweep, but the Lightnings became separated from the B-25s in poor weather. The 25th Sentai reported engaging ten aircraft near Jiujiang, shooting down one P-40 for no losses.[29] Such weather put a halt to interdiction activities for the rest of March and most of April.

Near the end of March, something terrible happened: the squadron's mascot, Lieutenant Dinkey, went missing. Nobody knew what happened exactly, but it was thought that he fell prey to the Chinese villagers he so openly detested. Forrest Green commented: "I have a good idea as to what happened to Lt Dinkey. The Chinese eat dogs. I've seen Chinese carry dog carcasses in town. They preferred black dogs for some reason and they would leave a small tuft of hair on the tail of the skinned carcass."[30] Also at the end of March, Lieutenant Colonel McMillan went on detached service to India on the 27th, leaving Captain Barber in temporary command of the squadron.

Most of April was uneventful save for an occasional scramble at an enemy feint, or a mission aborted due to weather.

Right: Lieutenant Thomas Pugh. Steve Blake

Below: The probably fate of Lieutenant Dinkey. His enmity toward the Chinese people finally caught up with him. Jerry Doughty

On the 29th, however, the weather cleared enough for Barber to lead a final river sweep: nine P-38s escorting two B-25s. McMillan and Barber had set up a system whereby only experienced pilots would fly the most dangerous missions, allowing the novices to gain operational experience on missions less fraught with danger.[31] Barber believed this river sweep would be a "milk run," perfect for an inexperienced pilot, and flew with a recent arrival on his wing, Lieutenant Fred Roll. Six miles west of Jiujiang, however, ten Oscars from the 25th Sentai and four Ki-27 Type 97 Fighters, codename "Nate," from the 118th Flying Training Regiment jumped Barber and his men with a significant altitude advantage. Barber ordered the B-25s to head for home and brought the P-38s in behind for cover.

Tom Pugh with the Catholic missionary and Chinese people who helped him after he landed in a remote field on 10 March 1944. 14th Air Force Association

Lieutenant Fred Roll in the cockpit of his P-38. Roll was Barber's wingman on the 29 April river sweep in which Barber was shot down. Jerry Doughty

All was going well until Barber noticed his novice wingman had fallen behind. Two Oscars pursued Roll and aggressively attacked him. Barber called for him to dive for the deck, but Roll did not respond. Barber saw no choice but to make a head-on attack to distract the enemy long enough for Roll to get away. Bringing his P-38 around, he engaged the fighters targeting his wingman. As he pulled up into a steep ascent to take aim, however, his airplane stalled. The enemy planes quickly took advantage of the situation and shot his right engine, setting it afire. Lieutenant Robert Campbell came to Barber's assistance, shooting an enemy fighter off his tail, but Barber's Lightning was already severely damaged. He bailed out only four hundred feet above the ground.

Lieutenant Campbell saw another P-38 under attack and turned to assist when a Japanese fighter attacked him from behind, shooting out his left engine. Campbell's cockpit filled with smoke. Billie Beardsley saw Campbell's fighter in front of him as he exited the fight and radioed for him to fly west, out of enemy territory. Campbell replied that he could not climb over the mountains. The two flew around the small range, but two minutes later, Campbell lost his right engine. He kept the Lightning under control as it glided to an altitude of eight hundred feet, where it suddenly flipped upside down. Campbell bailed out. Beardsley watched as the airplane crashed and exploded and saw Campbell land on a hillside, parachute caught in the trees.[32]

For all the trouble that everyone went through to rescue him, Fred Roll *did* manage to return to Suichuan, though with a plane that looked like a sieve for all the bullet holes in it. His left tire had been punctured so that when he touched down, his P-38 veered off the left side of the runway. The Lightning fell into a ditch and the nose wheel collapsed, further damaging the nose and engines.

Two young Chinese boys found Rex Barber when he landed and quickly covered him with brush they had cut for firewood. Japanese soldiers searched the area with dogs, and one soldier even stood next to the brush pile as he lit a cigarette. He tossed the match on the pile, but by some miracle the brush did not catch fire and the Japanese did not catch Barber.[33] The Chinese smuggled him past roadblocks into Jiujiang, where he waited for the Japanese to give up the search. Suffering an arm smashed by gunfire and a leg broken in bailing out, Barber trekked five weeks to return to Suichuan. Meanwhile, Captain Moon took command of the 449th until McMillan returned from India.[34]

When Barber finally returned on 7 June, Father Cosgrove thought he looked "none the worse for the experience apart from a broken arm." The squadron had feared he had been captured, figuring he would endure the worst kind of torture because of his part in shooting down Admiral Yamamoto. Far from it, however, Barber declared, "It was the best vacation I've had in years. ... The guerrillas treated me swell."[35] According to Chennault's policy, after being rescued by Chinese guerrillas, Barber could not continue flying in China. Chennault had defied the AAF brass in allowing him to fly in combat again in the first place and anyway, his injuries required medical treatment in the United States. Thus in the summer of 1944, Rex Barber was sent home.

Operation Ichi-go

Casey Vincent's river interdiction campaign was a miserable failure. The Japanese timed their offensive perfectly to use poor weather as a shield against American airpower and when the weather did occasionally clear, the 5th Air Army offered stiff resistance over the Yangzi River. On 18 April, under cover of poor weather, 140,000 Japanese troops crossed the Yellow River in a drive to capture the last stretch of railroad between Beiping and Hankou. On flat terrain and without air support, twenty-one Chinese divisions simply melted away in the face of Japanese tanks, artillery, and mechanized units. By mid-May, the Japanese completed phase one of Ichi-go at a cost of only 1,061 killed for 21,643 deaths inflicted on the Chinese.[36]

Chennault and Vincent were frustrated by their inability to counter the Japanese thrust, but poor weather continued to hold them off until early May. On the 6th, Vincent sent fifty-four aircraft to strike Hankou. Since he could not get accurate reports on enemy movements, he would strike their largest concentration of supplies. The strike force consisted of six B-25s from the 11th Bomb Squadron and eight from the CACW, eight P-38s from the 449th, seven P-51s from the 76th, and twenty-five P-40s from the other squadrons of the 23rd Fighter Group. Tex Hill briefed the P-38 and P-51 pilots at Suichuan and Casey Vincent briefed the P-40 pilots and B-25 crews at Lingling and Hengyang. Led by Hill, the fighters from Suichuan rendezvoused with the rest of the formation over Hengyang.[37]

The P-38s and P-51s flew top cover at twenty thousand feet. Through the heavy haze they could see the bombers some five thousand feet below, surrounded by P-40s packed in tightly around them.[38] The 76th flew new P-51Bs, the first flight of which Casey Vincent personally led to China at the end of February.[39] The "B" model boasted the Packard-built Merlin engine, which provided more power and a higher ceiling.[40] Several of the 449th's aircraft were new P-38Js, with the intercoolers redesigned in a chin scoop (allowing the engines to safely produce two hundred more horsepower), hydraulic-boosted ailerons, and a revised cockpit layout.[41] While the new fighters still could not maneuver with the Japanese, they could outrun, out-dive, out-climb, and outgun them. As the armada approached Hankou, the 25th Sentai launched twenty-four Oscars to intercept.[42] Over Dongting Lake, approximately 120 miles southwest of the city, Major Charles Griffith from the 76th spotted the Japanese at two o'clock high. Tex maneuvered the top cover into a head-to-head attack.[43] With a significant altitude advantage, Major Sakagawa's Ki-43s had the jump on the Americans. Lieutenant Lee Gregg led his flight up into the Japanese formation, but the Oscars swarmed around and shot

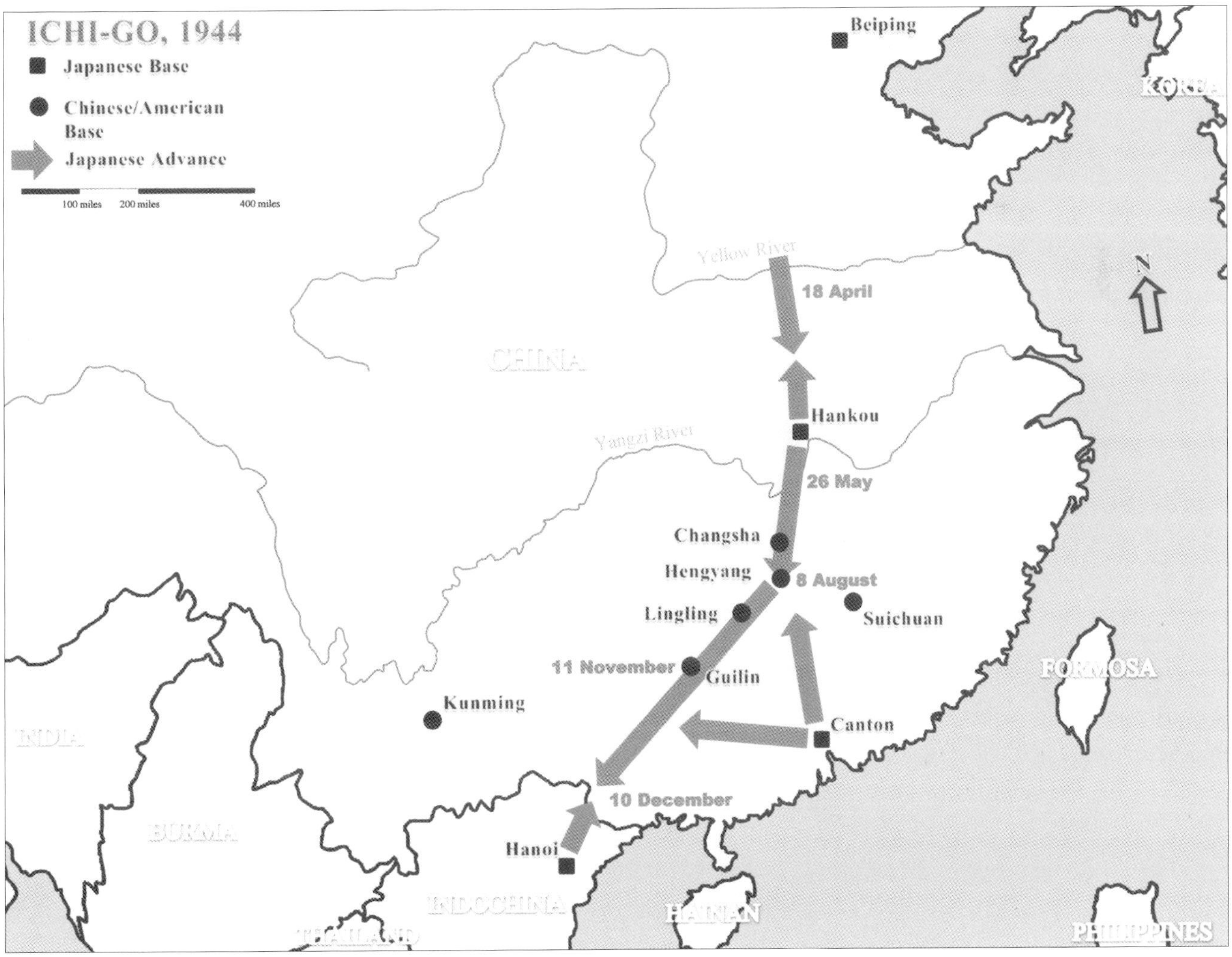

him down, along with Lieutenants William Jones and John Opsvig. Jones immediately bailed out, but Gregg was knocked unconscious as his fighter hurtled toward the ground.[44] Lieutenant Longueil dove away on one engine. The fight was intense. Fred Roll remembered it was "a real hair-ball fight, and all I could do was hang onto lead."[45] Lieutenant Morita flashed past the P-38s in his Oscar when he suddenly collided with Lieutenant Jones under canopy. The impact probably killed Jones and severely dented the wing root of Morita's fighter.[46]

Meanwhile, Tex Hill fired a short burst at an Oscar that quickly flashed in front of him. He searched in the haze for another target, and found one in a clear patch of sky below. He dove on the fighter and fired, sending it plummeting.[47] Lieutenant Glen Beneda and his wingman, Lieutenant Wendell Stoneham, were the last element of the last flight of P-51s. When the Ki-43s attacked, the two immediately tried to release their drop tanks, but Beneda's left tank would not detach. Beneda saw an Oscar in front of him and called for Stoneham to follow as he dove after it. Suddenly, another Oscar hit him from behind. He tried to dive away, but as he rolled his fighter, it snapped around viciously. He managed to break away from the fight, but his engine quit, forcing him to bail out. Stoneham continued diving to five thousand feet. He could not find Beneda, but saw two Oscars at ten o'clock, two thousand feet above him. He turned into them and made a pass on the leader, after which he broke away and continued searching for his element leader. He saw a parachute drifting toward the ground, but suddenly two P-38s flashed past with four Oscars on their tails. Stoneham engaged the Oscars and cleared the Lightnings' tails before breaking off for home.[48]

Fred Scudday lost track of his wingman during the fight, but continued toward Hankou with the main strike force. He was a popular man in the 449th, not only because of his big-hearted, easy-going Texas personality, but also because he was utterly unflappable in combat. He had gained considerable experience flying with the RAF Eagle Squadrons in 1941 and the South African Air Force in 1942. By the time he transferred to the AAF and arrived in China, he already had two confirmed and one damaged enemy aircraft to his credit. Over Hankou, he coolly maneuvered his P-38 in and out of the mass of Oscars, fighting for every inch of progress as he turned back toward home. By the time he finally disengaged, he found that his compass had been shot. He circled a small town about sixty miles north of Suichuan until the warning net reported his position and a fighter controller guided him home over the radio.
Much of the squadron was watching for him, especially the enlisted men, with whom he had made a point of spending time each day – helping them with maintenance and armament, asking and answering questions, and swapping stories. One of the mechanics finally spotted him when he was about ten miles away. He came directly for the runway – no buzz job and no victory roll. As he touched down, both of his engines quit, and the plane coasted to a stop. There was not a drop of gasoline

On 6 May 1944, Lieutenant Longueil returned to Suichuan on one engine, lucky to be alive. Michael Bates

remaining in the fuel tanks. The men had to fuel his plane in the middle of the runway just to taxi it to the dispersal area.

Back at the alert shack, one of the other pilots commented, "Boy, are you lucky, Scud!"

"Luck?" Fred Scudday leaned against the shack with a sandwich in his hand and a big grin spreading across his face. "Brothers of the 449th, one and all, that was skill. Had my fuel supply figured out to the last drop!"[49]

Though outnumbered, the top cover had done its job, distracting the Japanese long enough for the B-25s to escape and hit their targets. Casey Vincent was frustrated by the Japanese ambush and commented that, "Bombing was excellent – fighters disappointing."[50] Lieutenant Moritsugu Kanai claimed two of the three P-38s destroyed. Major Sakagawa claimed three P-51s and the rest of the sentai claimed two more. Tex Hill claimed one Oscar and Lee Gregg was credited with two. In reality, the Americans lost just the three P-38s and one P-51. The 25th Sentai reported losing no Ki-43s, but three were severely damaged and one pilot seriously injured.[51] A possible explanation for the 449th's poor performance could have been contaminated gasoline. Lieutenant Hammond turned back soon after takeoff because of water in his gasoline and other pilots complained about a loss of power.

Lieutenant Moritsugu Kanai, of the 25th Sentai, claimed a total of thirty-two enemy planes shot down, including three 449th P-38s. Yasuho Izawa via Steve Blake

In spite of accurate bombing, the 6 May mission failed to stop the Japanese. The High Command was nevertheless concerned about American airpower and charged the 5th Air Army to "annihilate the U.S.-China Air Force and attain air supremacy in order that it might cooperate directly with the ground operations whenever necessary."[52] Toward this end, it determined to wipe out the airbase at Suichuan and sent over one hundred bombers and fighters on 12 May (known as "liquidation day" to the Americans) in three waves beginning at 0100 and lasting until 1600 hours. The first attacks occurred too early for P-38s to intercept, but since the night raids in February, the ground echelon had collected enough twin fifty-caliber machine guns from wrecked B-24s to construct four gun pits around the field. The moon was low and the Japanese bombers difficult to see as they came in one at a time to bomb the field. Each time, officers and enlisted men manning the guns opened fire, but could not seem to bring anything down. Eventually, one Lily came over whose crew forgot to turn off the light above its bomb bay doors. Three gun positions poured lead into the bomber until it erupted in flame and plummeted into the ground. They found the twisted metal wreckage near the field in the morning.[53]

The second wave arrived at 0630: six Ki-48s from the 90th Sentai escorted by eighteen Ki-43s from the 48th and thirty-five from the 25th.[54] Bob Kruidenier from the CACW remembered that eight P-38s "took off with a roar and climbed up to altitudes that a P-40 can never get to. There also were four P-51As, and they took off just ahead of our nine [P-40s]."[55] Fred Scudday claimed one Oscar and the Warhawks and Mustangs claimed another three. The Japanese erroneously reported shooting down two P-38s, but lost Sergeants Katsuji Kurosaka and Nobuyuki Hoshi of the 48th Sentai. Despite being outnumbered two to one by the Japanese fighters, the Americans managed to disrupt the attack. The third wave arrived at 1400: twelve bombers and sixty fighters. Suichuan launched seven P-38s, three P-51s, and several P-40s but managed to shoot down only one Lily, claimed by Wendell Stoneham. The other Lilys dropped a string of bombs directly over revetments full of parked aircraft. In all, the Japanese believed they destroyed seven airplanes in the air and thirty-eight on the ground. After the attacks on 12 May the Japanese press boasted: "Forward base of Fourteenth Air Force Wiped Out."[56] In truth, they destroyed one P-40 in the air and one B-25 on the ground, also damaging three B-25s and four P-38s. No Americans were killed. The attacks did manage to deplete Suichuan's gasoline reserve, however, prompting Vincent to pull his B-25s from the field the same day.[57]

The pace of operations and intensity of the enemy attacks combined with insufficient supply to make life difficult for the ground crews of the 449th. Buck Burris recalled that the armament section did not have much in the way of modern equipment. Loading bombs on a P-38 required them to find unoccupied Chinese coolies to hold the bombs in place with a bamboo gurney while the armorers tightened the wing nuts to fasten them into place. Then, they would attach the bomb's fuse and tail unit. Fragmentation bombs were considerably easier to load, but also more dangerous.[58]

Armorers servicing the guns on one of the 449th's P-38s. Richard Maddox

449th Fighter Squadron armorers take a break from servicing one of the unit's P-38s to pose with a Yank magazine. National Archives

Jim Hyde described the lengths the crew chiefs and maintenance personnel would go through to keep airplanes in the air:

> Most of the time we kept one airplane stripped – it never got into condition. Something would go wrong and we'd have to rob it of the part. About the time we got that part in to fix it, something would happen where we would have to rob it for another one. We had one airplane that stayed down for parts for two or three months at a time.[59]

Maintenance was a nonstop job. Often crews worked twenty-four-hour shifts to keep the squadron fighting. A lighted mechanical revetment was set up at Suichuan to make it easier to work at night and ground crews cycled through in shifts to prevent complete exhaustion. The revetment was a circle of compacted earth about fifteen feet high to protect it from bombs. One side had an opening wide enough to move airplanes in and out. Jim Hyde remembered that one day in early May "We were working on another aircraft; one that I had been a crew chief for at one time named *Patches*, because it had been patched up so many times. It was in that revetment being worked on along with another aircraft." Suddenly, Hyde looked up and saw a bomb headed straight for them. "When you see bombs drop, if they look oblong or long you know they're going to miss you. When you see them and they look like a needle pointing at you they're going to be close." The bomb he saw looked like the latter. "I hollered 'Boys get out it's coming close.'" He and the other mechanics ran from the revetment and dove into a slit trench dug alongside. "The bomb hit on the end of that trench and showered dirt on all of us. It shook us up pretty good but it didn't hurt anybody. But it was a very close deal."[60]

Ground crewman guarding ordnance on the flight line, 1945. George Brabec

The early-model P-38s experienced more maintenance problems than any other standard American fighter. The guns would jam in turns of more than 3 1/2 Gs, refueling in the field would often take in excess of thirty minutes, carburetor temperatures would run too high, intercoolers would break easily, inspection panels were difficult to remove, and oil and coolant lines would often vibrate free and make a mess.[61] Despite these problems, Jim Hyde liked working on the P-38 and thought it was "pretty easy to maintain." According to Hyde:

> The Allison was a clean, sleek looking engine. I worked on both inline and radial engines and I prefer the inline because of the appearance – it was just a slicker looking engine – that old radial engine may have delivered pretty good horse power but it was a monstrosity to look at.[62]

Despite their poor aesthetic properties, radial engines were generally more robust than inline engines. Ground crews worked with what they had, however. Though conditions were ridiculous, Buck Burris commented that, "We didn't think about it, we just did it."[63] By keeping the machines armed and in good

Ground crew working in the open on a P-38's Allison engines. Jack Bowman

Ground crewmen inspect the tail section of a P-38 damaged in a hard landing. George Brabec

George Brabec in a slit trench at Mengzi in 1945. This is similar to the trench into which Jim Hyde jumped when the Japanese bombed the mechanical revetment at Suichuan. George Brabec

working order, they kept the squadron in the war, contributing just as much as the pilots to eventual victory.

Most of the pilots had a good relationship with the ground crewmen. Jim Hyde was, for a time, Jim Heitkotter's crew chief. Heitkotter remembered:

> One balmy Sunday Jim Hyde and I were sitting on a wing talking of many things. It came time to show pictures of family at home. When I saw his wife's picture I said, "Why, that's Inez Nyberg!" Very surprised (as was I) he asked, "How do you know her?" looking sternly inquisitive. "I went to high school with her in Fresno." Until then we did not know each other's home town. We were closer friends from then on.[64]

Unlike many squadrons, the 449th made little distinction between officers and enlisted men. They would often play cards or sports together but roomed in separate buildings. According to Jerry Doughty, "All of the ground crew and support personnel were superb. I will always be indebted to them. They were the back bone of the 449th and a great bunch of guys."[65]

Meanwhile, on 26 May, the Japanese launched phase two of Ichi-go; 250,000 troops crossed the Yangzi River and followed the railroad bed (the railroad itself had been destroyed by the Chinese) southwest along the shore of Dongting Lake to where it meets the Xiang River just north of Changsha. Marshall Xue Yue, who had three times before turned the Japanese back at Changsha, prepared to make a stand, but the Japanese bypassed the city, leaving only a token holding force, and continued on to Hengyang.[66]

Rather than targeting the JAAF, the 14th Air Force focused on close air support and interdiction as the Japanese ground forces barreled through ineffective Chinese opposition. The shortage of gasoline kept most of Chennault's bombers grounded, but his fighters remained heavily committed. Buck Burris commented: "You can't imagine how much bombing and strafing missions we did ... I've loaded enough bombs on them old P-38s."[67] The pace of operations took its toll. On 29 May, Lieutenant Walter Rose experienced trouble with his right engine on takeoff. He circled the field once and came in on the base leg with his wheels down. He could not land, however, because of a P-40 taking off. He raised his gear, circled again,

Ground crewman working on an Allison engine at Lingling, 1943 or 1944. 14th Air Force Association

Mechanics pull an engine from a P-38 for maintenance in 1945. George Brabec

but this time his left engine stopped. He crashed three miles from the runway. According to Curtiss Perry, "He was busted up real bad and died before they got him to the Suichuan hospital."[68]

At the beginning of June, Lieutenant Colonel McMillan called the squadron together. "Boys," he said, "You've always known I've never held anything back from you. The Japs are getting closer. They are pressing down on [Changde] and now they're starting a squeeze play by moving on us from the south. The jig is up. Our stay here now depends entirely on the Jap movement. Maybe it will be a day longer, maybe a week or more, but it's pretty sure sooner or later we shall have to move and move quickly."[69]

To McMillan and many of the other American personnel in China, it seemed as if many of the Chinese generals had already given up, unwilling to challenge the Japanese advance. Casey Vincent directed a new interdiction campaign to stymie the axis of advance along the Xiang River, but most pilots cynically thought of it as a wasted effort. Nevertheless, Vincent's new campaign was much more effective than his last one. Finally, better weather allowed P-40 and P-51 fighter-bombers to interdict traffic on the Xiang River, which effectively cut the flow of Japanese supplies in half. Additionally, the terrain in the Xiang River Valley funneled the Japanese advance to two land lines of communication. Pack trains moved along the railroad bed and truck convoys moved along a single roadway on the opposite side of the river.[70] Vincent assigned the 449th to interdict truck convoys. Sometimes the Lightnings would use parachute-suspended fragmentation bombs, but more often, they would strafe the convoys along the length of the column. According to Chennault, "When rains softened the road, convoys bogged down in the mud, making sitting ducks for the Lightnings' 20mm cannon. After the first week of fighting, this road was lined with charred chassis of burned trucks."[71] Eventually, the Japanese found that daylight movement of trucks was too costly and restricted their movement to nighttime only. While road interdiction further limited Japanese supply, the 14th Air Force's inability to conduct operations at night allowed the Japanese to continue operations.[72]

Interdiction of pack trains was somewhat more successful. During much of Ichi-go, the Japanese used horses in terrain that limited mechanized forces. On average, eight horses were required to replace each truck, making eight hundred horses necessary to replace one brigade, a column impossible to hide from the air.[73] Bruce Schultz remembered a strafing attack against Japanese motorized barges moving packhorses across a river: "I led the flight on a line astern pass and the carnage among the Japanese army and their horses left areas of red in the river."[74] While the 14th Air Force claimed only 2,739 horses killed, the Japanese admitted to losing over ten thousand to all causes – mostly to air attack. Between river, road, and pack train interdiction, the Japanese front lines received few supplies. Unfortunately, there was no anvil of Chinese ground troops against which the hammer of airpower could drive the Japanese and they survived on what supplies they carried or captured until they reached Hengyang.[75]

Jerry Doughty's crew chief in front of their P-38. Doughty considered the ground crews to be the backbone of the 449th. Jerry Doughty

The 5th Air Army also focused on ground attack. JAAF records state, "the main mission ... was cooperation with the ground forces," and went on to testify that their aircraft "sustained heavy losses during this operation and received little replenishment. It was compelled, therefore, to avoid air combat."[76] The Japanese possessed only 230 combat aircraft against a force they estimated to be upwards of 520. While Chennault possessed almost five hundred aircraft at that time, two hundred were required to defend bases for the B-29s arriving in China and 150 were assigned to support operations in Burma, leaving around 150 planes to oppose Ichi-go. Chennault estimated he faced over one thousand Japanese aircraft and believed the Japanese outnumbered him until early 1945. In fact, he achieved numerical superiority by June 1944.

Though both sides avoided air combat, they still met while operating over the same battlefield. On 11 June, fifteen Ki-43s from the 48th Sentai intercepted twelve P-38s on a ground attack mission near Anqing. Lieutenants Nunn and Frank each claimed an enemy aircraft destroyed, but the Japanese reported that all Ki-43s returned safely.[77] While escorting B-25s to Hankou two days later, Lieutenant Colonel McMillan and Lieutenant Newnom each claimed one intercepting Oscar. Of the nine Ki-43s from the 25th Sentai, Sergeant Kazuo Miyasaki was killed in action and another crash-landed at Senti. On 18 June, twelve Ki-43s from the 25th Sentai and four Ki-44s from the 9th met twelve P-38s escorting three B-25s to Anqing. The Tojos flew top cover while the Oscars dove to attack. Lieutenant Williams claimed one enemy fighter destroyed, but the Japanese shot down Lieutenants Bartlett and Roll. Billie Beardsley, who the next day would shoot down a dive-bomber near Changlokai, witnessed one of the two getting shot down and reported:

> A few seconds after the fight started I saw one P-38 going southeast trailing smoke. I dove down to see if the P-38 was being attacked, but could see no ZEROS after him. [The] pilot bailed out while I was still 3,000 feet above him. The ship crashed in the first foothills south east of [Anqing]. The pilot also landed in the first foot hills about one half mile from the crashed ship, apparently safe. [I] could not identify [the] pilot or ship no.[78]

In any event, both Bartlett and Roll made it safely back to friendly territory. The Japanese claimed five P-38s destroyed and reported no losses.[79]

As the Japanese advanced closer to Suichuan, the Americans feared they would have to defend the base themselves. On 14 June, the 449th received a shipment of M1 carbines, lightweight semi-automatic weapons that almost seemed like toys. Tom Monaghan, the squadron armament officer, was fooling with a carbine, showing the firing mechanism to Captain James Bledsoe, a recent arrival to the squadron. Fred Scudday was nearby, both hands on a table, leaning over some recently arrived pinups. Suddenly, a shot rang out and Scudday fell to the ground. Monaghan, for all his preaching on weapons safety, had not known the carbine was loaded. When he accidently fired the weapon, the thirty-caliber round went right through Scudday's neck, killing him instantly. Monaghan was mortified. There had not been a more popular man in the squadron than Fred Scudday, and the incident weighed on Monaghan very heavily.[80] The squadron's morale began another downward spiral.

Lieutenant Jack Frank in the cockpit of his P-38. Many of the ground crew considered him "a real character." Richard Maddox

The Japanese kept advancing closer and closer to Suichuan. On 17 June, Japanese troops took the towns of Shangli, sixty miles southeast of Changsha, and Fenghuoli, forty-seven miles northwest of Suichuan. P-38s bombed and strafed the towns, starting fires and causing considerable damage before sighting a reinforcing column of approximately two thousand troops and strafing it, inflicting an estimated four hundred casualties.

Lieutenant James Bartlett in the cockpit of his P-38. Bartlett was shot down near Anqing on 11 June, but bailed out and safely returned to the 449th. Jerry Doughty

While such attacks were devastating, they were never enough to stymie the enemy advance. Air attacks on troop columns could delay an advance, but they could never do enough damage to stop one. According to Chennault only an aggressive interdiction campaign combined with a stalwart Chinese defense could halt the Japanese.[81]

As the Japanese surged forward, the front lines blurred. Towns were taken faster than intelligence sources could report. Casey Vincent believed the best way to pinpoint the enemy's vanguard was to send forth patrols of fighters to engage it. On 24 June, he flew to Suichuan to confer with Lieutenant Colonel McMillan. The 449th had already begun evacuating the base two days previous, and when Vincent arrived McMillan was preparing to lead another bombing mission. Vincent wanted him to cancel the mission and instead lead a strafing and frag-bomb attack on a Japanese column reported north of Pingxiang. The weather was not good, and the low ceiling meant there would be a murderous reception by the Japanese troops. McMillan thought the idea was asinine and told Vincent as much. Vincent went into a rage and the two men had a heated argument on the flight line in full view of the rest of the squadron. Finally, Vincent threatened to court-martial McMillan. Frustrated, he replied that they would "fly the damn thing!" The armament crews quickly unloaded the five-hundred- or one-thousand-pounders and prepared the Lightnings with fragmentation bombs.

Pingxiang was a small town in mountainous terrain seventy miles southeast of Changsha. McMillan led a formation of eleven P-38s to the area, but near the town they sighted thousands of soldiers thirty kilometers south of where Chinese intelligence reported the enemy to be. McMillan was unable to tell whether the troops were Chinese or Japanese, and as he was unwilling to kill friendly troops by accident, he circled several times, eventually drawing intense ground fire. Though the Japanese possessed few anti-aircraft guns, they instructed their infantry to fire their nine-millimeter rifles in sequence (called pattern fire). When a fighter came in on a strafing or bombing run in Europe, the German or Italian troops would usually dive for cover, unwilling to sacrifice themselves to the awesome firepower of its machine guns. The Japanese, however, would stand and fight, knowing full well that some of them would die. For the airman, the protection that lay in the fear his machine instilled did not exist against the Japanese, whose bullets would reach up and perforate his airplane's thin aluminum skin.[82]

McMillan turned and dropped his canisters of fragmentation bombs. As soon as the canisters left the wing, a parachute opened and the bombs dropped straight down, exploding on contact with the ground.[83] As he dropped the bombs, however, small arms fire hit his right engine, which began smoking so badly that he thought he would have to bail out. He called on the radio: "Them little slant-eyed bastards got me."[84] He decided to get as far from the target area as possible and departed to the southeast. Lieutenant Arpin was McMillan's wingman and flew alongside him as they left the area. The Japanese also hit Arpin, and he feathered his right propeller and shut down the engine. Both of McMillan's engines were still running, but he told Arpin that the coolant in his right engine was leaking and that the left engine oil pressure was dropping fast. Jim Hyde explained that the Japanese probably hit the P-38's ethylene glycol radiator: "The thing went out of fuel and the aircraft caught fire."[85] Ten miles from Pingxiang, McMillan saw the Lu River and asked his flight: "How do these things land on water?" One of them answered, "Climb out of your parachute." According to Arpin:

> Right after this I started overtaking him and saw that he seemed to be removing his parachute shoulder straps. I passed him and saw that his left engine was froze and was losing altitude. When I looked back from about 500 feet the ship had crashed in flames about 200 yards south of the river bed. I saw no parachute in the area.[86]

George McMillan had been the squadron's greatest commander. According to Father Cosgrove, he "ran the squadron from top to bottom. He knew every movement and condition of each department. His thoughtfulness for others was daily seen at the field."[87] Now he was dead. His P-38 became his funeral pyre, burning brightly just two hundred yards from the banks of the Lu River. The Japanese infantry, who did not subscribe to the myth of his fighter's overwhelming power, sent bullets skyward that pierced his vulnerable radiators just as Pheobus Apollo's baleful shaft pierced Achilles' heel. Naturally, the squadron was distraught at his loss and morale plummeted. Buck Burris commented, "He was a good commander. I had the greatest respect for him and it hurt me very deeply when I heard he went down."[88] The 449th was not the only squadron to lose its commander in the intense spring and summer of 1944. Chennault wrote, "We lost four squadron commanders to flak in less than a month, among them ex-A.V.G. George McMillan who had returned to China to command the 449th Fighter Squadron."[89]

By 24 June, the Japanese were only forty miles from Suichuan. Most personnel had already been evacuated except for a skeleton crew to keep the P-38s flying. On 26 June, the fighters departed for Guilin and the remaining personnel set to destroying the base. Jim Hyde was part of the last group to leave and remembered blowing up the line shack and operations building. He and twenty others boarded six charcoal burning trucks loaded with tools, equipment, and supplies and "chugged away at about 20 miles an hour." The trucks stopped frequently to allow the charcoal burning stove boiler to generate enough gas to continue, which left them perilously close to the Japanese on a number of occasions. On 28 June, the convoy reached Guilin. Each week the P-38s would fall farther back, and each week the truck convoy moved to catch up. On 8 July, Hyde was told he would be in charge of the convoy all the way to Chenggong (near Kunming). It was a tough road from Suichuan: over rugged mountains where white men had never before set foot. Often, Chinese would line the road to see the Americans. Hyde "finally arrived at [Chenggong] and the 449th on August 3rd, a month and 7 days since we left Suichuan. The six who finally finished the trip were Sgts. Harold Reeder, Tony Anthony, Ray Bunton, Walt Ritterbush and Cpl. Clairborne and me."[90]

C-46 Commandos evacuate equipment and personnel from Suichuan in advance of the Japanese army. National Archives

Suichuan was not the only base evacuated, Chinese opposition melted away in the face of the Japanese advance. Hengyang was the only place where Japanese troops met significant resistance. There, sixteen thousand Chinese troops made use of the terrain and defensive fortifications to inflict 20,290 casualties on the Japanese. With the help of American airpower, the defenders of Hengyang held out for forty-seven days, by which time only 1,200 undersupplied and underequipped Chinese soldiers remained. The defense of Hengyang could have lasted longer had the defenders been properly supplied, but Chiang Kaishek refused to send equipment to generals he considered political rivals and instead horded it for eventual war with the Communists. Consequently, Hengyang fell on 8 August and cleared the way for a Japanese advance on Guilin. Despite fierce resistance from the 14th Air Force, Guilin fell on 11 November and American pilots found themselves striking targets they had occupied only weeks before.

Though the 449th evacuated Suichuan, the Japanese bypassed the area, leaving a pocket of territory in Chinese hands. In August 1944, Major John C. "Pappy" Herbst moved the 74th Fighter Squadron to nearby Ganzhou and in November, the 118th Tactical Reconnaissance Squadron moved to Suichuan.[91] Both bases were supplied entirely by air. According to Luke Kissick, intelligence officer for the 74th Fighter Squadron, "B-24 tankers supplied the gasoline over the Japanese lines. C-47s and C-46s supplied the logistics, some personnel replacements and supplies in order to fly sustained operations." The "guerrilla" squadrons proved a thorn in the side of the Japanese, accounting for two-thirds of the 14th Air Force's successes between November 1944 and January 1945 because they had access to targets unreachable from any other airbases. Vital to their success was intelligence and independence of operations. As intelligence officer for the 74th, Kissick, "had the Chinese guerrillas, Chiang Ching-kuo's [the provincial governor] communications net, OSS [Office of Strategic Services], SACO [Sino-American Cooperative Organization], 2 bribed Japanese Naval Officers on my payroll, Coast watchers and 2 P-38 Photographic squadrons all reporting to me." Using this information, Kissick and Herbst planned missions, usually without direction or consultation with group or wing headquarters, located several hundred miles to the west.[92]

The greatest mission of the guerrilla squadrons was the 17 January 1945 attack on Shanghai, a target previously untouched by the 14th Air Force. It took Herbst and Kissick thirty days to lay the groundwork for the raid, including feeding information to a known Japanese agent that suggested Shanghai was out of range of the squadrons' P-51 Mustangs.[93] On the morning of 17 January, twenty P-51s from the 74th and 118th departed for Shanghai.[94] John C. Conn, a pilot in the 74th, remembered approaching the city at ten thousand feet. Fifty miles out, the fighters began a steady descent to hit the Japanese airfields at high speed. Conn's flight was led by the 74th's incoming commander, Major Philip Chapman, and hit Longhua Airdrome. Japanese fighters were lined up next to the airfield, wingtip to wingtip. The raid was a complete surprise. According to Conn, "we shot them up on the ground." The fighters were full of fuel and "would start burning right away," limiting visibility because of the smoke.[95] In attacks on three airfields surrounding the city, the guerrilla squadrons destroyed an estimated seventy-three enemy planes, mostly on the ground. In mid-February 1945, the Japanese took Suichuan and Ganzhou, finally completing Ichi-go and forcing the guerrillas to evacuate.

Ichi-go was significant for several reasons, not least of which was the fact that Chennault lost most of his airbases in East China. Because the Allies defeated the Japanese advance in India, the Japanese did not completely drive Chennault out of China. While Ichi-go was clearly a defeat for Nationalist China, which sustained at least 310,000 casualties and lost most of its territory, it was not necessarily a victory for the Japanese. Despite the fact that Japanese forces in China and Indochina linked up on 10 December 1944, it took them months to make the rail corridor operational, by which time the war was nearly finished. Additionally, Ichi-go deprived Japan of troops at a critical time in the Pacific. U.S. Marines landed on Saipan in the Marianas Islands on 15 June 1944. Prime Minister Tojo considered the Marianas vital to the defense of the Japanese Empire, but because of Ichi-go, he had only forty thousand troops with which to defend Saipan.[96] By July, it was firmly in the hands of the United States, and Guam and Tinian followed in August. These islands served as airbases from which B-29 Superfortresses decimated Japan in 1945.

Ironically, Ichi-go also heralded the effective end of the JAAF in China. The 5th Air Army was unable to replace losses in China because of the need to reinforce the Philippines and was gradually reduced to impotence. By the time the Japanese took Guilin, the American air force outnumbered the 5th Air Army by more than five to one. By December 1944, the 25th Sentai had lost so many aircraft and pilots it virtually dissolved, and most other sentais in China operated at half-strength or less. By the summer of 1945, most Japanese fighter units in China had withdrawn to Taiwan or Korea.[97]

CHAPTER FIVE

Walkout

While the rest of the 449th was battling the Japanese in East China, Lieutenant Lee Gregg was undergoing a different ordeal. When last seen on 6 May 1944, he was out cold and his P-38 was hurtling toward the ground. As the plane plummeted, picking up speed, Gregg suddenly regained consciousness. Since his aircraft was damaged and uncontrollable due to high-speed compressibility,[1] he decided to bail out. He quickly disconnected his oxygen tube and radio equipment, and released his safety belt. Straining forward, he grabbed the emergency hatch release on top of the control panel. The canopy separated and the suction instantly pulled him from the cockpit. He pulled the parachute ripcord immediately, but so great was his speed that the opening shock fractured his twelfth vertebrae and again rendered him unconscious. He awoke sometime after hitting the ground and tried to stand up. In addition to his back injury, however, shrapnel had wounded his left ankle during the air battle. He collapsed and passed out.[2]

Meanwhile, Glen Beneda from the 76th Fighter Squadron was also having trouble. When he bailed out, his right leg struck the horizontal stabilizer of his airplane. Landing in a rice paddy, he stood with some difficulty and called to nearby Chinese farmers. He held up the blood chit he carried in his back pocket, a silk cloth with the American and Chinese flags and an inscription in Chinese promising a reward to anyone who returned the bearer to friendly lines. He yelled "Meiguo, Meiguo," which means "America, America," but the frightened Chinese would not approach him. Finally, one of the farmers pointed to a farmhouse in the nearby village and Beneda painfully began walking toward it. When he neared the house, a man walked out and they conversed through Beneda's pointie-talkie, a book with common phrases displayed side by side in Chinese and English. To communicate with the Chinese, the American had only to find the phrase he wished to convey, and point to the Chinese characters next to the English translation. Though much of the Chinese population was illiterate, the man opposite Beneda was somewhat educated and understood that he wanted to locate any nearby guerrillas.[3]

They set off, several hours later coming across Beneda's airplane outside the village of Luojia, seventy miles west of Hankou.[4] The P-51 crashed in a rice paddy and lay upside down, completely submerged. Chinese villagers crowded around, reaching into the water to salvage anything they could find.[5] At 2000 hours, Beneda and his guide finally arrived at a guerrilla outpost. With some trepidation, he looked over the guerrilla fighters, who wore no insignia and spoke no English. They brought him to a local command post where the unit's political officer informed him in broken English that he was under the protection of the Communist New 4th Army.[6]

In the 1920s, the Soviet Union sponsored the creation of the Chinese Communist Party (CCP), which demanded social and economic reforms from the ruling Nationalists. Chiang initially cooperated with the CCP, including working with them in the 1926 Northern Expedition against separatist warlords, but he soon came to realize that they represented the single greatest threat to his political survival. Without warning, he ordered the execution of CCP members in Shanghai in 1927 and in a series of extermination campaigns throughout the early 1930s, doggedly pursued them across China.[7] In 1934, what was left of their forces, under the charismatic leadership of Mao Zedong, set out on the "Long March," a retreat from the Jiangxi Province in south-central China, northwest to Yan'an, in the remote Shaanxi Province – three thousand miles over 370 days. The war against Japan prevented Chiang from destroying the remnant of the Communist forces.

The CCP was in a unique position with respect to the war against Japan. When they negotiated their nonaggression pact with Russia in 1941, the Japanese agreed to leave the CCP in control of three provinces in northwest China. Thus, the Communists were in no immediate danger of annihilation like the Nationalists. However, in the interest of garnering popular support for the inevitable resurgence of the Chinese Civil War, Mao led them in a guerilla campaign against the Japanese.[8] In reality, Japan only controlled the major cities and transportation routes in most occupied areas. Lee Gregg reported that while the Japanese supposedly occupied the area between Hankou and Yichang, the chances were good for an American to evade capture.[9] Mao's strategy was to establish bases behind enemy lines to "convert the enemy's rear into an additional front. Thus the enemy will never be able to stop fighting."[10] Coupled with this military strategy was a political one; the large pockets between occupation forces left a power vacuum the CCP was eager to fill. As the Nationalists fell back in the face of overwhelming military power, the Communists filled-in behind. By 1940, Mao's forces had gained so much popularity and support from occupied China that he dramatically expanded his operations, establishing the New 4th Army for operations in the Yangzi River Valley.[11] Thus in many ways, the CCP was the true winner of Ichi-go. While the Japanese spread their troops across China instead of responding more effectively to American advances in the Pacific, their campaign had a devastating effect on the Nationalists' military and political strength. To the peasantry, it appeared as if the Communists were the only Chinese group fighting the invader. Consequently, while in 1937 the Communists controlled only thirty-five thousand square miles of territory and one and a half million people in the poorest regions of China, by 1945, they controlled 225,000 square miles and sixty-five million people.[12] At the end of World War II, they were the most powerful political and military entity in China, paving the way for their takeover in 1949.

Both Glen Beneda and Lee Gregg ended up in the care of the New 4th Army. After bailing out, Gregg awakened to find four Chinese farmers carrying him toward Lake Hou. Though they could not understand when he tried to tell them he was an American, he suspected they recognized him as such based on his appearance. Two of the Chinese stripped the insignia from his uniform while the other two went to fetch a boat. For the next four days, he lapsed in and out of consciousness, sometimes finding himself in a house or on a boat, and at others, being rushed through the night on a stretcher. On the fifth day, he awoke to find himself in the care of an inexperienced medic with a small detachment of Communist troops. The medic tended to the shrapnel wound in his ankle, but could do nothing to mend his back.

Lee Gregg spent three days recuperating with the detachment before the Japanese closed on his position. Escaping in the night, the guerrillas took him by boat across the swampy lowlands to the southeast. They told him to lie in the bottom and remain silent until they arrived at a farmhouse at 1000 hours the next day. Sentries reported the Japanese approaching again only one hour later. The guerrillas picked up Gregg and ran, taking fire from troops only one hundred yards away. Rushing behind a house, the Chinese hid him underneath a haystack and turned to confront the enemy. Gregg remembered taking cover for what seemed like three hours as the two parties exchanged rifle fire and grenades. Finally, the guerrillas drove off the Japanese, killing two of them and taking no losses. They boarded a boat and traveled through the rest of the day and night. Arriving at another farmhouse, a Communist soldier brought a parachute, pointie-talkie, and identification card to Gregg, telling him the owner was found deceased. The articles belonged to Lieutenant William Jones. Gregg was upset at learning of his friend's death. The lack of blood on the parachute made him think that Jones had drowned. In all likelihood, Jones probably died when he hit the wing of Lieutenant Morita's Oscar.[13]

Lieutenant Glen Beneda with his P-40 before the 76th Fighter Squadron transitioned to P-51s. Glenn Beneda

Meanwhile, Glen Beneda and his guerrilla escort travelled north, followed closely by the Japanese. He rode on horseback from town to town, finding refuge in the local Communist headquarters. When the guerrillas received intelligence that enemy troops were closing in, they would evacuate. The guerrilla intelligence nets were well organized and pervasive. According to Mao, "Every person without exception must be considered an agent – old men and women, boys driving ox carts, girls tending goats, farm laborers, storekeepers, schoolteachers, priests, boatmen, scavengers." Consequently, the Communists often knew every detail of a Japanese advance and simultaneously prevented the enemy from collecting information on their own activities. In order to preserve the strength of his forces, Mao instructed his guerrillas to disperse in the face of enemy strength and concentrate to attack enemy weaknesses. He realized that his guerrillas "must move with the fluidity of water and the ease of the blowing wind. Their tactics must deceive, tempt, and confuse the enemy. ... They must strike, then rapidly disperse."[14] Thus, as the Japanese pursued Beneda and his escort, the Communists dispersed, always staying one step ahead.

Moving primarily by night, Beneda continued toward friendly territory. On the night of 13 May, his party crossed the Han River, the next day arriving at the 3rd Regimental Headquarters of the 5th Division, New 4th Army. The following morning he was the focus of a big party thrown by the guerrillas. They showered him with food and gifts in appreciation for America's role in the War of Resistance Against Japan. The 3rd Regiment then provided him an escort of a platoon of forty-five troops and sent him on his way. On the 16th, the same day Lee Gregg learned of Jones' death, Beneda's horse threw and kicked him and the guerrillas fashioned a stretcher with which to carry him the rest of the way. At 2200 hours on 22 May, the group had just stopped to rest under a moonless sky when "I heard, 'tat tat tat tat tat' and I looked over and saw the muzzle flash of machine guns." Though his leg had been hurt when he bailed out of his fighter and the vicious kick of his horse left him worse off than before, he suddenly found that his legs worked much better. He got off the stretcher and ran, hiding behind a mound of earth in a nearby wooded area.[15] The Chinese fought a fierce battle, but as time passed, the shooting gradually died out. Beneda feared the Chinese had been vanquished, but soon heard the voice of Xiao Deng, one of his escorts, calling to him. The guerrilla took him by the hand and led him to a nearby village, where the rest of the group was waiting. According to Deng, "No one had been lost. Everyone was beaming with joy, and they waved the Japanese guns and swords back and forth. It appeared that our small troop had won this battle."[16] Continuing onward, the platoon delivered Beneda to General Li's (later State Chairman of China) 5th Division Headquarters at Da Wu Mountain on 27 May. The guerrillas told him that Lee Gregg was some number of days behind and he would wait there for him to catch up.

On 18 May, Lee Gregg arrived at the 3rd Regimental Headquarters of the 5th Division, where he remained for seven days recovering from his injuries. Every day, the Chinese changed his ankle dressing and applied heat packs to his back. While recuperating, Gregg spent time talking with the regiment's political officer and horseback riding to build his strength for the coming journey. Despite his painful injuries, he was impatient to continue. On the 24th, he wrote in his journal, "I'm getting mad – will I never get started?" It was not until the next afternoon that he and a battalion of three hundred guerrillas got underway. The guerrillas were equipped with rifles, mortars, and machine guns, marching in a single file line over a mile in length. At 1700 hours, a formation of three Japanese bombers flew overhead, unnerving Gregg, but not phasing the Communist troops.[17]

That night, the battalion crossed the Han River, continuing northward. Gregg's body was a mass of pain from the day's riding and he rigged a brace from his jungle kit to support him in the saddle. For the next several days, he rode in immense pain, needing morphine shots just to fall asleep at night. His ankle and bruising seemed to improve, but his back did not. Day after day, it became increasingly stiff and Gregg became more convinced that it was broken. At 2100 hours on the night of the 31st, as the party prepared to cross the Hankou-Yichang road, they came across an enemy patrol. According to Gregg, "Our commander challenged them and the answer was a shot. The bullet barely missed me, so close I could almost feel it." He bailed off his horse into knee-deep water in a rice paddy while more bullets zipped by. The guerrilla battalion responded with positive action: "Our men charged right into the face of their fire and used hand grenades and rifle mortars. We finally mounted the horses and ran like hell across the road and across some wheat fields while the soldiers covered us." Within an hour, the Communists drove off the Japanese and continued onward.[18]

After crossing the Hankou-Yichang, Shasi-Hankou, and Anlu-Hankou roads, the battalion turned due east to cross the Hankou-Beiping Railroad on 3 June. They waited several miles from the railway until dusk. At 1800 hours, the first half of the battalion crossed the tracks when suddenly, "here comes a train hell bent for election." Two locomotives pulled the train and the guerrilla commander supposed that it carried Japanese officers. The Communists had just enough time to set up their machine guns. As the train passed, "they really let them have it," taking only light return fire from the train cars. After it passed, the rest of the battalion crossed the tracks and they regrouped a quarter mile away. "We got about a mile from the railroad when I heard what I thought was a flight of geese. Just as I looked up there was a hell of an explosion about 100 yards ahead and to the right of our column. The bastards had come back and setup a heavy mortar." Fortunately, a strong wind kept the Japanese mortar team from hitting their mark and the guerrillas made good their escape. The next day, Gregg and his party finally arrived at Da Wu Mountain and the headquarters of the 5th Division, only a few miles east of the railway and approximately seventy miles north of Hankou. Beneda had been waiting eight days for his arrival. Gregg "was sure glad to see him,"[19] and, according to Beneda, "we talked all night."[20]

After a day of rest, Gregg and Beneda proceeded farther into the mountains to visit the 5th Division's military academy. It was 6 June 1944, the same day the Allies stormed the beaches of Normandy. For hours, they climbed a winding trail up a mountain until finally they reached the top. Before them was an arch made of pine boughs with a sign that read "Welcome to our alliance Lt. Gregg and Lt. Beneda."[21] A twenty-boy bugle corps trumpeted their arrival to a crowd of over two hundred students and soldiers, including twenty Japanese from the Anti-War League. Both pilots were startled to see Japanese soldiers at a Communist military academy and inquired as to the nature of their organization. Apparently, many Japanese taking part in their nation's "sacred war" became disillusioned after seeing combat in China. On 7 November 1939, Zhu De, Mao's military protégé, established the Japanese Anti-War League and began actively recruiting defectors. Mao and Zhu both saw propaganda as an important cornerstone to the Communist cause. Mao claimed that because of the barbarity of the war in China, many Japanese opposed the policies of their government. By propagandizing the enemy troops, "treating his captured soldiers with consideration, and by caring for those of his wounded who fall into our hands," the Communists could "further our mission of destroying the enemy."[22] By 1944, most Communist divisions had a detachment of ten to twenty Japanese defectors who provided intelligence by intercepting phone calls and other methods of espionage, created anti-war newspapers to distribute to enemy troops, taught Japanese language to Chinese intelligence personnel, and wrote stories, poems, and novels that demonstrated Japanese brutality in China.[23] Gregg and Beneda found the organization fascinating, and spent time talking with members of the league through their interpreter, Mr. Wang. The Communists asked both Gregg and Beneda to prepare a speech, which they delivered to the assembled crowd at the academy. Gregg thought, "It was pretty good – I surprised myself." Afterwards, they attended a party with General Li and returned to headquarters at Da Wu the next day.[24]

Early on the morning of the 8th, the two pilots and their escort of one hundred guerrillas departed for Nationalist lines. Before they left, General Li gave them a letter and a Japanese officer's saber to present to General Chennault. Doubling back a bit, the guerrillas led Gregg and Beneda back across the Beiping-Hankou Railroad. For four days, they traveled westward, greeted by grateful Chinese in every village and town. On the 11th, however, Gregg woke up "with the worst toothache I've ever had." After several hours of travel where every step of his stretcher-bearers "was a hit in the mouth to me," the guerrillas tried to pull the tooth out with a string, but it broke. Finally, they managed to find a doctor, but he did not have a pair of pliers, only surgical scissors. He eventually gave up and administered two CCs of morphine to help ease the pain. Regardless, Gregg did not sleep well that night.

He woke up the next day feeling much better and learned they were to remain at their present location while the guerrillas sent a messenger to contact the Nationalists. Four days and three messengers later, however, the Americans began to worry. As it turned out, the Nationalist 69th Division, actively engaged in operations against the Communists rather than the Japanese, stood between the two pilots and friendly lines. Despite the fact that both the Nationalists and Communists were fighting the Japanese, they did not cease fighting each other, making it a delicate procedure to hand off rescued airmen. While perhaps surprising, this was characteristic of Chiang, who believed that while the Japanese represented a disease of the skin, the Communists were a disease of the heart.[25] Worried in light of improving Communist fortunes and expansion, Chiang levied an embargo on CCP-controlled territory in 1940.[26] He also stockpiled American lend-lease equipment for a future showdown with Mao rather than commit it against the Japanese. This bewildered many Americans, who angrily reported "acres and acres of new vehicles: jeeps, carry-alls, weapons carriers, 6x6 trucks and gasoline tankers parked neatly, row upon row,"[27] while poorly equipped Nationalist troops melted away in the face of the Japanese advance in East China. One of the guerrillas told Gregg that the Nationalists probably thought that the messengers were trying to draw them into an ambush and therefore executed them on the spot.[28]

Despite their physical condition improving, (Gregg, for example was finally able to walk for extended periods), Gregg and Beneda became increasingly impatient as time wore on. On the morning of 16 June, the two woke up to the sound of heavy engine noise. In the early morning light, Gregg saw six B-29s pass overhead. That night, forty-seven B-29s had raided the Yawata Imperial Iron and Steel Works on the island of Kyushu in the first attack on the Japanese Home Islands since the 1942 Doolittle Raid.[29] The B-29s Gregg and Beneda saw were stragglers returning to their forward base at Chengdu. The bombers

A CACW B-25 Gunship at Liangshan in 1945. Robert Crozier

had recently arrived to begin Operation Matterhorn, General Arnold's plan for bombing the Japanese mainland from China. Arnold directed his B-29s to target the steel industry in Japan and Manchuria as the first step in bringing about the downfall of Japanese industry. Like the 308th Bomb Group, the B-29s were supposed to fly their own fuel and supplies into China, but in reality they fed off the supplies coming over the Hump at a time the 14th Air Force could least afford it. Chennault complained that between the B-29s and the six P-47 squadrons assigned to defend their bases, the 14th lost 1,500 tons of its gasoline allotment in March alone – before the Superfortresses even began operations![30] Stationing B-29s in China was temporary, however, as Arnold intended to move them to bases in the Marianas as soon as possible.[31]

Gregg was excited to see the large bombers, and speculated that perhaps they had bombed Tokyo itself. However, he had little time to dwell on the issue before the guerrilla band began moving westward once more. The next day, they arrived at the residence of Mr. Yen, a retired "gentleman" robber baron who had become rich off his captured spoils. Because the Nationalists would not deal with the Communists, they decided to hire Mr. Yen to make the exchange. For $13,000 Chinese, he escorted them to a nearby patrol of Nationalist soldiers. With their new escorts, the two pilots bedded down in a small village for the night. In the morning, just as the Nationalist platoon left the village, they received word of a nearby Japanese patrol. They immediately left the road and took off across the rice paddies, but soon were enveloped by rifle fire. Gregg and Beneda ran as fast as they could from the fight. According to Gregg, "Some of the soldiers split to cover us and we kept on at a run. Just as we got over a hill, machine guns cut loose ... so I guess it was quite a battle." With only a token escort, the two pilots walked for three hours before arriving at a field headquarters for a unit of the Nationalist 69th Division. The Chinese "treated us like kings," and a "sharp escort" of twenty Nationalist troops finally delivered them to Laohekou on 24 June.[32]

Gregg and Beneda hoped to ride the first plane out of Laohekou to the airbase at Liangshan. They found a B-25 headed that direction, but learned that it had to take pictures of the Japanese base at Yichang on the way. Praying the Japanese would not shoot them down again, they boarded the plane, finally arriving at Liangshan at 1430 hours. The local 14th

Air Force hospital treated both men. Gregg's injuries were too serious for him to remain in China and he was shipped back to the United States. Beneda could not fly in combat anymore because of Chennault's policy to ground airmen that had been rescued from behind enemy lines, but he elected to stay with his unit in an administrative role in hopes of being promoted to captain.[33] He delivered the letter and saber from General Li to Chennault and Chennault sent a reply asking Li to "convey to your guerrillas our admiration and our regards. Thank you very much!"[34] In fact, though the Nationalists remained locked in combat with the Communists, even as both parties fought the Japanese, Chennault convinced Chiang to let him work with them regarding the rescue of his downed airmen. He did not agree with the CCP's political philosophy, but saw them as a valuable ally and took advantage of their increasing influence in light of catastrophic Nationalist casualties and the ineffective Japanese occupation. The Communists were happy to cooperate, for they saw the efforts of the 14th Air Force as a very real contribution to the struggle against Japan.

A P-38 making a low pass over Chenggong. Joseph Fodor

Hainan Island

While Gregg and Beneda were walking back to friendly lines, the 449th made good its escape from the Japanese advance in East China. After the evacuation of Suichuan in June 1944, Casey Vincent moved the squadron to Er Tong Field near Guilin. They flew only one mission from that base, a B-25 escort on 1 July, before Chennault transferred them to Chenggong, under the command of Colonel John Kennedy and the 69th Composite Wing. By 8 July, most of the squadron had arrived.

Chenggong was 6,250 feet above sea level, in the same broad valley as Kunming. The six-thousand-foot-long, crushed-gravel field was located on the eastern shore of Lake Dianchi, twelve miles southeast of Chennault's headquarters. From the field, dark mountains loomed in the distance on all sides, bearing witness to the ruggedness of the Hump, even at its terminus. Between the airfield and Lake Dianchi was a small, terraced hill, approximately a mile wide, on which were located the American offices and barracks. Chenggong was a busy airfield. Two other squadrons of the 51st Group were stationed there, as well as elements of the 308th Bomb Group and squadrons of B-25s, P-61 night fighters, and C-46 and C-47 transports.[35] The high volume of traffic often exceeded the airport's capacity, especially with large numbers of transports coming and going. Oftentimes, bombers and transports were stacked in the landing queue at five hundred foot intervals from the runway nearly to the stratosphere![36] Joe Chiara, a pilot who joined the 449th in 1945, called it "an impossible chaos" and recalled that "a simple taxi trip down to the end of the runway for us was usually a 30 minute wait, while being stuck behind about 15 of them clearing their takeoff and check list chores!"[37]

As at most American airbases in China, the Chinese War Area Service Corps (WASC), under the command of Major General Huang, provided all the food and facilities. Chennault figured that by contracting these functions he was able to devote more personnel and supplies to prosecuting the air war. In fact, because of the WASC, the 14th Air Force functioned effectively with half the number of personnel and one quarter the amount of supplies that an air force its size would normally require.[38] The facilities at Chenggong were typical: officers and men lived in one-story mud brick hostels with red tile roofs. A mess hall was on one end of the officer hostel and the operations section and pilot ready room were on the other end. There were no buildings on the flight line, however, and the ground crews performed all maintenance and armament work in the open. The squadron dispersed its P-38s around the general area, some protected by compacted-earth revetments. The facilities were the best China could furnish their American compatriots, and although some personnel believed the facilities were acceptable, others remembered them as far less than perfect. Forrest Green recalled: "It was pretty primitive really. I don't think there was any indoor water and I also remember it seemed like it was built in a graveyard because it had some

P-38s on the flight line at Chenggong. The nearest one is P-38J-15 #312 (42-104335), which flew as Grover Stubbee's Queen of the Sky and Dan Church's My Achin' Ass. Note the older P-38Hs in the background. James Heitkotter

Jim Heitkotter standing next to one of the graves surround the squadron barracks area at Chenggong. James Heitkotter

Gravity-fed shower system at Chenggong. James Heitkotter

The road from Chenggong to Kunming. Chenggong was about twelve miles south of Chennault's headquarters. James Heitkotter

Street markets in Chenggong. James Heitkotter

Chinese coolies labor in Chenggong. China's lack of heavy equipment was made up for in manpower. James Heitkotter

old tombstones around there."[39] He also remembered the large number of rats infesting the barracks, which pilot Jack Bowman described in detail:

> One thing we did after going to bed was shoot rats. We all had flashlights and 45 automatics. After we turned the lights out we could hear the rats running along the boards going around the room at the top of the walls. One guy would shine his light and find a rat and everyone would shoot, trying to kill it. We used bird shot so there were no bullets flying around. After two or three guys started shooting at the same rat, it would normally be hit and mortally wounded.[40]

Though not perfect, Chenggong would have to do; for the next year, the 449th Fighter Squadron would call it home.[41]

With the new location came a new commander, Captain James L. Bledsoe (promoted to Major in August). Captain Bledsoe was another old China hand, having served under Chennault as an instructor at the Kunming flying school before the United States entered the war. He returned to China after the war to fly for Civil Air Transport, Chennault's relief air transport line.[42] The men had mixed feelings about him. Jerry Doughty respected the fact that he had a lot of flying experience, but thought it was "Maybe too much for us. He seemed quite a bit older than the rest of us and rather reserved." Unlike most squadron commanders, "He thought nothing of flying through a cloud formation with his flight. Upon breaking out of the cloud cover, he was always on course." Meanwhile, "We younger troops with little or no weather experience looked like a three ring circus upon breaking into the clear. He would patiently regroup his flock and continue on with the mission." Overall, Doughty's assessment was that Bledsoe "was a nice guy and kind of a father image to us new troops."[43] Jim Heitkotter, on the other hand, had a strongly negative opinion:

> Captain Bledsoe was not very popular with the pilots, as he came from a transport command and knew little of fighter tactics. His most horrifying demonstration of this came when he had twelve of us stacked in a beautiful echelon right, then went into a right turn. It was extremely lucky that none of us collided in suddenly finding we had nowhere to go.[44]

For better or worse, Bledsoe was in charge of the 449th. Despite reservations held by some of the pilots and crews, he led the squadron through some challenging missions, the most famous of which was an escort mission to the Japanese stronghold at Sanya Bay, Hainan Island, on 29 July 1944. Hainan was a mountainous tropical island with lush greenery and white sandy beaches, which lay across the Gulf of Tonkin from Hanoi in French Indochina. Sanya was an important link in Japan's shipping route to Southeast Asia and the Dutch East Indies and was a favorite target for the 308th Bomb Group's

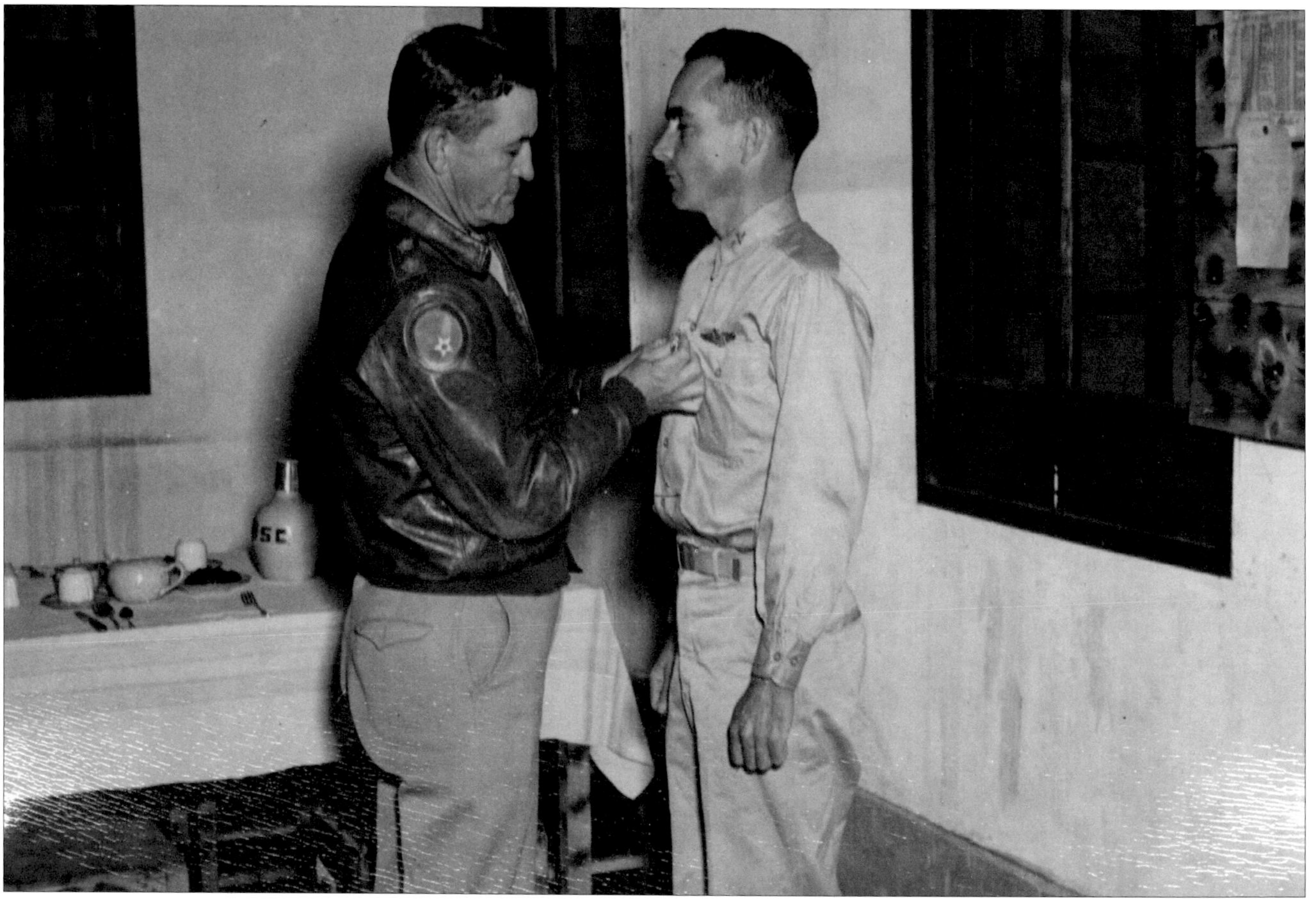

General Chennault presents Major Bledsoe with the Distinguished Service Cross, 1 November 1944. National Archives

Standing by a squadron jeep at Chenggong are, left to right, Jim Heitkotter, Jim Bledsoe, Joe Fodor, and Bob Jones. James Heitkotter

B-24s, including about thirty new aircraft equipped with radar bombing equipment for low-altitude anti-shipping raids in poor weather and nighttime.[45] The B-24s would typically sweep the gulf to Sanya Bay, then north to Hong Kong, however Zeros of the 254th Kokutai at Sanya made the route hazardous.[46] On the 29th, Chennault dispatched twenty-five B-24s and fourteen B-25s to hit the airfield and dock facilities in hopes of making the area safer for shipping strikes. At 0645 hours, seventeen P-38s departed Chenggong for Nanning, 370 miles to the southeast. One fighter turned back because of trouble with its propeller control but the remaining sixteen arrived at the forward staging base without difficulty. The P-38s carried 165-gallon external fuel tanks for the long journey ahead.

When the Lightnings arrived at Nanning, they waited for the bombers while the ground crew topped off their fuel tanks. According to Bob Jones, "Finally, we received word by radio that the bombers were on the way. We took off and headed south over the Gulf of Tonkin." Of the sixteen P-38s that arrived at Nanning, one did not take off because of engine trouble. Two others turned back soon after takeoff. "About a half hour into the flight, the 24's came into view. We joined up and continued to fly south. (I never did see the B-25's.) Our three flights of P-38's zig-zagged back and forth to keep from over-running the heavily laden B-24's." Suddenly, Jones discovered a problem: "My left main wing tank was half empty. I was operating out of my external tanks. How could this be? I checked my gas tank selection switches and found them to be correct." It turned out that a faulty valve was siphoning gas from his wing tanks to his external tanks. "I had to make a decision. I had as much gas as the other fighters but when I reached the target I would have to drop the external tanks. There would not be enough fuel to make it back. I decided to abort." Jones flew "a long lonely hour and twenty minutes over the waters of Tonkin" and arrived safely back at Nanning.[47]

Twelve P-38s piloted by Major Bledsoe, Captain Dowis, and Lieutenants Stubbee, Mahon, Yorston, Frank, Robinson, Rogers, Weber, Robertson, Calder, and Burrell remained to escort the B-24s to their target. Rather than approach Sanya Bay directly, which would lead the formation over the length of Hainan Island in plain view of the Japanese, the Americans planned a less conspicuous approach. They would parallel Hainan's coast from about thirty miles offshore and pass south of the island in order to hit Sanya Bay from the west. The approach worked; the formation did not encounter enemy fighters until it was directly over the target. The P-38s crossed the coast in three flights, one at 20,000 feet, one at 23,000 feet, and one at 26,000 feet. They spotted eighteen Zeros from the 254th Kokutai, several of which were taking off and two of which had climbed to 25,000 feet. The B-24s bombed the dock area and turned left toward the sea. John Charlton,

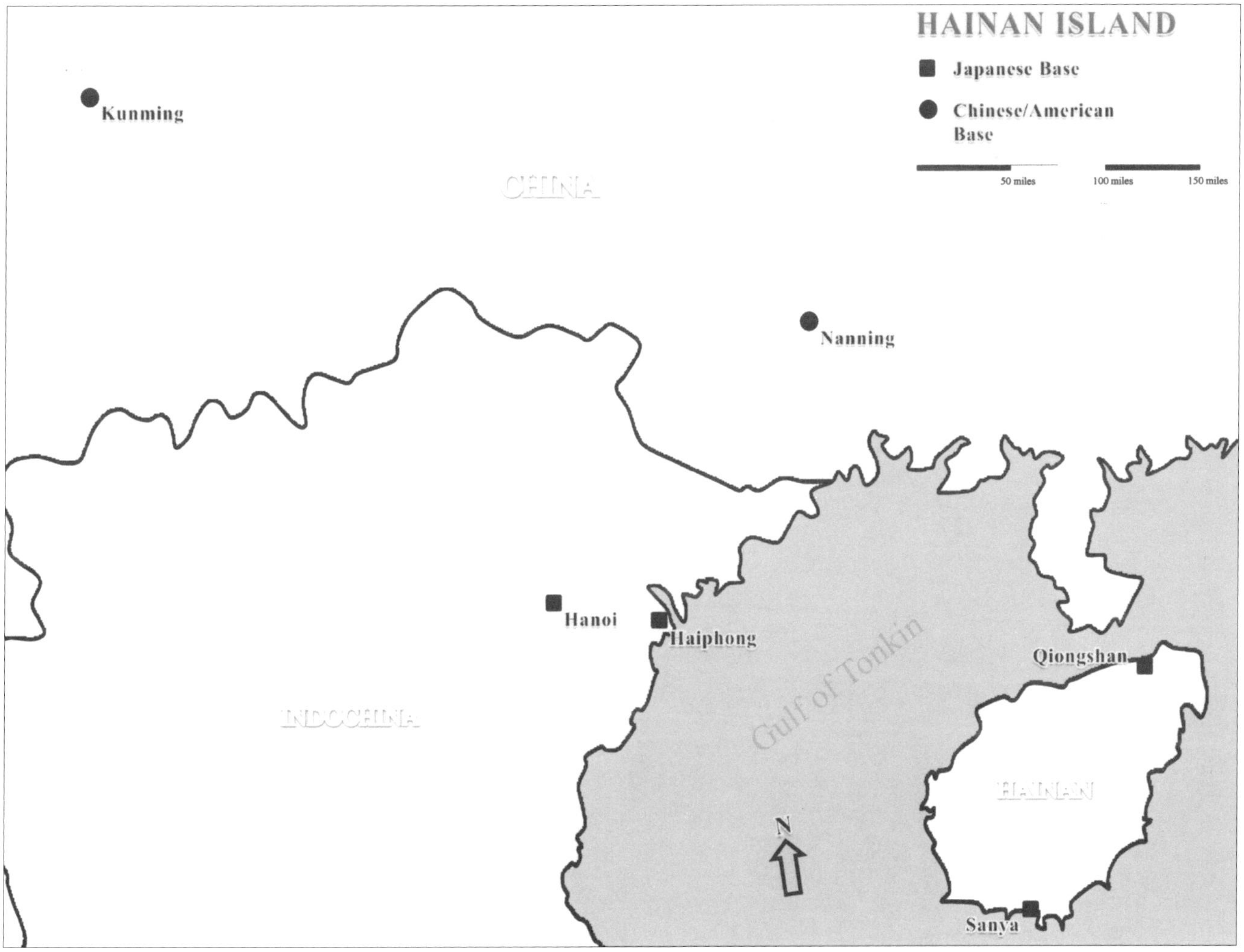

William Robertson in the cockpit of his P-38. On 29 July 1944 over Hainan Island, Robertson turned a Japanese fixed-gear fighter into a no-gear fighter. Jerry Doughty

navigator on the lead B-24, remembered, "Jap fighters were making passes from our front at one time. They always tried to knock down the lead plane. They pressed us relentlessly. Our gunners got two of them and damaged another." Though the situation appeared desperate, "The P-38s covered us front and above. I saw the Japs falling out of the sky, burning. I have never been on a mission where our escorting fighters took better care of us."

The sky over Hainan Island quickly became the scene of a chaotic dogfight. Lieutenant Stubbee was flying east when a P-38 dove in front of him with a Zero on its tail. Stubbee turned behind the fighter, firing all the way, as he closed within two hundred feet. He observed hits on its wing roots and fuselage before it caught fire, rolled, dove to three thousand feet, and exploded. Lieutenant Frank witnessed a Zero attempting to initiate an attack on a P-38 which had just broken from a pass on another enemy fighter. "I was not sure whether he saw me or not so I feinted a turn away from him and down and then continued pressing my attack." He closed to about one hundred feet, pulled up on the Zero's tail, and fired. His initial burst hit the wing root. "The enemy pilot tried to rack it in and the whole left wing tore loose."[48] Back in the lead B-24, Charlton looked on as "A Jap made a pass from high overhead." He alerted the gunners, but "A P-38 also sighted him and gave chase." When the enemy fighter came within range of the bomber's fifty-caliber turrets, "our gunners opened up. He passed to our left, smoking, the P-38 on his tail. They went down to the sea where the Jap hit and exploded. Our P-38 pulled up, and I can swear that twin-engine plane had a grin on its face."[49]

The mission was a huge success. The B-24s started eight large fires in the fuel storage areas, with thick columns of smoke reaching five thousand feet into the air visible from forty miles away. None of the bombers were damaged.[50] Stubbee and Dowis each claimed two enemy fighters shot down and Lieutenants Frank, Yorston, and Mahon each claimed one for a total of seven destroyed, five probably destroyed, and three damaged. Lieutenant Robertson even reported shooting the fixed landing gear off a Nate, forcing it to belly land on the field. The 254th Kokutai testified to losing three Zeros and one pilot. In turn, the Zeros erroneously claimed two P-38s destroyed and five B-24s damaged.[51] The *CBI Roundup* reported on the mission's success:

> Outstanding mission of the week was the strike at [Sanya], big Jap base on Hainan island, by a large flight of B-24's with P-38 escort. Ninety percent of the bombs hit the target area, causing large fires and secondary explosions, while the Lightnings claimed seven confirmed and eight probables of 16 Jap interceptors.[52]

General Chennault was so impressed he wrote a commendation for the participating Lightning pilots:

> 1. Pilots of the 449th Fighter Squadron who flew escort in the [Sanya] Bay mission on 29 July 1944 are worthy of high commendation.
>
> 2. Though attacked by a force of enemy interceptors that outnumbered them nearly two to one, these pilots scored a brilliant victory. Seven enemy planes were shot down, five probably destroyed and three damaged. Few of the interceptors were able to penetrate the escort screen, and the bombers' gunners were able to cope easily with

the few that did get through. As a result of the excellent work of these pilots none of the bombers or fighters sustained serious damage.

3. The work of these pilots was a demonstration of their superiority over the enemy fliers and adds great credit to their records.

/s/ C. L. CHENNAULT[53]

It seems that General Chennault was finally changing his attitude toward the 449th, and for good reason: the feats performed in the air over Sanya Bay were truly praiseworthy and helped clear the way for the radar-equipped B-24s. With only minimal harassment from Japanese fighters, in twenty-one sea sweeps in August the 308th claimed 69,000 tons of shipping, further constricting the noose around Japan.[54]

CHAPTER SIX

The Salween Campaign

General Joseph Stilwell arrived in the CBI Theater on 25 February 1942, only ten days before the port of Rangoon fell to the Japanese. Chiang Kaishek immediately placed him in command of seven divisions of the Chinese army in Burma, but he could not stem the tide of the Japanese advance. By May 1942, the Japanese had overrun all of Burma and Stilwell and his staff escaped in a harrowing 140-mile walkout to India. Stilwell remarked to the press, "I claim we got a hell of a beating. We got run out of Burma and it is humiliating as hell. I think we ought to find out what caused it, go back and retake it."[1] To Stilwell, a land supply route through Burma seemed the only way to save China and was his focus (his "obsession," according to Chennault) for the rest of his time in the CBI.

In November 1943, Roosevelt, Churchill, and Chiang met in Cairo, Egypt. Stilwell had launched his American-trained Chinese divisions ("X" Force) from India into Burma the month before, and at Cairo, the Allies decided to support his effort with a British amphibious invasion in the south and a Chinese drive from the Salween River in Yunnan Province ("Y" Force) to link up with X Force in the north. Stilwell's objective was to build a new road from Ledo, India, to connect with the old Burma Road north of Lashio. Chiang was to launch his forces from Yunnan in December 1943, but immediately after Cairo, Roosevelt and Churchill proceeded to Tehran, where Stalin guaranteed them he would enter the war against Japan after the defeat of Germany – provided they open a second front in Europe. With Stalin's commitment came a dramatic decrease in the importance of the CBI and a renewed emphasis on Europe. In light of this, Britain cancelled its amphibious operation in Burma. It fell to Stilwell to deliver the unpleasant news to Chiang that once again the Allies reneged on their commitments. Stilwell had already committed X Force, however, and needed Chiang to launch Y Force from Yunnan if he was to have any hope of success. Chiang refused. He felt that he could better employ his soldiers against the Japanese (or the Communists) in China, rather than committing them to an operation of little importance to the Allies. Stilwell was frustrated and decided to coerce Chiang through his control of Lend-Lease supplies. His manipulation and blatant disrespect angered the Nationalist Chinese leader, who remained obstinate. Finally, Stilwell appealed to President Roosevelt, who, gradually becoming disillusioned about Chiang, sent an ultimatum telling him to either launch his forces across the Salween, or risk the end of American aid to China. Chiang relented and, on the night of 10/11 May 1944, Y Force began crossing the Salween River.[2]

The Y Force commander, General Wei Lihuang, set his initial objectives as the capture of Tengchong and Longling, with subsequent action to be determined based on the situation. Unlike Longling, Tengchong was not on the old Burma Road. However, Wei hoped to open the Tengchong Cutoff, a 124-mile trail that ran directly from Tengchong to Myitkyina (Stilwell's next objective in Burma). If developed, the cutoff would greatly shorten the distance convoys had to travel from Ledo to Kunming. The twelve-thousand-foot-tall Gaoligong Range loomed ominously between the Chinese and their objectives, however, rising steeply to eight thousand feet over the narrow Salween River Gorge. The Japanese 56th Division made use of the difficult terrain and was well entrenched in four critical mountain passes. By 5 June, twenty thousand Chinese troops had descended into the precipitous gorge and reached the base of the range on the west bank of the river. Wei decided to attack Longling first, as its fall would cut Tengchong off from Japanese reinforcement. Initial progress was promising: the 28th Division contained Songshan, a multi-peaked mountain fortress overlooking the Burma Road and Huitong Bridge site (the Chinese had destroyed the bridge itself during the Japanese conquest of Burma) while the 87th and 88th divisions swung around the road to the south and assaulted Longling. By 8 June, Chinese troops breached the city's outer defenses, but the Japanese rushed reinforcements from Tengchong and vigorously counterattacked. The ten-thousand-man Chinese force failed to consolidate its initial gains and only 1,500 Japanese troops

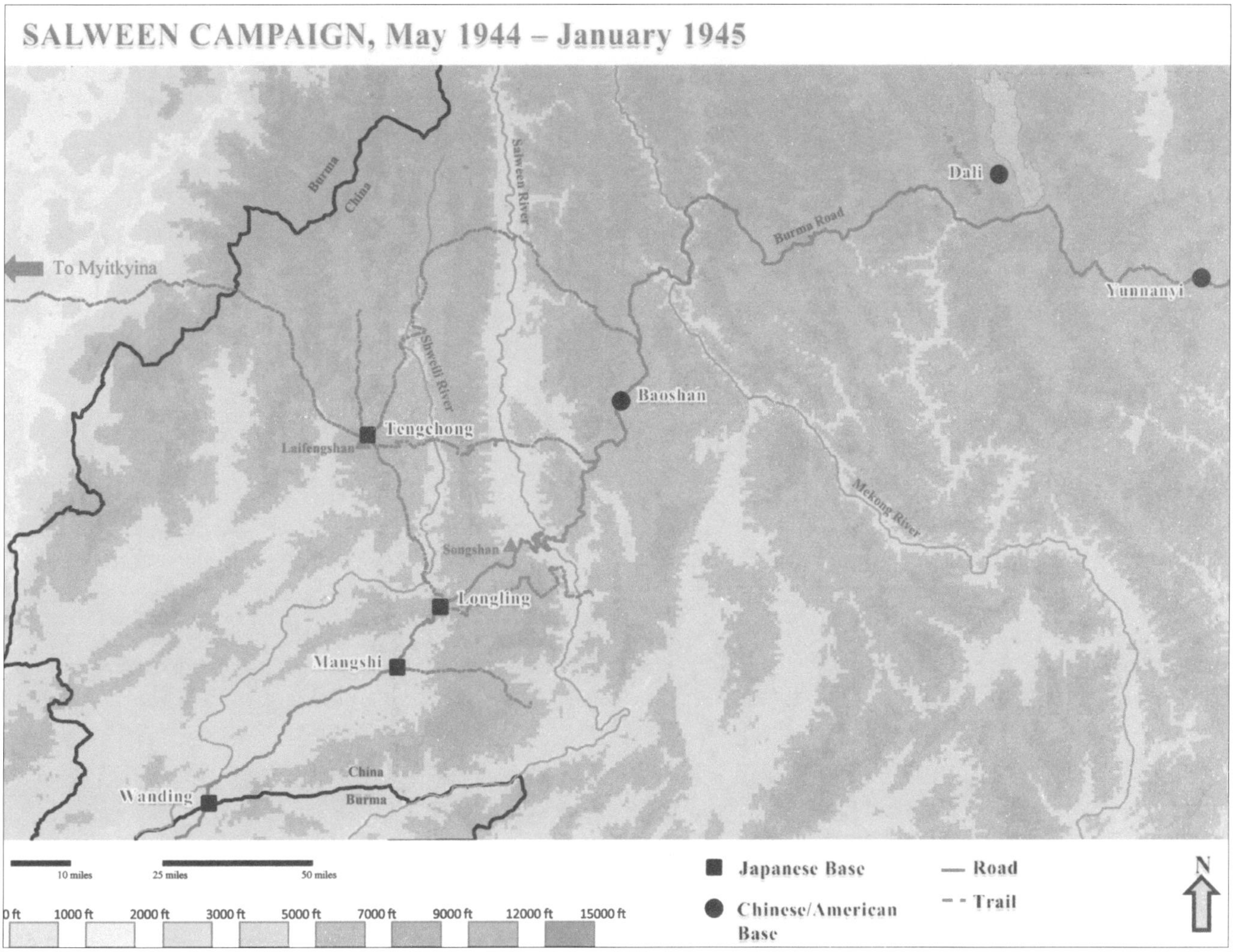

pushed it from the city. Meanwhile, on 17 May, Stilwell's X Force reached Myitkyina and took the airfield. His tired forces failed to take the town before Japanese reinforcements arrived, however, precipitating a siege that lasted until 4 August.[3]

Attached to General Wei's Y Force was an American liaison team led by Brigadier General Frank "Pinky" Dorn, a survivor of Stilwell's epic walkout from Burma. The team had no command function, but gave advice, coordinated logistical support, and provided air-ground liaison for the Chinese. Chennault established a detachment of the 69th Composite Wing at Yunnanyi under the command of Major A. B. Black to provide air support. The airfield at Yunnanyi was 6,100 feet above sea level, six thousand feet long, and oriented northeast to southwest. It was in a small valley surrounded by low mountains, through which passed the Burma Road, 130 miles west of Kunming. The detachment included fighters, bombers, transports, and light aircraft. Twenty-two P-40s from the 25th Fighter Squadron provided close air support. Nineteen B-25s from the 22nd Bomb Squadron carried out battlefield interdiction and heavy support missions. Fourteen C-47s from the 27th Troop Carrier Squadron provided aerial resupply. Ten L-5s from the 19th Liaison Squadron at Baoshan and Yunnanyi performed special support missions, including courier missions, medical evacuation, artillery spotting, and occasionally airborne forward air control.[4]

Close air support on the Salween Front was very important and well coordinated. Chinese troops found it impossible to lug heavy artillery over treacherous mountain trails and instead depended on P-40, and later P-38, fighter-bombers to act as heavy artillery for them. According to Joe Fodor, the Chinese "needed a little backup help from the aircraft, which is what we did."[5] Chinese troops often called on fighter pilots to support them with bombs, parafrags, rockets, napalm, and machine guns. As each flight crossed the deep chasm carved by the Salween River and approached the front, they radioed an American air-ground specialist who talked them onto the target, sometimes utilizing cloth panels (difficult to use in rough terrain) or mortaring smoke shells near the target.[6] On one occasion, three P-40s bombed and strafed a Japanese gun emplacement only twenty-five yards in front of Chinese troops hugging the ground with panels on their backs for identification. The Japanese abandoned the position and none of the Chinese soldiers were harmed. The three pilots received commendations from Dorn.[7] As in East China, terrible weather was the primary limitation for air support on the Salween Front.

By late June, Wei found he could not maintain land lines of communications to his forces besieging Longling because the Japanese still controlled Songshan – despite his best efforts to take it. Several times his infantry dislodged the Japanese from outer positions only to be driven back in counterattacks. To the north, Chinese patrols ferociously fought their way over the Gaoligong Range and began sealing off the entrances to the Tengchong Valley, while XX Group Army prepared to assault the city itself. Tengchong was once the largest trading center between China and Burma, specializing particularly in jade. The Japanese had conquered it on 10 May 1942, as a postscript to their campaign in Burma. Most of the twenty thousand Chinese villagers fled to the mountains, but returned when the Japanese threatened to burn down their homes. Once back in the city, the Japanese gave them quotas of food and labor to provide; if they did not supply the prescribed amount, Japanese troops entered their houses and seized what they needed. The Japanese executed many villagers after forcing them to build defensive fortifications so they could not leak information to the Allies. They shot Chinese who tried to escape labor gangs. Japanese Army troops also took Chinese women as forced prostitutes until Korean "comfort women" arrived in 1943.[8]

Finally, in July 1944, Y Force troops arrived to liberate the city. Japanese commanders did not think Chinese troops could battle their way across the mountains encircling the city, but by the second week in July, the Chinese had them surrounded. The XX Group Army took the adjacent villages and Japanese hill fortifications, often taking advantage of heavy rainstorms to sneak into enemy positions. Tengchong itself was a harder nut to crack. Lieutenant Lu Caiwen, a graduate of the Huangpu Military Academy and an intelligence officer attached to the XI Group Army, reconnoitered the city before the battle and reported on the Japanese defenses. Having grown up in Tengchong, he vividly remembered the forty-foot tall, twenty-foot thick wall made of compacted earth and stone blocks that surrounded the city. The wall was the dominant feature of the town, built during the Ming Dynasty, when more than four thousand cities boasted such fortification.[9] He also reported that the Japanese had constructed pillboxes around the outside of the wall, as well as opened embrasures in it, and built barriers behind it. Thus, "As one old Chinese saying goes, when one person holds the position, even hundreds of soldiers cannot break through."[10] Chinese ground troops operating with few supplies and no heavy artillery had little chance of taking the city.[11] By mid-July, the campaign to reopen the Burma Road had settled down to four sieges: Myitkyina, Longling, Songshan, and Tengchong.

With the 449th ejected from East China, and the Salween Campaign bogged down in siege, Chennault decided to add firepower and long-range capability to his forces supporting Wei by moving a detachment of P-38s to Yunnanyi. He did not intend it to be a permanent base; a detachment would operate there as long as Y Force needed them. On 22 July, three officers and thirty-two enlisted men from the 449th flew to Yunnanyi via transport aircraft. The enlisted men quickly established the requisite facilities and on 25 July, eight P-38s flew in from Chenggong. P-40 pilot Clifford Long remembered that when the P-38s arrived they demonstrated the capabilities of their twin-engine fighters: "They would come back with one prop feathered and the engine shut down just to show us that they could fly on one engine. That was quite a sight to see ... a flight of four P-38s come back with just one engine."[12] Immediately

A view of the mountainous terrain from a P-38 high above the Salween Front. Joseph Fodor

following their arrival, the commander of the 25th Fighter Squadron, Lieutenant Colonel Henry Amen, led Captain Bledsoe and Lieutenant Yorkston on a strafing mission to Songshan to introduce the Lightnings to combat on the Salween Front.

The next day, the Yunnanyi detachment began flying missions to Tengchong. The siege could not be broken until XX Group Army somehow scaled the city's massive walls, but the 1,800 Japanese soldiers manning strong points along the walls and inside the city made the fortress unassailable to infantry with nothing but primitive wooden ladders. Unlike most Chinese cities, Tengchong paralleled the terrain to the southwest, the wall being oriented to the northwest instead of to the north. General Huo Kuizhang, commander of XX Group Army, planned to assault the southeast wall, where the valley broadened to offer the most open terrain, thus denying the Japanese strong defensive positions and enabling more effective air support. The Japanese, however, had positioned their artillery on Laifengshan, a mountain looming eight hundred feet above the surrounding terrain, immediately southwest of the city. From the top of Laifengshan, Japanese artillery commanded the entire valley. Huo called on the 14th Air Force for aid. At 1200 hours on 26 July, the first of four waves of P-38s and P-40s arrived to hit targets in the area.[13] Four P-38s and four P-40s found cloth panels southeast of Laifengshan directing them toward fortified positions on the mountain. The P-40s attacked first, rolling into a dive-bombing attack and releasing their bombs at five hundred feet. All four bombs hit the target. The P-38s attacked next, each carrying two five-hundred-pound demolition bombs. Four bombs hit the target, and four fell short. The next two waves of fighters attacked targets in Tengchong while the final flight of four P-38s scored six direct hits on Japanese positions at the apex of the mountain.[14] While the fighters attacked from

The east side of the Salween River (called Nu Jiang by the Chinese) at the widest point in the gorge where Chinese troops crossed on their way to retake Tengchong. Author's Photo

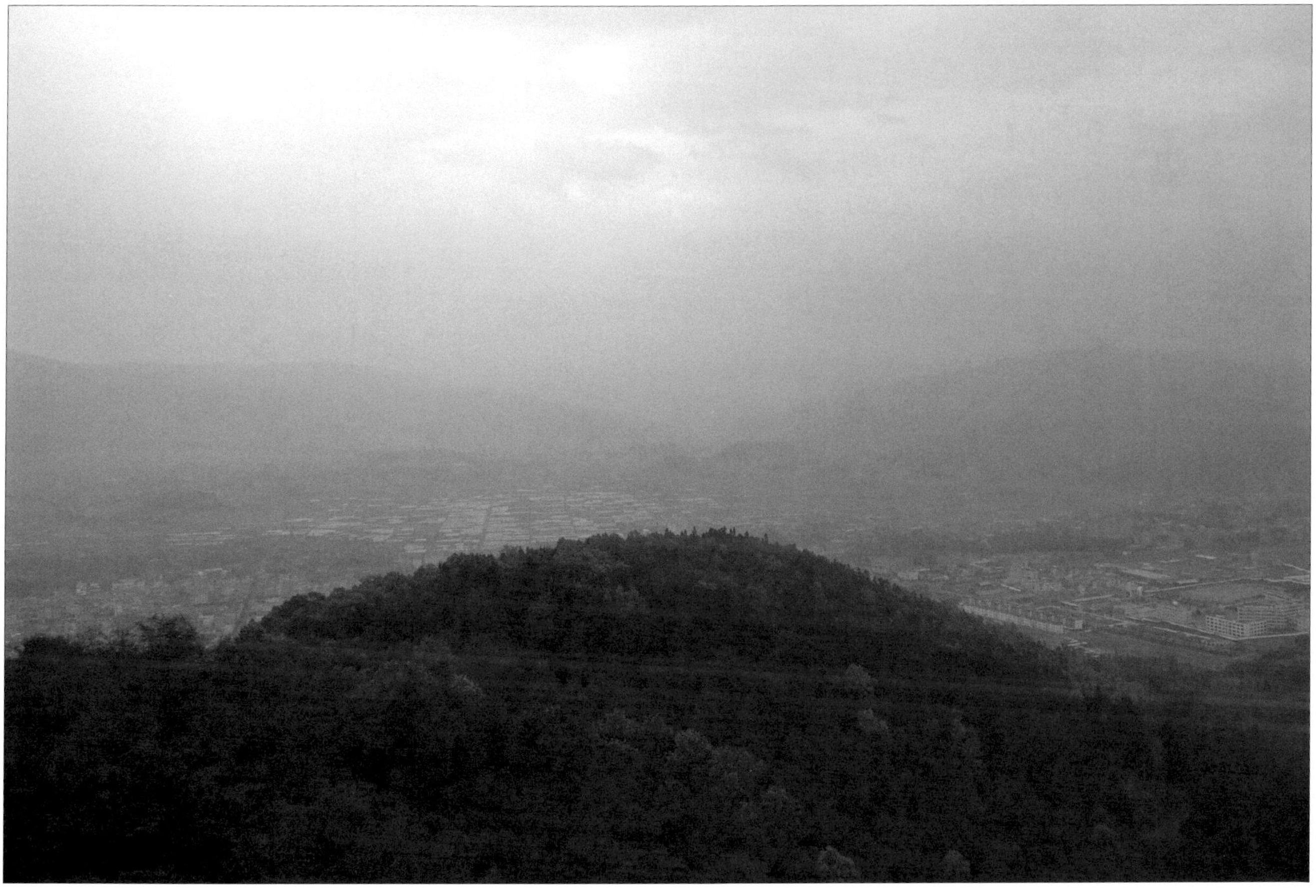

The view from Laifengshan demonstrates how the Tengchong Valley broadens toward the southeast. Author's Photo

above, artillery and mortar fire covered the Chinese infantry as they used American Lend-Lease flamethrowers to burn the Japanese out of their bunkers and trenches. By evening, the Chinese had reached the top of the mountain, having killed some 380 Japanese while taking 1,200 casualties themselves. The next morning they mopped up the remaining resistance and repelled a counter-attack from the city.

Simultaneous with the attack on Laifengshan, Huo's troops attacked the southeast wall of Tengchong. B-25s bombing from medium altitude found it difficult to hit the face of the wall, however, and failed to breach it. Chapman Hale, a pilot with the 22nd Bomb Squadron, remembered making an attack with two other B-25s. According to Hale, "Low bombing in those mountains was extremely hazardous" because "it was so tight in there that the bomber just couldn't maneuver very well."[15] All three bombers missed the wall, instead sending their bombs crashing into the city. The P-40s supporting the operation bombed at low level with five-hundred-pound demolition bombs. One bomb by itself did little damage to the massive wall, so the Warhawk pilots planned to hit the same spot with one after another until the wall crumbled down. To prevent damage to the low-flying fighters, the bombs had a seven-second delay fuse, but according to Clifford Long, "when the plane in front of me hit the wall with the five-hundred-pound bomb, it hit the wall and rolled back away from it" without doing any damage.[16] Consequently, with the wall intact and the preponderance of Chinese troops focused on Laifengshan, Huo's attack on the city failed.

Over the next several days, P-38s from the 449th attacked Japanese positions outside the wall and strong points inside the city. Every day the detachment flew multiple missions to Tengchong and to bridges and supply centers in Burma to wear down the Japanese. For many of the men the missions blurred together. Jerry Doughty only remembered a lot of "strafing and skip-bombing and dive-bombing."[17] Ed Mark, an armorer with the 25th Fighter Squadron, recalled that the 449th and 25th

Above: Two 22nd Bomb Squadron B-25s climb away from Tengchong after bombing the city wall. National Archives

Opposite
Top: Bomb damage assessment photo after a strike on Tengchong. National Archives

Bottom: An American fighter-bomber attacks the Tengchong city wall in preparation for the Chinese assault. U.S. Army

Fighter Squadrons would sometimes launch fifty sorties and drop more than sixty five-hundred-pound bombs in a single day.[18] The Japanese repeatedly told Chinese villagers that the aircraft overhead were Japanese. On 2 August, however, nine flights of "Japanese" P-40s and P-38s attacked the city. The Warhawks approached perpendicular to the wall, racing up the open end of the valley from the southeast. To bomb the wall from low altitude, 25th Fighter Squadron armorers fashioned twelve-inch long, two-inch diameter steel spikes to screw into the front of the bombs. Flying at 250 miles per hour only ten feet above the ground, the pilots pulled the bomb release and lifted over the wall in one smooth maneuver. According to William Mitchell, the wall became "a kind of dartboard." If everything worked as planned, the bombs would "hit the wall and stick." Mitchell remembered, "The attack was all over in minutes, and the results were much as planned. The wall kind of crumbled down, but the effect was far less than an open door to the city."[19] Meanwhile, twelve B-25s skip-bombed the southeast wall and three P-38s with two five-hundred-pound bombs each bombed Tengchong's east gate (situated in the center of the southeast wall), scoring two hits on the gate and four in the city. The American planes managed to breach the wall in five places, including a fifteen-foot gap through which the Chinese infantry could attack. The Japanese covered the breach with intense machine gun fire, but five waves of P-40s and P-38s arrived every twenty minutes to strafe the Japanese

defenders, allowing the Chinese to use their ladders to climb the remnants of the wall. The Japanese tried desperately to push the Chinese from the city, but a lone platoon determined to scale once more unto the breach and held out through the night of 3/4 August. The next morning more Chinese troops poured into the city and took a pillbox. The Japanese resisted fanatically. House-to-house fighting erupted, drawing the battle out for more than a month and keeping the 14th Air Force busy hitting enemy strong points in the city.[20]

Throughout May and much of June and July the JAAF was absent from the Salween Front, distracted by the Japanese offensive in India, 10th Air Force fighter sweeps in Burma, and rotating its sentais from combat to re-equip with the latest fighters. In June, the 64th Sentai rotated to Saigon in French Indochina to re-equip with the new Ki-43-III with a more powerful engine and methanol injection, leaving the 50th and 204th Sentais at Meiktila, Burma. On 28 June, Captain Takemura led four Ki-36 Type 98 Direct Cooperation Reconnaissance Planes, code name "Ida," from the 83rd Sentai escorted by six Ki-43s of the 204th Sentai on the first of ten supply drops to the encircled garrison at Songshan.[21] Each Ki-36 carried a bamboo container covered with lacquer-stiffened cloth with a capacity of two thousand bullets or fifty grenades. Only five such drops were successful; the rest fell into Chinese hands.[22] On 26 July, Major Kanemitsu, commander of the Songshan garrison, requested air support to deal with Chinese artillery battering his positions. While two Ki-51s dropped supplies to the Japanese, eight Oscars from the 50th Sentai machine-gunned the Chinese artillery and crews, delaying offensive action for a week. Chinese anti-aircraft fire hit Corporal Tasuo Koyasu's Oscar and he crashed into a Chinese position.[23] In August, the 64th Sentai arrived back at Meiktila, but the 50th rotated to Saigon to reequip with the new Ki-84 Type Four Fighter, codename "Frank," and the 204th withdrew to Thailand and prepared to move to the Philippines. The Japanese decided to stop Y Force by interdicting its supply lines and ordered the 64th Sentai to prepare to bomb the newly rebuilt Huitong Bridge. What the Japanese did not realize was that Y Force depended almost entirely on air drops from the 27th Troop Carrier Squadron because of the difficulty of establishing land lines of communication over the rugged terrain.

It was to the troop carriers' credit that they were able to supply twelve Chinese divisions on a one hundred mile front with only fourteen airplanes. Nearly every day, C-47s dropped over fifty tons of supplies (over one hundred tons on some days) to Chinese troops in spite of bad weather.[24] According to C-47 pilot Melvin Waymire, "The weather was usually pretty treacherous especially in the drop areas. We would run into

A C-47 drops supplies to Chinese troops on the Salween Front. U.S. Army

thunderstorm after thunderstorm outbound and inbound. It was bad. I had never experienced such terrible weather." Usually the transports flew through the weather on instruments, but about twenty percent of the time, they turned back or were grounded.[25]

Each transport crew flew two missions per day to deliver enough supplies to Y Force. Dorn's liaison group radioed drop zone information and supply needs to 69th Composite Wing staff at Yunnanyi, who in turn briefed the transport crews. The C-47s carried only enough gas for the mission, plus an hour's reserve, and flew about one-and-a-half hours to the drop zones where they descended to five hundred feet above the valley floors. Pilot Robert Jones remembered, "The C-47 was a pretty good old airplane;" despite the high altitude and limited maneuvering room over the Salween Front, "at the speeds we were flying it was still maneuverable enough" to "make your circles, and keep away from the mountainous terrain."[26] The Chinese arranged colored cloth panels and smoke to mark the drop zones. The C-47s usually made several passes while "kickers" in the back released the five thousand pounds of cargo by freefall (if delivering rice) or by parachute. According to pilot Jerry Disharoon, rice was sewn tightly into seventy-pound bags and then placed in loose outer bags. "When the bags were dropped from a very low altitude, the inner bag would break and the outer bag would hold."[27]

Occasionally, the Japanese would try to trick the transports by mimicking drop zone panels, though the colors were hard for them to reproduce. Disharoon remembered one particular mission when his C-47 arrived over the drop area at twilight. It was hard to see the drop zone because of a low-lying fog covering the valley floor, but his crew "located a target on a knoll that looked right." The first and second passes went alright, but blue smoke from mortar rounds began drifting over the drop zone. On the third pass, one of Dorn's liaison teams radioed that Disharoon and his crew were dropping rice to the Japanese, who were firing at them with an artillery piece. "By this pass, the blue smoke was bad and just as we came over, a round from the field piece hit just in front of us. As we poured on the coal to climb out, we could see the rounds from the field piece hitting the mountain on the outside of our turn."[28]

Normally transports had no direct communication with Dorn's teams and travelled in complete radio silence without fighter escort. On 6 August, however, a C-47 witnessed six Oscars strafing Chinese positions near Songshan. Two pursued the transport, but it escaped into the clouds. On 18 August, "a beautiful day," according to Clifford Long, thirteen 64th Sentai Oscars took advantage of the favorable weather to make an attack on the Huitong Bridge.[29] Sergeant Toshimi Ikezawa, a pilot with the 64th Sentai, dropped two fifty-kilogram bombs in a diving attack on the bridge. He and the other pilots missed, and Warrant Officer Kazuo Shake was shot down by anti-aircraft fire, but as the Oscars circled to reform, Ikezawa saw two C-47s over the Salween River returning from drop zones near Tengchong and Longling.[30] He broke formation without permission and attacked the transports, sending one crashing down

27th Troop Carrier Squadron "kickers" dropping rice to the Chinese. U.S. Army

with the loss of all aboard. The other evaded by diving to ground level just above the river.[31] Lieutenant Long, Captain Robert Bell, and Lieutenant Colonel Henry Amen had just finished a rocket attack on a Japanese strongpoint near Tengchong when they received word of the attack. Long remembered, "All of the sudden I saw the colonel drop his rocket tubes from the plane. I knew what was going to happen so I dropped my rocket tubes and [Bell] dropped his rocket tubes. We were going to get in a dogfight." The Warhawks found the Oscars only five minutes to the southeast and dove to attack: three P-40s against twelve Oscars. Ikezawa saw the P-40s above him and turned away, escaping to the west. In accordance with Chennault's instructions, the P-40s attacked the rest of the formation from above, dove away, then climbed and attacked again. Long covered Amen on three attacks and remarked, "The dogfight was very intense for a while" until "I broke away and almost instantly was hit by enemy fire." He looked over his shoulder to try to

The rebuilt Huitong Bridge in the Salween River Gorge. U.S. Army

see his attackers when one of them dropped on his tail and sent a hail of bullets into the right side of his airplane. "One of the shells came through the canopy and knocked the goggles off the top of my head." Long put the nose down and pushed the throttle forward but another burst of gunfire hit his right wing, severing the aileron cable.

The two Oscars pulled up and away as Long's P-40 spiraled toward the ground. Corporal Ryuzo Yamamoto claimed it as destroyed. Long almost bailed out but found that he could fly level if he kept the stick fully to the left and the airspeed above 170 miles per hour. In this condition, and without hydraulics to lower the landing gear, he determined to make a crash-landing on the grass airstrip at Baoshan, in a valley six miles wide east to west and fifteen miles long north to south just east of the Salween River. Baoshan was one hundred miles closer than Yunnanyi and though his engine was running fine, he did not wish to incur further risk. Reaching Baoshan, Long descended toward the field at 180 miles per hour with his gear up. When he neared the ground, his propeller hit and sheared off, spinning off to the right and sending his plane ballooning into the air. "I worked it down close to the ground again and noticed the rice paddies were coming up at me. I had a lot of airspeed and was near the ground so I just pushed the stick forward to dive the plane right into the ground." The right wing hit first and his plane cartwheeled across the field, knocking him unconscious. When he awoke he found the plane upright, but totally destroyed. After some difficulty opening the canopy, he walked away with only minor injuries.[32]

Left: Sergeant Toshimi Ikezawa, Oscar pilot in the 64th Sentai. Hiroshi Ichimura. Right: 25th Fighter Squadron pilot Lieutenant Clifford Long at Yunnanyi, 1944. Clifford Long

The favorable outcome of their dogfight against the P-40s emboldened the Japanese to further action and on 3 September, ten Oscars raided the tiny airstrip cleared for liaison planes near Tengchong. Ikezawa remembered Captain Hideo Miyabe leading the raid. They spotted two L-5s in the air near the city; one flipped over in a hurried landing, but the other evaded the Japanese planes. Ikezawa commented that the slow and nimble plane was difficult to shoot down, though it eventually crash-landed on a mountainside and the crew escaped into the woods. The Oscars strafed and set fire to two more L-5s parked next to the airstrip.[33]

25th Fighter Squadron P-40Ns at Baoshan, December 1944. Clifford Long

A small tent city which served as living quarters for the small contingent of Americans at Baoshan. Clifford Long

Above: Lieutenants Robert Binzer and Tom Quigley in front of a 27th Troop Carrier Squadron C-47 at Yunnanyi. Robert Binzer

Below: Lieutenant Don Forsythe in front of the P-38J-15 (42-104023) Sonnova Beast he flew on 8 September 1944. Jerry Doughty

Right: Don Forsythe in the cockpit of his P-38. Jerry Doughty

The Japanese attacks added a considerable amount of tension to operations on the Salween Front. According to Jack Engle, the C-47 crews kept "our heads moving in the cockpit, eyes searching the sky for single-engine aircraft. One man kept vigil in the navigator's dome, constantly alert for specks in the distance ... Nerves were on edge; we had no desire to dog-fight a Zero in a C-47 – Who does?"[34] P-38s began regular patrols to guard against enemy Oscars. If attacked, transports broke radio silence with a phrase like "Buicks at mike niner" and the friendly fighters rushed to assist (the entire area was plotted on a grid overlay, lettered north to south and numbered west to east, thus "mike niner" described the transport's position). C-47s rarely received close escort, but Bob Binzer remembered one time "waving at the P-38 pilot that had come up to ride on my left wing for a bit."[35] On 8 September, Lieutenant Binzer was co-pilot for Captain William Peters on an airdrop mission to Longling. Binzer's squadron commander asked for fighter cover for the mission because of the recent Japanese activity in the area. Binzer's C-47 departed west from Yunnanyi at 1415 with four P-38s flown by Lieutenants Rea, Heitkotter, Calder, and Forsythe twelve minutes behind. The faster Lightnings planned to rendezvous with the transport over Baoshan and cover it to the drop zone.

Peters and Binzer arrived at Baoshan and circled, waiting for the fighters. Below them, eight Air Transport Command (ATC) C-47s unloaded Chinese troops flown from the Indo-china border to reinforce Wei's troops attacking Tengchong and Longling. Peters became impatient and noticed a line of thunderstorms west of Baoshan. He figured the P-38s would not be able to accompany him through the weather anyway and decided to proceed without them. They prepared the ship for turbulent weather: wheels down, speed reduced, seats lowered, headsets removed, seat belts tightened, and carburetor heat "on." Binzer recalled, "It was the worst storm I had ever been in. The first updraft sent us up way too far to be flying without oxygen. Then suddenly we were in a downdraft, all accompanied with extreme turbulence." As Binzer's C-47 disappeared into the thunderstorm at 1510 hours, twenty 64th Sentai Oscars descended out of the overcast at eight thousand feet to strafe Baoshan. Ikezawa saw a C-47 over the field and again broke formation to attack, sending it down in flames.[36] The rest of the formation saw a smorgasbord of targets before them and fell upon the C-47s on the field.[37]

Meanwhile, Rea led the P-38s to the rendezvous at Baoshan. The reason for situating an airfield there was apparent, as the valley was the only reprieve from the continuous mountainous terrain between Yunnanyi and the Salween River. The airfield was in the southwest corner of the valley at 5,495 feet above sea level. The vibrant green of the rice paddies in the valley contrasted with the red-brown tinge of the surrounding mountains, evident through the dark green of the pine trees and scrub. As the P-38s approached the valley from the east, "Douglass" (the controller at Baoshan) radioed to them that at least eleven Oscars were attacking the field.[38] According to Jim Heitkotter, the Lightnings climbed to just below the overcast, dove on the unsuspecting Oscars, "and then all hell broke loose."[39] Rea closed on Warrant Officer Tadashi Kinoshita's Oscar from behind and fired, causing it to explode in flame. Tadashi managed to steer his crippled plane into a parked C-47, killing himself and destroying the transport. Another Oscar climbed from below to make a pass on Rea, but Calder attacked it and noticed pieces flying off the wings and fuselage

A view southeast across the Baoshan valley in 2009. Author's Photo

as he fired. The Lightnings used the speed they built up in the dive to zoom back to the base of the clouds and turned to make another attack.[40]

On the ground, Technical Sergeant Matthew Blaszko, a pilot with the 19th Liaison Squadron, was refueling his L-5 when the Japanese attacked. He had just barely made it to a drainage ditch when the P-38s arrived and noted that after the first pass several of the Japanese went into a Lufbery Circle, a defensive maneuver in which several fighters fly a tight circle so that if one is attacked, another will immediately be on the tail of the attacker.[41] The Lightnings made a slashing attack, intending to dive through the Lufbery Circle and climb back to altitude, but Rea noticed two Oscars heading toward him and turned to confront them head-on. He fired his guns and the Oscars broke off. One Oscar pulled up, but the other broke laterally. Rea fired a burst into the latter's exposed underside and saw heavy smoke trailing from the plane as it winged over and dove for the ground.

In this photo taken at Chenggong in 1944, are, from left to right: Calder, Forsythe, Masterson, unknown, Robinson, and Hyde. James Heitkotter

Meanwhile, in the swirling mass of airplanes, another Oscar got on Rea's tail and hit his right engine, landing gear, aileron, and hydraulic system. He immediately departed for Yunnanyi on one engine. Heitkotter damaged Rea's attacker and covered his escape before getting on the tail of another Oscar. As he pursued this target west to the edge of the valley, the Oscar rolled into a split-s from less than one thousand feet above the ground. Heitkotter rolled into a ninety-degree bank and saw he did not have enough altitude to follow it through the maneuver. Upon looking up, however, he noticed the Japanese pilot had left him heading straight for a mountain! "I continued to roll and just got over the top of the hill. We both climbed while coming around to meet again in a head-on pass." Heitkotter admitted, "Both of us must have been a little chicken, with a little left rudder to avoid a collision, which also aimed our guns aside as there were no hits. We just looked at each other as we passed within fifty feet." Heitkotter climbed away and noticed the scattered Japanese elements regrouping as they departed to the south. He lined up behind them to note their heading for the debriefing when he "realized that I could climb a little into the cloud cover and catch them unseen for a real turkey shoot." Heitkotter's "judgment of speed and distance was the

Lieutenant Jim Heitkotter in front of his P-38G-10 #301 (42-13437) Black Lace at Chenggong. Heitkotter flew this aircraft during his first encounter with enemy fighters on 8 September 1944 over Baoshan. James Heitkotter

The mountains west of the airfield at Baoshan, into which Jim Heitkotter nearly crashed his P-38. Author's Photo

basis for a huge disappointment," however, "for as I descended out of the clouds I found myself right beside their formation unable to turn into them without colliding." Heitkotter looked over at the drab green Oscars, each marked with a colored fuselage stripe and downward diagonal arrow on the tail, white for the 1st Chutai, red for the 2nd Chutai, and cobalt for the Headquarters Chutai. Low on fuel, he turned away and headed back to Yunnanyi. He "wondered later about the wisdom of that tactic. My miscalculation might have had me descending into the middle of their formation or perhaps a little in front – then imagine my disappointment!"[42]

Peters and Binzer knew nothing of the air battle behind them since they removed their headsets to fly through the thunderstorm. The weather cleared over Longling and as they descended to make their airdrop, the radio operator told them to put on their headsets and listen to the commotion. Binzer remembered, "We listened as we flew the drop mission and realized that had we been circling a little longer we could have been in the middle of that battle, the Japanese fighters had arrived about the same time as our fighter cover." Binzer flew north for ten minutes to avoid Baoshan on the return trip to Yunnanyi and landed safely. Other transports were not so lucky; the Japanese fighters shot down two ATC C-47s and destroyed two more on the ground (including the one Kinoshita crashed into). The Oscars also jumped two C-47s from the 27th returning from airdrop missions, but the timely intervention by the 449th allowed them to escape into the clouds. One of the C-47 pilots who witnessed the battle claimed that, "When the P-38s fired at a Jap fighter, it looked like the whole nose of the P-38 was spitting fire."[43]

Trouble for the 64th Sentai did not end when it left the P-38s behind at Baoshan. The 449th shot down only one Oscar in the battle (Rea claimed two destroyed) and damaged four, but on the return trip to Burma the remaining aircraft flew into the same thunderstorm Peters and Binzer encountered and four of them crash-landed.[44] Rea made a successful emergency landing at Yunnanyi. According to 27th Troop Carrier Squadron records, had it not been for the P-38s arrival "shortly after the attack began, the total of 4 ATC ships destroyed would have been much greater."[45] Sergeant Blaszko was also grateful for their intervention, as no planes from the 19th were damaged and no personnel injured, and said he "would like to thank [the] flight of P-38s that came to our rescue over [Baoshan]."[46]

The next day, 9 September, Chinese troops in Tengchong captured several Japanese soldiers and Chinese collaborators, including a Taiwanese interpreter named Bai Tongshi who told them that the Japanese planned to airdrop supplies to their embattled garrison the next morning. The Chinese relayed the information to Yunnanyi and waited in eager anticipation. The air brimmed with tension and excitement. The Chinese soldiers realized that victory in Tengchong was near and that the defeat of the enemy's last desperate attempt at resupply would crush the spirit of the Japanese.[47] Acting on the Chinese intelligence, the 69th Composite Wing provided its resupply mission the next morning with a double escort. Four P-38s, three P-40s, and one P-51 escorted the C-47 to Tengchong. At 0900 hours, south of the city, they encountered twelve Oscars and three Lilys conducting the resupply mission for the Japanese. The Lightnings released the five-hundred-pound bombs they had planned to drop on Japanese positions in the city and attacked the enemy fighters. The Chinese on the ground watched as the twin-fuselage fighters, known to them as *shuangshengzi* ("the twins"), roared into the enemy formation. Lieutenant Russell Robertson shot down the Japanese formation leader, Captain Fumio Kitazawa, and claimed another as a probable.[48] Meanwhile, Lieutenant Colonel Amen led the Warhawks and Mustang against the Lilys, unpainted except for the red "meatballs" on their wings. Captain Charles Dundas, one of the 27th Troop Carrier Squadron's senior pilots, made a shallow turn to get his C-47 out of the line of fire and in doing so witnessed Amen dive in to shoot down one of the Lilys.[49] Captain Bell fired a burst into another Lily's left engine, which burst into flame. He ruddered right and shot another burst into the Lily's right engine. The bomber-turned-transport dove into the side of Laifengshan.[50]

The Chinese reported that the plane exploded into thousands of pieces, instantly killing the crew of four. "To the east lay a head, to the west, a hand. Here were chunks of skin, there pools of blood. The enemy had planned to come wreak havoc on our army, but they reaped what they had sown."[51] The Americans shot down all three Lilys and a second Oscar crash-landed in Japanese territory.[52] Having suffered greatly for little gain in combat against Lightnings, Warhawks, and Mustangs, the JAAF withdrew from the Salween Front and focused on defending Japanese forces in Burma.

The Chinese peasants enthusiastically gathered the Japanese medicine and ammunition scattered across the countryside and Chinese soldiers captured two surviving Japanese crewmen. Bi Shixian, who as a boy of ten saw the two prisoners marched away to headquarters, also reported that one of the Lilys crash-landed in a nearby river. The crash fatally injured one of the pilots, but the other survived. A local farmer ran to the plane and, opening the door, took the pilot's pistol, watch, and fountain pen. He then dragged the pilot out of the plane and took him to his home. Realizing a golden opportunity when he saw one, the farmer fed the pilot and then made him work in his fields. This went on for two weeks before the Chinese 198th Division finally found the captured Japanese in the peasant's home when they were passing through the village. They were surprised at the farmer's audacity and took the pilot into custody. They sent him to a prison camp in Tengchong and then to Chongqing, eventually repatriating him after the war.[53]

By 14 September, due in large part to the air superiority established by the 449th and support from the 14th Air Force, the Chinese cleared the last remnants of the fierce Japanese defenders from Tengchong. Of the 1,800 Japanese troops, all but fifty fought to the death. Bi Shixian commented that, "the reason we won the battle in Tengchong was because of our American ally's support ... the people of Tengchong owe the American people a debt of gratitude we shall never forget." In fact, all across the Salween Front Chinese efforts finally began to meet with success. Chinese troops took Songshan on 7 September after American engineers tunneled under the main position and blew it up with six thousand pounds of TNT. The Chinese also entered Longling for the first time in two months and occupied a portion of the city. Japanese infantry from Lashio attempted to break through to reinforce Longling, but Chinese troops controlling strategic hill positions along the Burma Road turned them back. With the two initial objectives of the Salween Campaign in hand and Japanese resistance crumbling, it appeared only a matter of time before Y Force could link up with the Allies in north Burma.[54]

Raising Hell in Southeast Asia

Japanese reinforcements and supplies for the Salween Front moved from Indochina to Burma along a rail corridor beginning in Hanoi and stretching through Saigon, Bangkok, and Chiang Mai to the old Burma Road at Lashio.[55] Though Thailand was a major conduit of Japanese supply, America considered it a "reluctant ally," colluding with the Japanese only to avoid being invaded by them. Besides providing bases and rail facilities,

American engineers detonate six thousand pounds of TNT in mines underneath Japanese positions on Songshan. U.S. Army

Thailand's only military contributions were a brief and unsuccessful attack on Indochina in early 1941 and a limited invasion of the Shan States in eastern Burma in 1942. For this reason, the United States never formally declared war on Thailand, though Chennault's planes had attacked Japanese bases in the country since the early days of the AVG. In the fall of 1944, the 10th and 14th Air Forces flew into Thailand to disrupt supply lines feeding the Japanese war machine in Burma. Though the 449th continued to support Y Force as it advanced to Mangshi, the next Japanese stronghold on the Burma Road, it left the bulk of close air support to the 25th as it flew an increasing number of rail and road interdiction missions along with 22nd Bomb Squadron B-25s and (occasionally) 308th Bomb Group B-24s. The destruction of strategic railroad bridges in Southeast Asia could potentially halt the flow of supplies for days at a time and therefore became the primary objective for American aerial interdiction.

For the 449th this not only meant fighter sweeps and escort missions to protect bombers, but also bridge busting missions for the fighters themselves (late-model P-38s could carry up to four thousand pounds of bombs). Dive-bombing was the most common method used for bridge busting, though it was not always effective, depending on the terrain and enemy defenses. Jim Heitkotter remembered "a lovely suspension bridge" that escaped destruction because of a gun emplacement on the bank. He was flying tail-end Charlie and the three fighters in front of him missed the bridge because they were distracted by the gun. Heitkotter rolled into his dive and "became more intent on the rising tracers from the gun than on the bridge. I missed the bridge, but made a direct hit on the gun. I should have been first!"[56] Another method the Lightnings used was skip-bombing. According to Joe Fodor, from high altitude the P-38s would "pass the target on the way down" and then "drop down on the deck." Just before reaching the bridge "you dropped your bombs and then they would skip into the abutments of the bridge." The

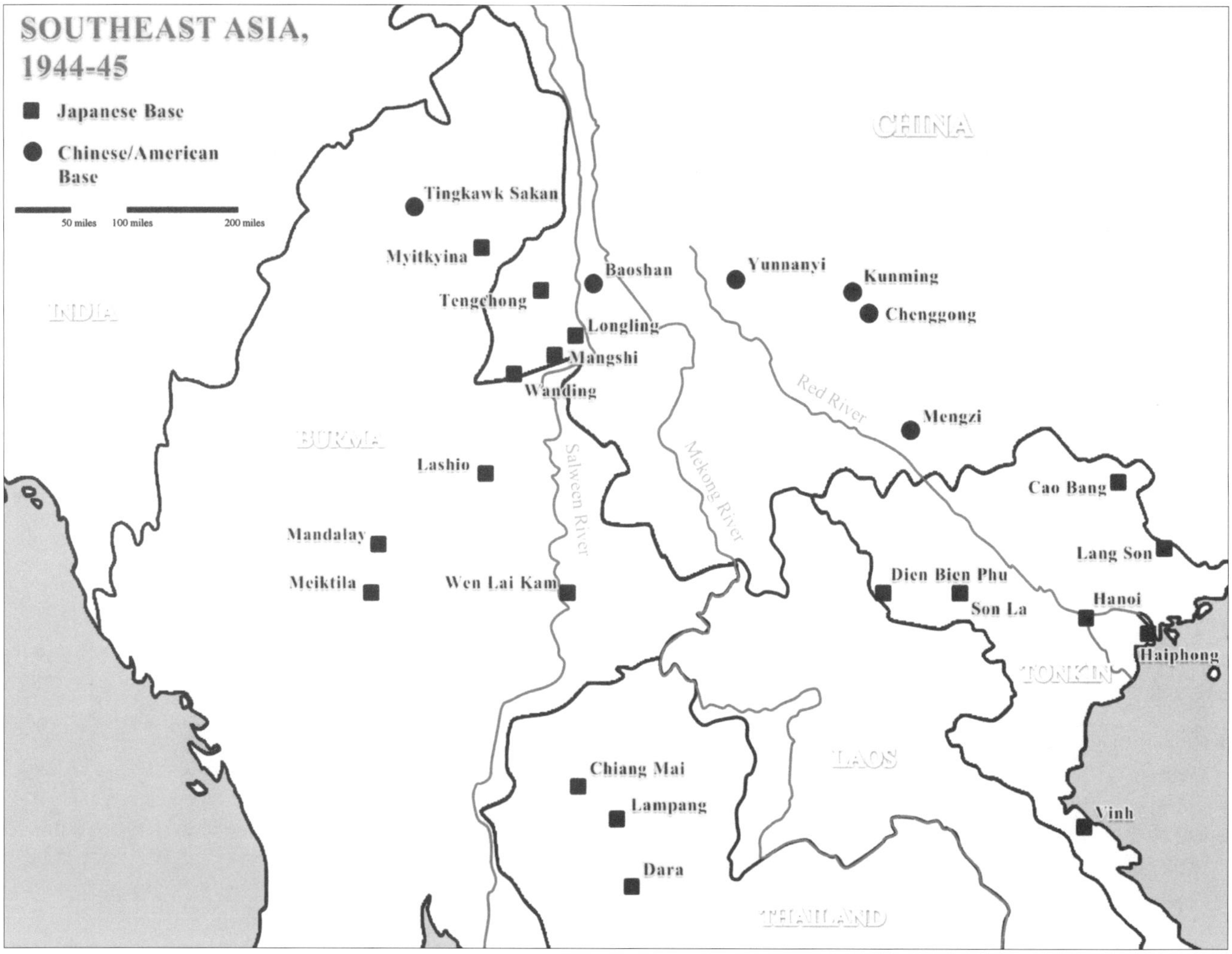

bombs had a three to five second delay fuse, "not much time to get your ass over the bridge and back down on the deck." Fodor claimed the method was very accurate because "you just aim the damn airplane towards the bridge and let her go."[57]

Skip-bombing was also popular with the B-25s because bombing bridges from a medium altitude with few planes rarely achieved good results. The Mitchells met their match however on 26 September when four P-38s led by Major Bledsoe escorted six B-25s to attack the Dara Bridge in Thailand. Chapman Hale remarked that such close escort on missions was rare, but "the P-38s flew along with us, I guess maybe because they didn't have anything better to do." When the B-25s arrived at Dara, midway between Chiang Mai and Bangkok, they encountered a 360-foot long bridge with concrete pillars and a steel superstructure rather than the flimsy wooden bridges they usually struck. Hale remembered, "It was a bridge built by Americans and it looked just like an ordinary American bridge." This presented a problem similar to the walls of Tengchong; when the B-25s skip-bombed the bridge "the bombs would usually hit those pillars and bounce off." When they exploded "it looked like you knocked the bridge out, but it would still be standing."[58] The B-25s turned for home but the four Lightnings remained to search for targets of opportunity. On long missions, P-38s carried two 310-gallon external fuel tanks, but on short or medium range missions they often carried a one-thousand-pound bomb under each wing or a bomb under one wing and a fuel tank under the other. Doughty remarked, "It was not unusual to escort B-25s with our P-38s loaded in one of these configurations. After escorting the B-25s to their destination, we would peel off for our target."[59] Repeated attacks by the 22nd Bomb Squadron failed to destroy the Dara Bridge, which finally fell on 3 November to a large formation of 10th Air Force B-24s. The bridge's sturdy construction was simply too much for fighters or medium bombers to handle, but this proved to be the exception rather than the rule.

The 449th's interdiction efforts not only included bridges in Thailand, but also bridges and shipping in Indochina. On 9 November, Major Bledsoe led four P-38s southeast of Hanoi to strafe shipping along the coast. After expending their ammunition, he instructed his flight to assemble into tight formation to climb through the low overcast. Upon breaking into the clear at five thousand feet, however, he realized that Lieutenant James Nunn was missing. Nunn's radio had been malfunctioning for much of the mission, and consequently, efforts to contact him proved futile. As he was never heard from again, Major Bledsoe believed that he probably became disoriented in the clouds and crashed.

Joe Fodor in the cockpit of his P-38. Jerry Doughty

"Fearless" Forsythe and "Lonesome" Joe Fodor in front of Forsythe's P-38J. James Heitkotter

Right: Chenggong 1944. Standing left to right: Forsythe, Trumble, Robinson, Jones, Calder, unknown. Sitting on the bench is Henry Rogers on the left. Jim Heitkotter

The American built bridge at Dara, Thailand, which withstood multiple attacks by the 14th Air Force. Joseph Fodor

Reconnaissance photo of the airfield at Lampang, Thailand. Joseph Fodor

Left to right: Russ, Weinel, Stubbee, Desper, Robinson, and Sgt. Porfiro Lazaro (working on the jeep). James Heitkotter

A 449th Fighter Squadron P-38 attacks a Thai Ki-27 in this Thai painting. RTAF Museum

On 11 November, eight P-38s returned to Thailand on an offensive reconnaissance of the railroad and airfields between Chiang Mai and Dara. The Lightnings divided into two flights and left Yunnanyi at 0920 hours with nine P-51s from the 25th Fighter Squadron. Captain Desper led the first flight with Lieutenants Roll, Flomer, and Robinson. Lieutenant Conway led the second flight with Lieutenants Stubbee, Jones, and Fodor. Robinson returned to base shortly after takeoff because of engine trouble, but the remaining sixteen planes continued to Thailand at fifteen thousand feet. At Chiang Mai, the P-38s covered the Mustangs as they descended to sweep the airfield and continued at low altitude to Lampang, midway between Chiang Mai and Dara. There the Mustangs strafed a single plane on the field before the P-38s encountered five Ki-27b Nates (called "Ota" in Thai service) from the Royal Thai Air Force (RTAF). When the JAAF upgraded to the Oscar in 1942, it gave the RTAF its obsolete Nates, a small fighter with fixed undercarriage rarely encountered by the 449th. There was a big contrast between the fast, comparatively wide-turning P-38 and the slow, maneuverable Nate. Fodor remarked, "They were maneuverable as hell but slow as hell."[60] Desper's flight made a head-on pass at a Nate flown by Chief Warrant Officer Culadit Detkanchorn and shot it down. The fighter erupted in flames, but Culadit managed to bail out. Meanwhile, the other four Nates jumped the formation of Lightnings from above. Conway fired at a Nate he claimed as probably destroyed before his left engine was shot out by Pilot Officer Kamrop Bleangkam. Kamrop claimed Conway's fighter as destroyed, but in fact, he immediately turned for home and made an emergency landing at Simao, a small field only fifty miles from the Thai border, 180 miles southwest of Chenggong. Other American fighters hit Kamrop's Nate, forcing him to crash-land.[61]

After Conway left the battle, a Nate attacked Flomer from behind and sent him into a panic when it set his right wingtip gas tank on fire. Fodor remembered: "He was holding the mike button down and hollering: 'Somebody get this Jap off my ass!'" Captain Desper was upset that he was not observing radio discipline and, after chasing the Thai fighter off his tail, angrily told Flomer that if he wanted him to, he could stop his P-38 in midair and "I'll get out and piss on it for you." He "was madder than hell because he had to leave the fight and head back to base" with Flomer, but they made it back to Yunnanyi without further incident.

The P-51s also had trouble with the Nates. One of the Mustang pilots, Lieutenant Henry Minco, engaged one at low altitude and radioed: "I've got one trapped in the valley down here." After the mission, however, the 25th reported Minco as missing in action. According to Fodor, "that was the last we ever heard of him." Besides the loss of a P-51 and damage to two P-38s, the results of the mission were good. Desper, Flomer, and Roll all shared credit for one Nate destroyed, while Jones claimed one destroyed and one probably destroyed, Stubbee claimed one destroyed, Conway and Fodor each claimed one probably destroyed, and the P-51s claimed two destroyed. Four of the five Thai pilots survived the combat, but the RTAF admitted losing all five Nates. This convinced them to avoid Allied fighters for the rest of the war and thus the 11 November mission cleared the skies over Thailand for the American interdiction campaign. The Thais (erroneously) claimed one P-38 destroyed and three P-51s damaged.[62]

449th Fighter Squadron P-38J at a forward staging base, 16 November 1944. J. Forrest Green

Throughout October and November, the 449th flew several missions a day to Burma, Indochina, and Thailand, patrolling for enemy fighters, providing close air support, and striking at enemy supply lines. The Lightnings consumed a large amount of fuel and bombs, which prompted Chennault to implement a practice called shuttle bombing, whereby P-38s and B-25s attacked targets in Burma, landed at Tingkawk Sakan, seventy miles northwest of Myitkyina, refueled, and bombed another target on the way back to China. Tingkawk Sakan was no closer to most of the 449th's targets in Burma than Yunnanyi, but was supplied by the Ledo Road rather than the overtaxed Hump airlift. As far as Chennault was concerned, shuttle bombing gave him two missions for the price of one. Jerry Doughty vividly remembered the airstrip at Tingkawk Sakan, cut out of the jungle and just long and wide enough to land a P-38, "that is, if you held your elbows in and sucked up." The facilities were all in tents and a special crew hunted wild game for food. "At night, you were lulled to sleep by the wailing of the animals. It reminded me of the old comic strip, Terry and the Pirates." Doughty's first mission to the strip was on 4 December. He was flying Captain Wire's wing when they spotted the field and "made a fighter peel off for landing that would have made any fighter jock proud. We taxied in, cut our engines and climbed out of our ships like peacocks." A group of men met them at the flight line and asked what they were doing there. It turned out that Tingkawk Sakan "was about a half hour flying time north of us. We sheepishly gave our apologies and headed for our original destination. Sure was glad that I was only a naïve wing man!"[63] Because Tingkawk Sakan was in liberated Burma, it was privy to supplies not available to Americans in China, including white bread, spam, and beer. There were no eggs,

22nd Bomb Squadron B-25 at Tingkawk Sakan, Burma. 22nd Bomb Squadron Association

A 35th Photo Reconnaissance Squadron F-5 snapped a photo of this 449th P-38 as it drops napalm on the bridge at Wen Lai Kam, Burma. Note the napalm dropped short into the village on the left side. National Archives

P-38L-5 #308 (44-25434) in the air over China in late 1944 or early 1945. 14th Air Force Association

however, which abounded in China, spawning a burgeoning trade. Heitkotter explained: "The two economies soon became more equalized. After bombing on the return run, we flew at high altitude to cool the beer for those who eagerly gathered after landing. This went on for a couple of weeks or so and was a sought after duty."[64]

A somewhat unique shuttle bombing mission occurred on 20 November, when eight P-38s carried napalm to a highway bridge at Wen Lai Kam, 120 miles southeast of Lashio. Napalm is a firebomb fuel-gel mixture that readily adheres to most surfaces and was usually used against personnel, who would quickly die of immolation or asphyxiation, though the 69th Composite Wing thought it might be useful in burning down wooden bridges.[65] The 449th's first attempt at using napalm had not been successful: on 28 September, six P-38s flew to Kunming to be fitted with sway braces to accommodate the seventy-five gallon napalm tanks, but the maintenance crews had trouble adapting the braces to the P-38s. When the Lightnings tried to drop the napalm on a bridge near Lang Son, Indochina, many of the tanks would not release and others failed to ignite; none of them hit the target. On the return trip, one of the tanks shook loose while a P-38 was on final approach at Nanning and set a house on fire. For the mission to Wen Lai Kam, seven Lightnings each carried two properly-mounted 165-gallon napalm tanks and one carried two five-hundred-pound incendiary cluster bombs. An F-5 from the 35th Photo Reconnaissance Squadron, which had arrived in July 1944 to help the over-extended 21st, accompanied the mission to record the results of the bridge attack. Reconnaissance pilot Sterling Barrow remembered flying many bomb damage assessment missions to bridges in Burma, sometimes taking photos before, during, and after a mission.[66] This time, the napalm ignited and completely covered the bridge, but according to Heitkotter, "the constant high humidity there had the timber so saturated they did not ignite." The napalm burned furiously for eight minutes without doing any damage to the bridge, which frustrated many of the pilots. Heitkotter claimed that, "One five-hundred-pounder would have done it. We had our own brand of snafus you see."[67] Napalm proved much more effective against entrenched troops, as it would flow into the trenches and foxholes and the Japanese would emerge engulfed in flames.[68] Four of the P-38s that attacked Wen Lai Kam flew on to Tingkawk Sakan and the remainder returned to Yunnanyi. Photoreconnaissance kept the 69th Composite Wing apprised of the status of bridges throughout Southeast Asia so that those repaired or undamaged could be returned to repeatedly in what became a never ending contest between American airplanes and Japanese engineers. By December 1944, the 449th had helped knock out "most of the bridges along the Burma road in Japanese held areas and down to Mandalay," according to Dick Conway.[69]

The interdiction campaign in Burma was particularly successful because Y Force kept steady pressure on the Japanese, forcing them to expend ammunition and supplies they could not replace. This was the anvil on which Chennault envisioned the hammer of airpower grinding the Japanese into oblivion. On 20 November 1944, Y Force took Mangshi, allowing the 27th Troop Carrier Squadron to land supplies on its airfield, and advanced to Wanding on the China-Burma border. Wanding was the only remaining Japanese position on the Ledo-Burma Road after Bhamo fell to X Force on 15 December. In a far cry from its amateur performance early in the campaign, Y Force attacked Wanding on 19 January in a well-coordinated air, artillery, and infantry assault which left the Japanese defenders decimated. The next day, Chinese forces found that the Japanese had evacuated the town.

On 21 January, William Mitchell and Cliff Long of the 25th Fighter Squadron circled over the flag raising ceremony in Wanding with two other P-40s. Suddenly, as a small brass band labored through an unrecognizable tune, mortar shells crashed in from the surrounding hills. Dignitaries and generals dove for cover and called on the P-40s to provide close air support one last time. The Warhawks dove down and silenced the Japanese in a series of strafing attacks. Despite substandard musical support and the startling interruption to the ceremony, the Burma

Clifford Long's P-40N flown over the flag raising ceremony at Wanding, 21 January 1945. Clifford Long

Road was finally open. Though the first truck convoy into China traveled from Myitkyina to Kunming via the Tengchong Cutoff, by the end of the war only sixty-five vehicles used this route because it was a more difficult road to travel than that through Wanding and Longling.

Ironically, General Joseph Stilwell, the man most responsible for the construction of the Ledo-Burma Road, was not present at its opening. Stilwell's lack of tact and respect in coercing Chiang to commit his forces to the Salween Campaign angered Chiang greatly, and prompted him to demand Stilwell's recall. Roosevelt was upset that Chiang put very little effort into resisting the Japanese, depending instead on the Americans to win the war for him, but he was also worried that if he did not give in to Chiang's demands the Chinese might negotiate a separate peace with the Japanese, freeing countless Japanese soldiers to fight the Americans in the Pacific. Thus on 19 October, Roosevelt ordered Stillwell to return to the United States and split the CBI Theater in two. Lieutenant General Dan Sultan commanded the new Burma-India Theater and Lieutenant General Albert Wedemeyer commanded the new China Theater. Chennault and Wedemeyer both claimed the Ledo-Burma Road had been a waste of men and material, carrying only six thousand tons of supplies into China in May 1945, by which time ATC was delivering over forty thousand tons a month over the Hump. Had more effort been put into defending China instead, neither man believed Ichi-go would

XX Bomber Command B-29 at Chenggong, October 1944. Jim Hyde was the refueling boss and had great difficulty filling it up. James Heitkotter

have been as successful. What the Burma campaign did accomplished, however, was to allow ATC to fly the southern Hump route over Myitkyina, which was shorter and safer and contributed to the greater tonnage flown into China.[70] Additionally, Chinese troops on the Salween Front liberated twenty-four thousand square miles of Chinese territory and proved that with air support and numerical superiority they could defeat a well-entrenched Japanese Army, a feat never accomplished in the history of Sino-Japanese warfare.[71]

Perhaps more important to improving Chennault's supply situation was the end of Operation Matterhorn. Matterhorn was a flawed program from the beginning. Arnold's concept of a self-sustained strategic air force, incessantly bombing Japan from airfields in China, was simply not feasible. B-29s made poor transports and could not supply themselves as originally planned, instead depending on Hump supplies meant for Chennault. Additionally, most of Japan was out of range of Chengdu, the B-29s' forward staging base west of Chongqing, and the lack of supplies allowed for relatively few missions which made the operation ineffective against Japanese industry. To make matters worse, Chennault had no authority over the B-29s despite the fact that they operated in his theater and he was obligated to provide fighter defense for their bases. He repeatedly asked Arnold for permission to use B-29s to oppose Ichi-go, but Arnold denied his requests until Wedemeyer insisted on a raid in December 1944. On the 18th, eighty-four Superfortresses fire-bombed Hankou, decimating the city, but far too late to make a difference. Thus, throughout much of 1944, Chennault supplied and supported a massive project that did nothing to stop the Japanese from conquering East China. By early 1945, however, the B-29s began withdrawing from China to join those stationed in the Marianas Islands. The Americans first started construction of the B-29 base on Saipan on 30 June and the first bombing raid from the field was in November. Saipan was five hundred miles closer to Japan than Chengdu and did not suffer from China's supply problems. Thus, by spring 1945, Operation Matterhorn, the Salween Campaign, and Ichi-go all ended, leaving Chennault free to redefine the strategic situation in China.[72]

CHAPTER SEVEN

Back to Sanya Bay

On 25 December 1944, despite the holiday and poor weather, the 449th returned to a familiar target: Hainan Island. Lieutenants Mahon, Rogers, Burrell, and Flight Officer William Jones took off from the forward staging base at Luliang, sixty miles east of Chenggong, under a heavy overcast. Keith Mahon led the mission and was upset for several reasons, "not the least of which was the thought of missing Christmas dinner." He questioned whether the 449th was capable of undertaking a mission under such conditions, considering they had neither the equipment nor qualified pilots to fly in poor weather. "I contacted a friend at 14th Air Force Headquarters who worked with us a lot and asked him to try to persuade someone to postpone this crazy mission until at least the next morning." Mahon's friend informed him that Chennault himself had ordered it to demonstrate to the Japanese that on a holy holiday he was willing and able to strike a strategic target on a long-range mission. Aircraft from Hainan continually harassed American bombers and submarines attacking merchant shipping and Chennault wanted to show that he was willing to retaliate. Exasperated, Mahon picked three volunteers, briefed them, and took off at 1300 hours.

The four Lightnings flew east over Indochina at five hundred feet above the ground until they found a break in the overcast near the coast and climbed to twenty-two thousand feet. Halfway to Hainan, Jones pulled up beside Mahon's plane so as not to break radio silence and signaled that one of his engines was overheating. Mahon remarked that, "the condition was visible, because there was a thin, wispy white trail of engine coolant from a pressure relief valve. ... I didn't like being down to only three, but we chugged along." Despite Mahon's reservations about the weather, his navigation was perfect. The flight arrived over the island and descended through a break in the clouds. Mahon described it as "just like the parting of the Red Sea for Moses. We looked down and the clouds had parted. ... I gave the signal and we slowed up, dropped our external fuel tanks, put down our dive brakes, and headed down." The three P-38s flew low to avoid detection for the remaining twenty-five miles to Qiongshan Airfield, on the northeast coast of Hainan. As they neared the field, they encountered as many as seventy-five machine gun positions and Mahon noticed tracers arcing up toward his airplane, but "no large shells were bursting around us (yet), so it was not too distracting." He picked out a radar unit ahead of him and fired into it, getting "good strikes all over it so it didn't require any more attention." He noticed two fighters parked by the side of the runway as he passed, but "When I came back around one of the others had beaten me to them. They were both on fire, but I now had a good view into a large aircraft hangar in which there were several more airplanes. I directed that we concentrate our firepower through the open hangar doors." All three Lightnings flew low over the field and fired into the hanger from the southwest. "You can imagine what damage could be done with all the .50-caliber armor-piercing incendiaries and our 20mm cannon's high-explosive incendiaries bouncing and zigzagging around and exploding inside that hangar. WOW – it was a dream target! We probably made four passes."

After eight minutes over the field, a large gunboat in the harbor began firing exploding white phosphorous antiaircraft shells at the P-38s. Normally, the fighters flew beneath the burst height of such shells, but this time the Japanese had their altitude and Mahon decided it was time to leave. The Lightnings departed at low altitude to the west and Mahon instructed them to climb one at a time through the overcast and assemble on top. He looked back for a final damage assessment: "The radar unit was burning merrily, so were three aircraft along the runway, and the hangar was a roaring inferno." When he looked forward again, however, he "was headed straight for a haystack!" Without thinking he yanked back on the controls, managing to clear all of it save for slicing through the very top with his propeller tips. There was no permanent damage, but "there sure was a big hay storm!" Everything happened so quickly that Burrell and Rogers had no time to yell over the radio. "I told them later what they were thinking – that the fool was too close to the ground to be looking anywhere but straight ahead." The flight continued low offshore until they found and attacked a 250-foot gunboat ten miles from Hainan. Burrell became separated from the others on the second pass and climbed through the overcast to twelve thousand feet. He could not find Mahon or Rogers and so returned to Luliang on his own. The other men landed several minutes later. Though the raid by three fighters was hardly decisive, it demonstrated that Chennault would keep the pressure on Hainan no matter what the conditions.[1]

Mahon's mission to Hainan was not his last. On 29 December, Major Bledsoe left the 449th for a staff job at 51st Fighter Group Headquarters, leaving Captain Ralph Wire, who had scored three kills and three probables with the 49th Fighter Group in the Pacific, in command of the squadron. On 5 January 1945, Wire and Mahon led two flights of Lightnings followed by twelve 26th Fighter Squadron Mustangs back to Sanya Bay, site of the 449th's successful mission on 29 July 1944. Sanya was now home to a detachment of the 901st Kokutai, a Japanese naval air group specializing in convoy escort and anti-submarine warfare in the South China Sea. It was equipped with 170 G3M Nell bombers, H6K Type 97, codenamed "Mavis," and H8K Type 2, codename "Emily," flying boats, and A6M Zero fighters. The Nells were equipped with radar or magnetic devices to locate submarines, which they would either bomb or call on other planes or ships to attack.[2] In early January, photoreconnaissance showed a large concentration of the 901st's planes on Hainan and Chennault characteristically directed a strike while conditions were favorable. In addition to Wire and Mahon, the P-38 pilots on the mission included Captain Rogers and Lieutenants Roll, Heitkotter, Tribby, Mercer, Huber, and Christy. The Lightnings departed Chenggong at 1215 hours and the P-51s from Kunming at 1220. To Hainan and back was a round trip of almost 1,300 miles – a stretch for the fighters' range, even with drop tanks. Huber and four P-51s aborted because of engine trouble, leaving eight P-38s and eight P-51s to carry out the raid. The American fighters flew down the Red River Valley, past Hanoi and Haiphong, and across the Gulf of Tonkin to Hainan Island. The Lightnings flew at twenty thousand feet until five miles from the target, when they jettisoned their belly tanks and began a steady descent, reaching the Japanese airfield at Sanya thirty minutes ahead of the Mustangs.

Keith Mahon standing next to his P-38L-5 (44-25084) Eula D II, named after his mother. Mahon became an ace when he shot down two aircraft over Hainan Island on 5 January 1945, bringing his total to five. Steve Blake

William Jones in the cockpit of his P-38. Jones's aircraft had coolant problems on the way to Hainan on 25 December 1944 and he was forced to abort the mission. Jerry Doughty

Mahon led Orlando Blue Flight in the first attack, passing to the west of the field and attacking from the southwest at nearly five hundred miles per hour. Heitkotter remembered the attack was "a near surprise." Blue Flight witnessed several Zeros taxiing for takeoff and almost two hundred personnel scattering across the field. Mahon strafed parked aircraft on

P-38s and P-51s depart Chenggong on a joint mission in early 1945. Bruce Carnachan

1: CAPT ROBINSON
2: MAJ BLEDSOE
3: CAPT MASTERSON
4: CAPT ROBINSON
5: CAPT MAHON
6: CAPT KELLY
7: LT MOORE
8: CAPT HARRIS
9: LT WEBER
10: LT CHAMBERLIN
11: LT HUBER
12: LT ROLL
13: LT HEALY
14: LT FORSYTHE
15: LT BARTLETT
16: CAPT ROGERS
17: CAPT MERCER
18: LT PRITCHET
19: LT JONES
STANDING 20: MAJ WIRE

Jerry Doughty

Opposite
Pilots of the 449th Fighter Squadron at Chenggong, 1944. James Heitkotter

Right: Reconnaissance photo of the airfield at Sanya Bay, Hainan Island. National Archives

449th Fighter Squadron P-38s fly in formation over Southeast Asia on a mission in 1945. Michael Bates

Lieutenant Carroll Huber aborted the 5 January 1945 raid on Hainan because of engine trouble. Jerry Doughty

the flight line. On the left, his wingman strafed the hangers. Rogers, on the right, strafed aircraft preparing to take off from the runway, and Heitkotter, Rogers' wingman, "had no target except a truck, rumbling along a burm on the far edge of the airfield." By the time he lined up on the truck, however, "I was past him. At that speed the ground seemed like a huge roller because whatever I saw ahead of me was under me so quickly." The first pass left one Zero destroyed and three damaged on the ground.[3]

As Blue Flight passed to the northeast, Wire led Green Flight from over the mountains two miles from the shoreline. The airfield was located on the flatland between the mountains and the beach. As they began to strafe the field, however, eight Zeros attacked from above. Tribby was flying tail end Charlie and noticed one diving from three o'clock high. He tried to warn Wire over the radio, but his transmitter failed. Taking the situation into his own hands, he turned into the attack and made a pass on the enemy plane at a high deflection angle. Neither plane hit the other, but as the Zero flashed past, Tribby dropped his nose and found himself on the tail of another one, just having taken off from the runway. "His wheels were up but some flaps were down and he had not gained much flying speed. A short burst at the wing root caused [him] to nose down and crash on the beach just below." After seeing the Zero crash, he pulled around to the right and lined up on another. "This was about a 10° deflection shot at very close range. I could see the cannon shells tearing up the fuselage just below the cockpit and smoke was starting to be quite visible in the cockpit. At this time I took a hit directly in the battery and of course everything electrical quit – no guns, no radio receiver and no electrical instruments." In addition to Tribby's one confirmed and one damaged, Wire shot down two and the rest of the flight damaged four. Blue Flight made a sweeping 180-degree turn back into the air battle and Mahon shot down three more.[4] Both Wire and Mahon became aces.

Meanwhile the P-51s barreled in on the field at low altitude led by Lieutenant Shirley "Daddy" Wilson, who had finished his combat tour but wanted one more mission before he returned to the States. The first Mustangs arrived in time to become embroiled in the massive dogfight, now joined by eleven Zeros. In the confusion Heitkotter "saw a '38 on the tail of a P-51 and it must have seemed like he was firing at it – mistaking it for a Jap. I hollered out on the radio 'That's a '51 you're shooting at!'"[5] Low on gas, at 1520 hours, the Lightnings pulled out of the fight and headed for home. Most of the P-51s arrived after the P-38s departed, however, and took over the combat. Lieutenant Jerry Ravenscroft was a pilot from the 26th Fighter Squadron who was friends with 449th pilot Fred Roll, whom he had flown to visit at Chenggong on occasion. He started in on the airfield when he saw a single Zero leaving the area to the east. "I don't know why I left the formation," wrote Ravenscroft, "whether it was because I wanted to test my aerial talent, or feared that this single [Zero] could disrupt and do damage to the mission, or what." None of the other Mustangs from his flight peeled off so he approached the fighter alone. "I dove below the Jap fighter, cut back on my speed, approached real close, gained

Sanya's modern airport is built between the beach and the mountains atop the old World War II field. Author's photo

Lieutenant David Tribby (left) standing with another pilot in front of his P-38J-20 (44-23309) Ruthie. Steve Blake

Tribby (left) with his crew chief, Technical Sergeant Boyles. Steve Blake

altitude until I was directly behind him, and started firing short bursts from my machine guns." His first burst may have killed the pilot, because the Zero continued flying without evasive action. "I pulled up higher and to the side, [but] he still wasn't showing any evasive action, and I started to machine-gun the engine. Soon, there was smoke and fire so I peeled off to go back to the runway." Flying west, Ravenscroft discovered a single flying boat parked at a dock in the bay. He made several passes on it before continuing toward the airfield.[6]

Smoke covered the field from the Japanese planes on fire and more Zeros were in the process of taking off. Ravenscroft began strafing when suddenly four enemy fighters set upon him from above. "We had ourselves a good go-around. Head-on passes, from behind, sideways, they were all over and I was doing my best, and enjoying the activity." Ravenscroft had heard that Zeros could not pull down and to the left as well as the Mustang because of their different engine torque, thus "I made many pull downs to the left whenever I knew someone was on my tail, which was often." The chaotic dogfight continued without another American fighter in sight. In amongst the twisting, turning action, Ravenscroft saw a Zero begin to smoke and then saw a parachute. He looked down at his gas gauge and realized it was time to go. He received credit for one confirmed, one probable, and one damaged while the rest of the 26th claimed an additional four fighters in the air and five bombers on the ground.[7] The Japanese reported losing eight Zeros and three pilots, including Captain Akira Sugiura.[8] Rear Admiral Horiuchi Shigetada, commander of the 901st Kokutai, admitted that constant air attacks like the one on 5 January steadily depleted his forces until he withdrew them to Shanghai in April 1945.[9] Daddy Wilson, who was never seen again after calling for his Mustangs to form up and go home, was the only American lost on the raid.[10]

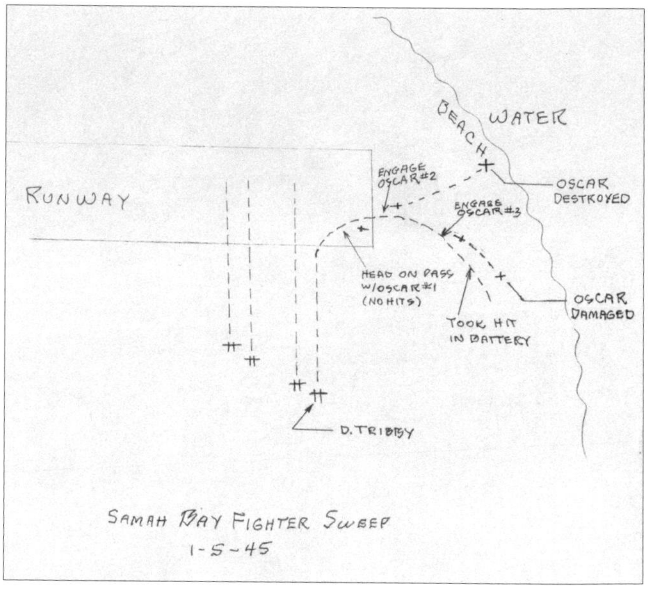

David Tribby's diagram of the 5 January 1945 mission to Hainan showing his P-38 breaking off from the strafing attack to engage Japanese Zeros (erroneously depicted as Oscars). Steve Blake

For many of the pilots, the return trip to China was more dramatic than the dogfight over Hainan. The last radio transmission Tribby heard before his battery was shot out was Rogers

26th Fighter Squadron pilot Jerry Ravenscroft in front of a P-51C at Kunming. Jerry Ravenscroft

Ravenscroft in the cockpit of his P-51. Jerry Ravenscroft

Robert Christy in the cockpit of his P-38. Christy's fighter was damaged over Hainan on 5 January 1945, but he managed to bailout safely over southwest China and walk back to Chenggong. Jerry Doughty

saying: "I think I've taken a hit in the wing, am heading home." Tribby realized that without his electrical system he would not be able to access the 120 gallons of gas in his leading edge tanks and would not be able to make it back to Chenggong. He saw Rogers off his right wing and decided to follow him back as far as possible.[11] Heitkotter and Christy also found themselves in trouble. Heitkotter recalled, "In regrouping for the flight home, Lieutenant Christy found that he could not maintain much speed and I found that my wingtip tanks of seventy gallons had siphoned out. The trip would now have to be made at ultra economy cruise."[12] Apparently, "There was something wrong with the caps on those 'J' models – get in a high speed turn and it would start siphoning."[13] Minus four P-38s, the formation returned to Chenggong at 1800 hours, two of the five remaining Lightnings badly damaged. Ravenscroft made it back to Kunming, despite most of his squadron landing at different forward airbases for lack of fuel, and discovered over 250 bullet holes in his Mustang. His crew chief was upset that the plane had to be scrapped, but at least Ravenscroft made it back alive.[14]

One hour and twenty minutes after departing Hainan, Tribby's right engine ran out of fuel. Rogers pressed on ahead and landed safely at Chenggong, but twenty minutes later Tribby lost his left engine. He found himself two thousand feet over a small valley surrounded by rough terrain and decided to bail out. "I pulled the canopy release after trimming the ship for 120 mph glide, released my harness and safety belt and found myself pulled out of the cockpit. The tail of the ship passed 12 to 15 feet below me. After 10 or 12 seconds, I pulled the rip cord and the chute opened instantly." Tribby watched as his P-38 crashed into the hillside; "It was no consolation to watch the 120 gal of fuel that could have gotten me home burn uselessly." As the sun set, he landed on a slate shelf pointing forty-five degrees upward from the side of a hill. "It was very fortunate that I was wearing paratroop boots. As it was it peeled off a patch of skin from the top of my left boot half way up my thigh."[15]

Meanwhile Heitkotter and Christy flew slowly into the darkening night. Approximately 110 miles due south of Chenggong at 1815 hours, Christy radioed, "This warning light's been on so long it must be standard equipment! I'm gonna bail out." Heitkotter eyed his gas gauges, which read empty, and answered: "Pick a good spot. I'll be right behind you." He zipped his maps into his jacket, grabbed the first aid kit, and jettisoned the canopy. "All these proceedings had not bothered me much ... but then I saw in the blackness the impact and explosion of Christy's plane. I prayed that he got out okay and was then genuinely frightened." Heitkotter slowed his P-38, put his butt and parachute on the right wing, and slid head first on his back toward the tail. As he slid off the back of the wing, one of the counter-balances on the horizontal stabilizer tore open his left calf. To Heitkotter, it was "the most shocking and painful of anything I had yet experienced." As he hurtled toward the ground, his first thought was that his left leg must have been cut off. "My second thought was 'How the hell will I walk back to the squadron now?' and my third thought was 'Open the parachute!'" He landed safely, but unable to move, propped himself against a tree until morning.[16]

That night, Tribby managed to stumble upon a Chinese farmer returning home from the fields and spent the night at

The Lutheran mission where Jim Heitkotter was cared for. James Heitkotter

his house. The next day, he traveled by pony to the crash site but nothing of value remained intact. By 1600, he and his farmer friend arrived in a small town with a field telephone. He called a nearby American outpost, which dispatched a Jeep to pick him up. The next morning an L-5 liaison plane landed at the outpost and flew him to Chenggong. "There was some de-briefing and a session with the flight surgeon to take care of the contusions and abrasions on my left leg. He did recommend the Purple Heart, and it was awarded later. I had flown missions which required more time in the air, but this was to be the longest elapsed time."[17]

Local Chinese found Heitkotter on the morning of 6 January and carried him to a nearby Lutheran mission. On the way, "I was carried through where my airplane crashed. It had almost totally buried itself in the soft earth. I saw one wheel and what appeared to be the leading edge of a wing and it had hit just outside the edge of the village. No wonder they were alerted to something wrong." Just before dark, the party arrived at the mission and was met by one of the German missionaries, Mr. Pretel, who spoke fluent English and told Heitkotter he would be well cared for. Heitkotter was weak from loss of blood and was delirious for the next several days, but Mrs. Pretel sat by his bed "and maintained a constant vigil. Mr. and Mrs. Dietrich, whose mission was a few miles away, also spent considerable time caring for me." Heitkotter's room was crudely plastered, with only one high window that prevented looking outdoors. Often, visitors or missionaries would come to pray for him. "Actually, they prayed with me. I did a lot of praying for myself and for the missionaries."[18]

A Chinese runner brought word of Heitkotter's predicament to a German convent ninety miles away, which radioed 14th Air Force Headquarters. On 10 January, an L-5 flew Captain (Doctor) Julius Pomeranze over the area, but could not find a suitable landing site. The next day, he and Captain Amil Stafford drove eighty-three miles from Kunming to the convent. Upon arriving, they learned that Heitkotter was ninety miles away over rough mountain trails – a five-day walk. The local magistrate provided them with six soldiers, one coolie, and packhorses for the trip. Stafford radioed 14th Air Force Headquarters, giving

Kneeling is Captain Amil Stafford; behind him are the Dietrich children and behind them, standing left to right are: Mrs. Pretel, Mr. Pretel, Captain Pomeranze, and Mr. Dietrich. James Heitkotter

them Heitkotter's position and requesting contact by air on 16 January for a possible medivac. After days of trekking through the rugged mountains, Stafford and Pomeranze found Heitkotter well cared for at the Pretel's mission. Upon examination, they found he was running a temperature of 103 degrees and that his left leg had an infected laceration exposed to the bone. Penicillin and drainage brought his temperature under control and Pomeranze gave him two thirds of a quart of blood plasma to make up for the blood he had lost.[19]

Mr. Pretel and 150 children from the mission school cleared a landing strip on a flat area near the Red River and Stafford set up panel and smoke signals for searching planes. On 17 January, Stafford saw and heard aircraft overhead, but they were too high and too far away to see his signals. Heitkotter remembered: "What a thrill to hear the sound as the first one disappeared upriver. The next day, another one came and went, which was, to say the least, very disheartening." On 19 January, Captain Wire himself set to searching for Heitkotter and located the makeshift strip. He dropped a streamer from his P-38 with a note that informed them that an L-5 would arrive the next day.[20] Major Greenwood and Sergeant Dewey

Two L-5s parked on the improvised landing strip near the Lutheran mission. James Heitkotter

Dewey Mosier's L-5B ambulance plane taking off from the makeshift airstrip. James Heitkotter

Mosier of the 19th Liaison Squadron reached the landing strip as promised. Greenwood landed first and then Mosier landed the L-5B ambulance plane. "The touchdown was smooth, and all was going smoothly when suddenly there was a hard bump and a loud explosion. The left wing dropped, the tail dragged, and the plane came to a jolting stop." It turned out that Mosier's left wheel had struck a rock, causing the tire to go flat and the tail wheel assembly to collapse. Mosier immediately set to fixing his aircraft, holding the broken wheel together with the tire and filling the tire with sand since it would not hold air. Mrs. Pretel, who spoke German, Chinese, and English "became my interpreter/foreman in organizing the group of mission people who furnished the muscle needed to lift the plane and prop it up so I could work on it." The fix worked and Mosier airlifted Heitkotter out the next day.[21] Though Captain Pomeranze had given Heitkotter a dose of morphine before takeoff, the P-38 pilot was still aware enough to notice that once the L-5 got moving, Mosier lifted the left wing and rolled on only one wheel. Upon landing at Kunming Heitkotter noted the same thing and commented about it to the sergeant pilot. Mosier responded: "I didn't want to tell you earlier, but I broke a wheel on landing there. Only the tire held it together."[22]

Jim Heitkotter's rescue became the subject of a sensational news broadcast in the United States. Jim's brother Bill sent him the transcript when he returned home:

> This is the story of four Germans and one American fighter pilot. In these terrible days of war, we are conscious of daily acts of medieval cruelty and barbarism. We have heard and seen unparalleled blows at racial and religious tolerance. Yet this day only serves to remind us that not all people carrying the national strains of the Axis powers are such sadists or bullies.
>
> This fine story of gallantry comes to us from [Chongqing]. Four German missionaries were credited with saving the life of an American fighter pilot forced down in the strange mountains of Japanese occupied China [sic]. Second Lieutenant James Heitkotter of Mountain View, California, was going homeward from a sweep over the Gulf of Tonkin, beyond the large French Indochina coast city of Hanoi, when he was forced to bail out of his P-38. His leg was slashed by the tail boom of the plane when he jumped, and it was laid open to the bone. Heitkotter landed on mountain slopes, which formed a mile deep gorge of the Red River. He lay there all night in terrible pain. He was saving his emergency morphine until the pain became so intense he couldn't bear it. The next day, Chinese peasants brought word of the American's accident to the missionaries on the other side of the mountain. After a long, all-night walk, the Germans, whose home had once been in Munich, found the wounded pilot and carried him back over the mountain to their home.
>
> Soon through German sisters at a mission station nearby, word of Heitkotter's rescue was sent to 14th Air Force Headquarters at Kunming. When an engineering and a medical officer arrived at the far off mission in the mountains six days later, they found the Germans personally tending to the pilot on twenty-four hour shifts, giving him their scanty supply of drugs and compresses. It seems the officers had set out in a southwesterly direction with only the name of the small village, which was not listed on the maps. They trudged over 8,500 foot mountains with only an armed guard carrying blankets, plasma and surgical kits. Remember too this all took place in Japanese-held territory where the slightest misstep might result in sudden death [Heitkotter claims the bit about Japanese held territory and sudden death is "sensational but untrue"].

> Immediately the Germans and 150 students at the mission school built a small landing strip on the bank of the Red River to allow a plane to fly Heitkotter out. Here's what the engineering officer has to say about the German missionaries: "We felt we were leaving people we had known all our lives. They had been away from Germany most of their lives. Their only interest seemed to be working with the Chinese and they hardly kept posted on the war." Thus, the tender hands of four old Germans kept Lieutenant Heitkotter, whose name isn't exactly Irish either, from the brink of death. There is a moral to be learned from such instance of bravery and gallantry in these days of death, destruction and bitter hatred.[23]

All three of the 449th's pilots who bailed out returned to Chenggong within a matter of weeks, owing to the help of the Chinese people – and in Jim Heitkotter's case, to the German missionaries who cared for him. While Christy and Tribby remained with the squadron, Heitkotter was sent back to the United States. His injuries prevented him from flying any more missions with the 449th. This was, however, in stark contrast to the three pilots lost by the Japanese. Ultimately, the 901st Kokutai was unable to protect Japanese shipping from American submarines and aircraft, owing to the vast distances involved and the unit's steadily shrinking supply of pilots and aircraft. In fact, Japan lost so many merchant vessels that by May 1945, 308th Bomb Group B-24s rarely found any off the China coast.[24]

Forrest Green standing next to his P-38L-5 (44-25132) Ranger. Note the outline of Texas beneath the cockpit. J. Forrest Green

Replacements

Despite losing pilots to death and injury, the 14th Air Force continued to grow beyond the strength of the Japanese 5th Air Army. The widening disparity between Japanese and American resources and differences in pilot training had a telling impact on the air war in China. The training philosophies of the JAAF and the USAAF were very different, each reflecting its respective nation's strategy for winning the war. In Japan, each trainee received nearly four hundred hours of flying training before assignment to combat. Such extensive training meant the JAAF was composed of a relatively small cadre of very experienced pilots, which mirrored the Japanese philosophy of winning the war by striking rapidly with a small, highly professional force and bringing the United States to a negotiated peace. America, on the other hand, mass-produced pilots like any other commodity in the "arsenal of democracy." Each pilot received only two hundred hours of instruction, but experienced pilots regularly rotated from combat to pass their insights to trainees, and the AAF increased the capacity of this program throughout the war. America's training program remained consistent as the war wore on, but the Japanese compromised and cut corners until they sent pilots into combat with fewer than one hundred hours of flying training. Despite desperate efforts, Japan only produced forty-six thousand pilots during the war, compared to 193,440 produced by the United States. Thus, in the battle of attrition over China, the 14th Air Force steadily grew, while the 5th Air Army steadily shrank. By early 1945, Japanese airpower in China was a shadow of its former self and hardly a threat to the Americans.[25]

Because of weather and supply problems, however, the 449th flew few missions compared to squadrons in Europe and the Pacific, making it harder for pilots to complete the requisite number of missions for a full tour of duty (which would allow them to rotate back home). In addition, relatively few of the 449th's personnel were killed in battle, thus few replacements were required. According to Jim Hyde, "We didn't actually lose a lot of personnel, so there wasn't a great turnover."[26] The 449th did receive replacements after their stay at Suichuan, when the high operations tempo left the squadron shorthanded, and during the spring of 1945, when many of the pilots and crews finally finished their tours. Two such replacements were Lieutenants John Forrest Green and Paul "Don" McCloud, who graduated from pilot training on 5 December 1943 at Luke AAF Base near Phoenix, Arizona. After awaiting assignment at McChord Field in Washington, both were assigned to the 327th Fighter Squadron, a replacement training unit (RTU) at Marysville, California, in February 1944. The purpose of the RTU was to prepare pilots for service overseas by teaching and practicing the most up-to-date fighter tactics. Flying P-39 Airacobras, Don and Forrest became proficient at skip-bombing, strafing, and especially formation flying. After a couple of months, most of the unit went into combat in the

South Pacific and Italy. Green and McCloud, however, were asked to remain as flight leaders for a year training new pilots. The unit soon moved to Chico, California, and received P-63 Kingcobras and later P-38s. Green and McCloud pushed their students to the limits in stalls, maneuvers, formation flying – anything and everything to teach the characteristics of the airplane and make them confident flying it. The two flight leaders became so well known at the field that the tower operators called them "the tight pattern boys." Finally, in March 1945, Green and McCloud travelled to China as replacement pilots for the 449th. Their tour as flight leaders at Chico almost kept them from seeing combat in the war, but when they did arrive, they felt well prepared to fly and fight.[27]

Don McCloud in the cockpit of his P-38 at Mengzi. Paul D. McCloud

Before they entered combat in China, the 14th Air Force sent new pilots to an operational training unit in Karachi, India, where for two months instructors (pilots whose combat tour had ended) prepared them for the unique demands of the China Theater in war-weary P-40s and P-51s. Jack Bowman "really enjoyed this training as our instructors were all loose and laid back and were giving us the straight poop about combat in China." A practice distinct from training in the United States was shadow gunnery, where an instructor made his shadow visible on the mud flats near the coast and students took turns shooting at it while he maneuvered to make it difficult to hit. According to Bowman, "The mud easily showed the pilot where his bullets were hitting, but in correcting his aim, he had to be very conscious of altitude and air speed since over correcting was easy and spinning at low altitude was almost always fatal." Sometimes pilots became fixated on the target, losing their situational awareness and crashing into the ground.[28]

Don McCloud (near the middle leaning to his left so that Crone can be seen) and other replacements visiting the pyramids on their way to Karachi in March 1945. Paul D. McCloud

After training in Karachi, pilots waited for transport over the Hump to China. Pilots and ground crews alike often made their first trip as passengers in cargo aircraft, but because of the supply situation, often waited several weeks. The Hump was dangerous; not only did enemy fighters routinely patrol the route, but the weather could turn foul at a moment's notice. Bob Barrett died during one of the squadron's first trips. Bruce Carnachan clearly remembered his first trip over the Hump. He was an armorer who arrived in China during the fall of 1943 and transferred to the 449th after serving seventeen months with the 54th Air Service Squadron in addition to flying fifteen missions as a gunner on B-24s and B-25s. When Carnachan boarded a C-87 (a converted B-24) for the trip to China, the pilot told him to charge a round into his rifle. He "told us that if he called out, to turn off the safety, pull the rubber plug from the windows and stick our rifle out ready to fire, and he would tell us which way the Japanese fighters were coming! Thank goodness, we never saw any."[29]

When Jim Heitkotter finally arrived in China after the retreat from Suichuan, he was dismayed to find the 449th had no P-38 for him to fly. When the squadron moved to Chenggong it had twenty-four pilots but only eight aircraft, so Heitkotter was sent to the 16th Fighter Squadron on the other side of the field. Heitkotter complained: "Five of us red hot P-38 pilots who came all the way to China to win the war for 'em, and they

Bruce Carnachan test-firing a machine gun from the left waist position of a B-24 over Lake Dianchi in 1944. Bruce Carnachan

Jack Bowman sits on the wing of his new P-38L after arriving in China. Jack Bowman

Dan Church and his crew chief standing next to their P-38 in 1945. Mrs. Judy Church

assigned us to P-40s. What a blow to whatever morale we had!" For pilots trained in twin-engine, tricycle-gear P-38s, the single-engine, tail-wheel-equipped P-40 could prove troublesome. On Jack Bowman's first mission in a P-40 he was leading Danny Church in another Warhawk. They taxied to the end of the runway where they ran up their engines to check the magnetos. "In the P-38 which had a nose gear, the mags were checked by pushing the yolk forward. The P-40, unless you pulled the stick back, tended to raise up the tail when power was added." Bowman was not thinking and did not hold the stick back. When he added power, the tail raised off the ground. "Church being a good wing man followed my lead exactly. In perfect formation and within seconds his tail came up too. We both hit our props on the tarmac bending the props the same (about 4 inches)." The propellers had to be replaced, but "I don't remember even getting bawled out as it was so ridiculous that everyone rode our ass, and the instructors apparently thought it funny too."[30]

After a week of moping around the barracks, the 16th Fighter Squadron commander ordered Jim Heitkotter to check out in a P-40. His instructor ran him through all the procedures and then jumped down from the cockpit, saying "Take it up, it's all yours." He then climbed back up and explained, "When it spins out from under you, just chop the throttle. It will head straight down for an easy pull out. Get to about 3,000 feet before you try to turn." Heitkotter took off and upon reaching three thousand feet attempted a turn. The Warhawk went into a spin, but the instructor's advice proved correct and he recovered safely. "Gradually I learned to turn fairly tight and hold coordination." The next day he was assigned to Blue Flight, which almost scrambled for a Japanese air raid from the southeast.

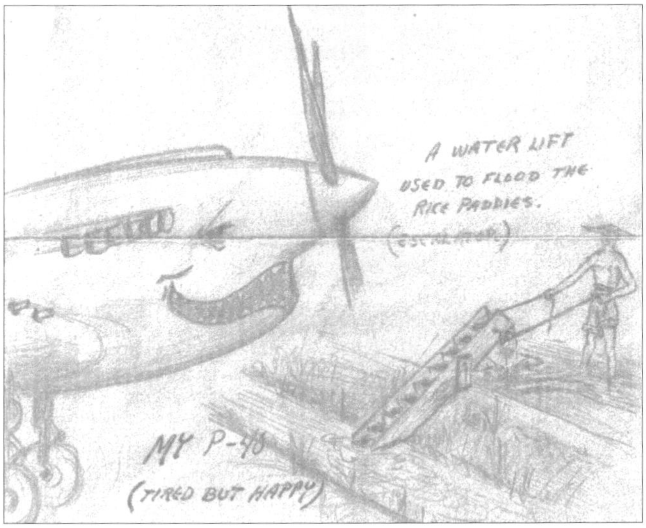

Top right: Jim Heitkotter drew this picture of his P-40 while stationed with the 16th Fighter Squadron at Chenggong. Several pilots from the 449th Fighter Squadron who arrived after the campaign at Suichuan flew P-40s with the 16th until enough P-38s arrived to replace those lost during the months of intense combat. James Heitkotter

Right: Lieutenant Jim Heitkotter with Black Lace, formerly the Golden Eagle. The six victory flags remain on the side. James Heitkotter

This rare photo demonstrates the red spinners and waxed fuselage of one of the 449th's new P-38Ls at Chenggong. Richard Maddox

"I determined right then that I would head northwest if they showed up. They did not, and after a few days more practice I grew to like the old machine." Just as Heitkotter settled in, two P-38 pilots assigned to the 16th died when they spun in on landing and the remaining twin-engine pilots were grounded. Instead, they were assigned as copilots for C-47s in the 14th Air Force's transport section until the 449th received replacement aircraft. Heitkotter remembered: "The next big news was very good news indeed. The 449th had acquired some P-38s and had rotated a few pilots home. So we, Huber, Jones, and I, were assigned to the squadron and even assigned our own airplanes. I promptly did a little nose art on mine renaming it *Black Lace*." Heitkotter inherited the battle-scarred *Golden Eagle*. He renamed the plane, and painted over the faded artwork, but left the six victory flags on the nose.[31]

For some replacement personnel, the road to China was longer than for others. Harold Franklin, an intelligence and operations non-commissioned officer with the squadron in 1945, remembered sailing across the Pacific on the troop ship *General William Mitchell*. On the way, the ship was damaged and limped into Wellington, New Zealand, but could not be repaired because the harbor was full of Allied naval ships damaged in recent battles with the Japanese. The *Mitchell* sailed to Sydney, Australia, to try to affect repairs, but that harbor was also full. Finally, they arrived at Hobart, Tasmania, and completed repairs before continuing to Bombay, India. After several weeks in Bombay, Franklin departed on a troop train to Calcutta, where he found he had been reassigned to Merrill's Marauders, an infantry unit fighting in northern Burma. Franklin served as a machine gunner for seven months before jungle rot infected his feet to such a degree that he was removed to a medical unit. Unable to march, Brigadier General Frank Merrill sent Franklin to Kunming, where he was assigned to the 14th Air Force and subsequently, the 449th Fighter Squadron.[32]

Though replacement personnel were few and far between, replacement aircraft were more common. Jim Hyde explained: "We got a fair amount of replacements over there. I would say that we weren't really kept destitute. Replacement aircraft were pretty much available."[33] Just like personnel, however, replacement aircraft had to be flown over the Hump. Pilots flew older P-38s to India, where they exchanged them for newer aircraft. The new P-38 "J" and "L" models featured

Left: Jerry Doughty with a P-38L in 1945. Jerry Doughty Right: Doughty's P-38L-5 (44-26099) Nina Gal, named after his mother. Jerry Doughty

Joe Fodor with his P-38 Patricia the Worry Bird, named after his wife. Joseph Fodor

Bill Dougherty standing next to a squadron standard at Mengzi in 1945. Dougherty led six Chinese pilots over the Hump on a ferry mission. Jerry Doughty

The P-38J-15 (42-104335) Bowman crash-landed on 17 June 1945 during a ferry trip through Burma. Jack Bowman

This late-model P-38 sports 320-gallon tanks, used either to haul gas or goodies. Bruce Carnachan

hydraulically boosted controls, dive brakes, and more-powerful engines. Jerry Doughty reported, "The 'L' model had a radar device that would alert the pilot with a buzzer, if an aircraft was within 1,000 feet and 20 degrees of your tail." Many of the new Lightnings' prop spinners were painted red, but the wings and fuselage remained unpainted. Doughty explained, "It was proven, waxing the fuselage and wings would increase our speed 10 to 15 miles per hour at all power settings. This was important."[34]

When flying the Hump to pick up new aircraft, P-38s often followed B-24s or B-25s because they had better navigation equipment. Joe Fodor remembered: "Flying the Hump was kind of treacherous but we made it alright. We had a B-24 escort us. It did the navigating while we kind of tacked on and just followed him in."[35] Oftentimes, an experienced pilot led formations of replacement aircraft, such as when Colonel Holloway led Harmon's flight over in 1943. Lieutenant Bill Dougherty led one of these flights, helping six Chinese pilots ferry their P-51s to China. According to Doughty, "They did not understand the importance of writing up maintenance problems on their aircraft when landing at the various enroute fields. Landing at [Chenggong], some of the P-51s were in pretty sad shape of repair. Bill Dougherty said it was an exhilarating and a challenging experience."[36] Jack Bowman recalled one experience when he was flying an old P-38 to India. On the way, his flight stopped in Burma for the night, but the next morning he lost an engine on takeoff. "It was too late to abort and too slow to fly so I pulled up the gear and bellied in." The rest of the flight continued to India, but "I had to stay another night so they could have an accident hearing the next morning. The whole board took about fifteen minutes and they got me on the next airplane going to India. I picked up a new airplane and returned to China with the flight."[37]

Trips to India for replacement aircraft also served as a "pleasant relief from the austere China living. They involved only three or four days being gone but we got to see civilization such as it was in Calcutta." The pilots also took the opportunity to stock up on supplies not found in China. Before departing China with war-weary P-38s, pilots collected money from the squadron to buy canned goods and alcohol in India. According to Bowman, "To haul them we had the three hundred twenty gallon belly tanks on our P-38s with the baffles cut out and the door in the side ... Depending on how many airplanes we had, usually four, and money available, we brought whole truck loads of cases of food to the airport to load and take home." Bowman was one of the smallest pilots in the squadron and was often tasked with loading the tanks from the inside. "If it was a hot day it was a real chore. The pilots outside handed me the cans to stack properly and fill as I went from both ends. When I finally finished, the load was awesome. The tanks would take over 20 cases of small cans and 13 cases of larger ones."[38] The pilots were very careful to avoid any abrupt turns and land gently on the return trip, but on one occasion William Jones accidentally dropped his tank of goodies while in the air. Doughty explained, "Lockheed was constantly changing positions of the switches with every new model. [On] this model, the mike and bomb switches changed position." Thus, when Jones tried to talk to the rest of the flight he dropped his tank of groceries. He felt terrible, but "The fellas took pity on poor Lt. Jones and did not ban him from the squadron."[39]

"Supply runs" boosted morale and kept the Americans' standard of living closer to that with which they were familiar, a luxury the Japanese did not enjoy. The fact that the 14th Air Force also received a relative abundance of replacement aircraft compared to the Japanese demonstrated America's superior industrial capability and the severe strain on the Japanese economy. Because Japan estimated that the war against the United States would be brief, it was unprepared for a protracted conflict against a nation with greater industrial potential and manpower. Consistent pilot training and superior production proved to be critical factors in Chennault's war of attrition over China and in America's victory over Japan.

CHAPTER EIGHT

French Indochina

In early 1945, with his eastern airbases occupied by the Japanese and the Ichi-go and Salween campaigns drawn to a close, Chennault arrayed the 14th Air Force along a 2,300-mile front to strike at Japanese river, rail, and road transport in preparation for a drive to Guangzhou by Wedemeyer and his American-trained Chinese troops. In Chennault's own words, his goal was "To paralyze Japanese communications in their newly won land corridor and rob it of all strategic value."[1] He assigned the 69th Wing, including the 449th Fighter Squadron, to attack lines of communication south of the 24th parallel and west of the 110th meridian, primarily Indochina and southwest China.[2]

Despite Indochina's status as a French colony, by 1945 it was firmly under Japanese control. After Japan blockaded China in 1939, it received forty-eight percent of its military supplies via the railway between Kunming and Haiphong. The Japanese demanded that the French close the railway, and rather than invite Japanese retribution, Governor-General Catroux conceded to their demands. In 1940, the French government sent Jean Decoux to replace Catroux and reverse his appeasement policies. In August of that year, the Japanese demanded that Decoux allow them to use bases in Indochina to block Allied supply routes into China and prepare for the conquest of Southeast Asia. He did not provide an immediate answer, which prompted them to make a coordinated land-air-sea assault on 22 September 1940. However, with only eleven thousand troops, fifteen modern aircraft, and one light cruiser at his disposal in north Indochina, Decoux quickly acquiesced and, under the direction of the Vichy government in France, negotiated a settlement whereby the Japanese could use four airbases in the Tonkin region garrisoned by a maximum of six thousand troops.[3]

Throughout the war, Japan gradually expanded its presence in Indochina until by 1945 it had forty thousand troops at bases all over Cochinchina, Annam, Tonkin (the three colonies that comprised Vietnam), Laos, and Cambodia. The Japanese left the French in administrative control of the colonies, which worked to both countries' advantage; the Japanese did not have to commit large numbers of troops to conquer or occupy Indochina and the French did not lose their profitable possessions. However, many of the colonists did not support Decoux's collaboration and openly celebrated the liberation of France and destruction of the Vichy government in the fall of 1944. The Japanese became wary of increasing pro-Allied activities, including sabotage, Allied intelligence, and rescue of downed American airmen. By the spring of 1945, Franco-Japanese relations were very fragile.[4]

Unfortunately, Captain Wire did not have the opportunity to lead the 449th on many missions into Indochina. On 2 February 1945, he and Mahon were practicing their combat skills when his aircraft developed mechanical trouble and spiraled out of control. He bailed out, but, like Heitkotter, struck the tail boom in the process. He survived the crash and learned of his promotion to Major that same day in the hospital – though he was subsequently sent home because of his injuries. Captain Henry Rogers, who had been with the squadron since early 1944, took command. There was a great contrast between Wire and Rogers. According to Jerry Doughty, Wire, "as his name seemed to imply, was wiry built and a live wire. He was mature for his age but not without a sense of humor." Rogers, on the other hand, "was a likable unassuming person. He seemed to be rather reserved but capable." Both Wire and Rogers were compassionate leaders and listened to their men. In turn, the pilots and ground crews liked and respected them.[5]

Rogers was ready to lead, but poor weather prevented missions throughout much of February. The total destruction wrought by the squadron's P-38s during the month amounted to one truck destroyed and one sedan damaged during a strafing mission on the 16th. Though the 449th was well suited to the task of disrupting Japanese lines of communication because of its experience in Burma and Thailand, targets deep in Indochina were beyond the range of P-38s stationed at Chenggong or Yunnanyi. In late February, the 449th established a new detachment

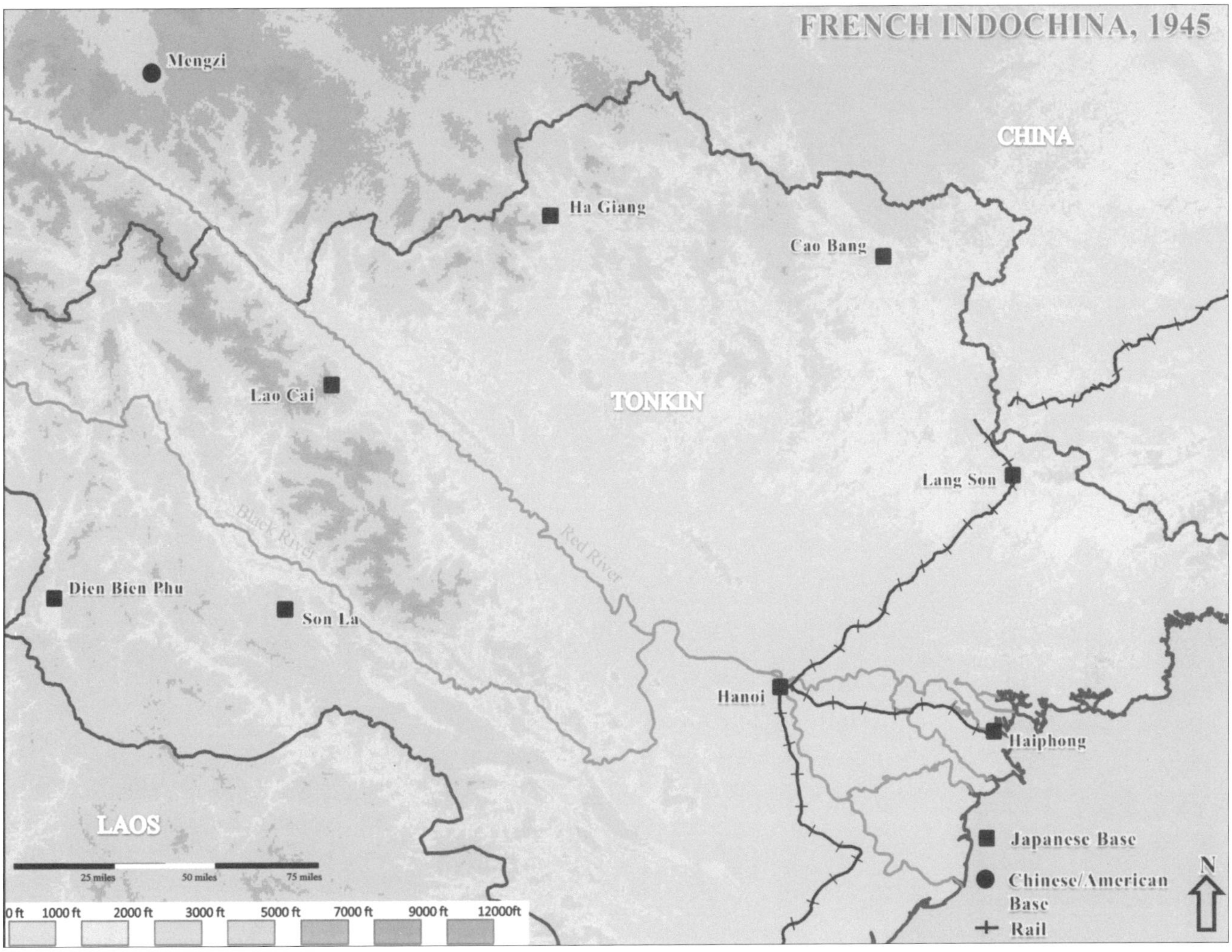

View toward French Indochina from Mengzi, which was about forty miles away. Bruce Carnachan

Headquarters tents at Mengzi. Bruce Carnachan

at Mengzi, one hundred miles south of Chenggong near the Indochina border, and shut down the detachment at Yunnanyi. Mengzi was a spartan base, with only one runway, no flight line buildings, and personnel quartered in standard sixteen-by-sixteen-foot tents instead of barracks. According to George Brabec, an armorer who had just joined the 449th, Mengzi "was like taking a step back in time of 200 years."[6] Forrest Green recounted that the airfield was less than a quarter mile from the walled city, where the flight surgeon had his offices, and that living conditions significantly worsened in poor weather. He also remembered that, "When the bad weather moved in it was very tenacious." It would usually rain for a week or two at a time "and our company streets were just quagmires." The Chinese-built runway, however, was made of crushed rock and useable in all weather conditions.[7] Despite its hardships, Mengzi contrasted sharply with the congested airfield at Chenggong. Jack Bowman commented that, "we were the only squadron at [Mengzi], and it was great."[8]

Left: Sergeant George Brabec showing off the accommodations at Mengzi. George Brabec. Above: Inside the ancient, walled city of Mengzi. Jerry Doughty. Bottom left: Forrest Green standing in the muddy quagmire outside his tent at Mengzi. J. Forrest Green. Below: Dan Church brushing his teeth outside his tent in Mengzi. Jack Bowman

The squadron flew its first mission from Mengzi on 5 March, during which five P-38s strafed the Japanese airfield at Tourane, destroying at least ten aircraft on the ground. No P-38s were lost, but the Japanese shot down a P-51 on a reconnaissance mission near Hanoi. The pilot, Ed Witzenberger, bailed out and was hidden from the Japanese by soldiers of the French Foreign Legion. The French underground helped Witzenberger reach Son La, and a few days later Foreign Legion pilot Lieutenant Hubert Cochard flew him to Mengzi in a Potez 25A2 biplane. The 25A2 was a two-seat reconnaissance version of what twenty years before had been the standard multi-role aircraft of over twenty air forces. But what had once been one of the world's premier airplanes was by then sadly antiquated. Besides the risk of making the trip in a rickety biplane, however, Cochard was also risking Japanese reprisals against himself and his family for helping the Americans.

Chinese "steam roller" pulled by up to two hundred coolies and used to make all-weather, crushed rock runways for the 14th Air Force. James Heitkotter

Bruce Carnachan remembered the air of excitement when the strange vintage plane landed at Mengzi and recalled that a 14th Air Force intelligence officer flew from Kunming to talk to Cochard about rescuing eight other airmen held by the French underground. The officer gave him a portable radio to coordinate the rescues but the old biplane crashed in poor weather on its return trip, destroying the radio and killing the Frenchman. Such weather prevented the 449th from carrying out all but two missions for the remainder of the month.[9]

On 9 March, the Japanese finally decided to end French collusion with the Allies and at 1800 hours gave Decoux an ultimatum accusing his administration of aiding downed Allied airmen, failing to recognize the Chinese puppet government in Nanjing, failing to provide funds and labor for the Japanese Army, and failing to contest Allied bombing missions. They demanded he give them proof of his intentions for a joint defense of Indochina in the event of an Allied invasion and gave him two hours to place French troops and infrastructure under Japanese control. Despite his previous collusion with the Vichy government and the Japanese, Decoux decided not to betray the Allies. He wrote a noncommittal reply neither accepting nor rejecting the Japanese demands. General Tsuchihashi Yuitsu correctly suspected that the response meant Decoux had no intention of acceding to Japanese demands. He immediately denounced the French for their "acts of treachery" and at 2121 hours broadcast the code "777" to the sixty-seven thousand Japanese troops in Indochina; a signal that the French had rejected his demands and for troops to seize government offices and communication centers, arrest French authorities, and attack police and military forces.[10]

The flight line at Mengzi. The 449th was the only squadron at the base, making it much less crowded than Chenggong. George Brabec

Above: Lieutenant Hubert Cochard getting in the cockpit of his Potez 25A2 biplane at Mengzi. Bruce Carnachan

Right: Sergeant Bruce Carnachan with Cochard's biplane at Mengzi. Bruce Carnachan

In Tonkin, thirty-two thousand French troops resisted the Japanese coup, but by morning, the Japanese had killed 2,100 Frenchmen and captured twelve thousand more. Generals Gabriel Sabattier and Marcel Alessandri, however, had been warned of the possibility of a coup the day before and had secretly left Hanoi. When the Japanese attacked, they escaped to the north. Alessandri's largest unit was the two-thousand-man 5th Foreign Infantry Regiment, whose men were an average of forty years old. The Japanese blocked Alessandri's men at Lao Cai and Ha Giang, and he lost seventy-five men to rear-guard actions and more to the brutal trek through the jungle. Sabattier lost contact with most of his men and escaped north along the Black River with a small band of survivors. The two generals joined again in a valley near the Laotian border called Dien Bien Phu, where Alessandri established his headquarters on 28 March. A British plane landed at a small airfield in the valley with messages from the leader of liberated France, General Charles de Gaulle, giving Sabattier civilian and military powers over what was left of French Indochina and instructing him to hold on whatever the cost. Thus, Dien Bien Phu became the scene of France's final stand against the Japanese in Indochina.[11]

When Chennault learned of the Japanese coup, he sent intelligence officers in liaison planes to coordinate airdrops of food and ammunition to the remaining French troops. According to Chennault, the 14th Air Force destroyed nine key bridges leading into Japanese-controlled Hanoi, despite the poor weather, causing a critical food shortage in the city and sparking riots amongst the local populace.[12] On 4, 7, and 8 April, P-38s flew missions to Dien Bien Phu, strafing Japanese columns entering the valley and escorting C-47s on airdrop missions. Paul Rittenhouse, a pilot with the 27th Troop Carrier Squadron, flew a C-47 to Mengzi on 9 April, but poor weather prevented him from taking off for Dien Bien Phu until the 12th, by which time the Japanese had a firm foothold in the valley. Two P-38s escorted Rittenhouse to the lush, green valley, where he observed two French biplanes (similar to the one flown by Cochard) on the airfield and cloth panels marking the drop zones. "Kickers" in the back of the transport dropped drums of gasoline and ammunition to the French below and the P-38s strafed buildings occupied by the Japanese.[13]

As the situation worsened, the 14th Air Force began evacuating French refugees. Joe Fodor remembered one particular mission for which four P-38s escorted a BT-13, four L-5s, and a C-47 to the valley. The L-5s and BT-13 landed to pick up refugees while the P-38s and C-47 circled overhead. The light aircraft took off again and the group flew back to Mengzi. The assortment of aircraft on the mission prompted Fodor to comment that, "It was kind of like a circus."[14] Unfortunately, Chennault's air support for the French soon ended. In a meeting with Wedemeyer and the U.S. ambassador to China, Patrick Hurley, President Roosevelt made it clear that the United States did not support colonialism and did not want France to control Indochina after the war. In fact, Roosevelt wanted Indochina

19th Liaison Squadron L-5 used for special missions in Indochina. Bruce Carnachan

George Brabec next to the 449th's BT-13, which participated in several missions into Indochina. George Brabec

Lieutenant Jack Bowman and crew chief Joe Butto with their P-38 Ripper's Reaper at Mengzi, 1945. Jack Bowman

to be an Allied trusteeship until it was ready for self-rule and saw the Japanese conquest as simplifying the problem of getting France to give up its colonies. Despite Roosevelt's death on 12 April, Wedemeyer ordered Chennault to carry out his policy. Chennault "carried out my orders to the letter but I did not relish the idea of leaving Frenchmen to be slaughtered in the jungle while I was forced officially to ignore their plight."[15] Leonard Logar, a pilot with the 19th Liaison Squadron, pitied the French and commented that, "the poor buggers didn't have anything except their reputations."[16] By 14 April, the French began withdrawing from Dien Bien Phu and headed for China. Jack Bowman recalled a mission to napalm Japanese mule barns in the valley after the French withdrawal. Dien Bien Phu was a major opium collection and processing center and the Japanese took advantage of the opium profit, just as Ho Chi Minh would do years later to fund his wars against France and the United States.[17] Bowman's mission was to eliminate the pack strings carrying opium from Indochina to Bangkok in an attempt to cripple the Japanese opium trade.[18]

Joe Fodor, Don Forsythe, and Palmer Foss outside the tent area at Mengzi. Joseph Fodor

Major William Moore sitting in a squadron jeep at Mengzi. Moore was on his third overseas combat tour. Paul D. McCloud

While providing air support for the French, the 449th simultaneously carried out a campaign against Japanese lines of communication. On 13 April, Major William Moore, a new arrival to the squadron, led seven P-38s to a highway bridge about two miles northeast of Cao Bang. The 449th had targeted the bridge three times before. On 2 April, they aborted the mission due to weather. The next day, one P-38 broke through the weather, but its bombs missed the target. On the 12th, three P-38s made bombing runs but did not damage the bridge. Thus on the 13th, Moore decided he would knock it out himself. The approach was tricky; three mountains formed a roughly four-hundred-foot-deep triangular gorge in which the bridge was located. Undaunted, Moore made a tight turn and steep descent, lining himself up with the target. He waited to drop the bombs until he could not miss. He *did not* miss: the bombs hit and dropped the span into the river, but damaged his P-38 in the process. Moore was so low that debris hit the underside of his aircraft and he was unable to lower the nose gear. He decided to land his damaged plane and radioed ahead to Chenggong to inform them of his predicament. He circled the airfield to use up as much fuel as possible so there would be less of a chance of fire if he crashed. Nervously chewing his cigar, he came in for a landing with the fuel gauges on empty. He made his final approach faster than normal and landed on his two main wheels to keep the nose off the runway as long as possible. He could not use the wheel brakes because they would pull the nose into the ground and instead intended to use the entire length of the runway to slow down. Brabec watched as Moore's Lightning slowed until the nose dropped to the ground. Moore had no control over the plane as it spun off the side of the runway. When it finally came to a stop, ground crewmen rushed to assist. The P-38 did not catch fire and they lifted Moore out of the cockpit. According to Brabec, "He was able to walk away from that one" and "the wad of a chewed cigar was promptly spit out."[19]

Other pilots were not so lucky. On 18 April, a flight of P-38s was returning to Chenggong when the left engine of Lieutenant Gilbert Schowengerdt's plane caught fire. Lieutenant Howard Boswell saw him bail out, "watched his parachute open, and saw him hit the water" in Lake Dianchi. Captain Melville Mercer, the flight leader, saw Schowengerdt "in the water near the chute, floating and moving his arms," but when a Chinese fishing boat arrived on the scene thirty minutes later, it found only the parachute. The squadron searched for Schowengerdt for days, hoping he had made it out of the lake and was sheltering in a Chinese village nearby. However, on the 24th they found his body washed up on the northeast shore.[20] The squadron also lost Captain Peter Bunce when both his engines quit over Indochina on 8 May.[21]

Meanwhile, Alessandri's Foreign Legionnaires slowly drifted into southwest China where the Nationalist Chinese detained them for their alleged collaboration with Japan. In late May or early June, Brabec was on a walk with three of his friends when he discovered a handgun by the side of the road. The gun was a MAB model "D" thirty-two caliber, semi-automatic pistol with a three-inch barrel and foreign words

Paper money on which the French officer scribbled a note to George Brabec. George Brabec

inscribed on the side. Brabec pocketed the pistol thinking he had found a good souvenir. Several days later, Moore told members of the squadron to keep a lookout for just such a pistol, as a foreign officer had lost it and, according to custom, would be executed if he did not return with it. Brabec went to Moore and confessed that he had found the pistol. Moore introduced Brabec to a French officer who had been waiting in his office and Brabec handed him the gun. Though the Frenchman could not speak English, he was filled with such gratitude that he wrote "En remerciement pour m'avoir rendu mon pistolet. En toute sympathie" (As thanks for having returned my pistol. With my best regards)[22] on a Vietnamese banknote and handed it to Brabec along with all the paper money he possessed (The money was, after all, worthless after the French government in Indochina collapsed). As the French officer departed, Moore commented, "Well George, for saving an officer's life there should be a medal in this for you." No medal was awarded, but Brabec kept the money as a souvenir of his time in China.[23] Eventually, about 5,500 French and Foreign Legion soldiers of various nationalities escaped into Yunnan from Indochina.[24]

The 9 March coup and subsequent campaign by the Japanese was a stunning defeat for the French, who blamed it on the lack of support from the United States. Even if Wedemeyer had not forbidden Chennault from supplying the French, however, poor weather restricted the flow of supplies to a trickle. Additionally, the Japanese killed or captured most of the French colonial garrison on the night of the 9th, leaving only a token force for further opposition. Regardless of the reasons, within less than two months the Japanese ended almost one hundred years of French colonial rule in Indochina.[25]

Move to Mengzi

Most of the 14th Air Force's intelligence on Indochina came from French colonial agents working with the Office of Strategic Services (OSS) – predecessor to the CIA. After the Japanese coup, however, Chennault found himself without any source of intelligence and wondering how he would recover downed airmen from behind enemy lines.[26] The lack of intelligence and poor weather also made May a slow month for the 449th. The unit's official records called it "the dullest month in the history of the squadron," because the P-38s flew only six missions and had little to report.[27] Jim Borge tried to keep himself occupied by teaching the flight surgeon how to fly in a light aircraft the squadron kept for training purposes. According to Bowman, however, "there was only one problem – it only had one set of controls." Borge decided the flight doc could fly after one demonstration ride and switched places with him after landing. Bowman recalled, "Doc wasn't quite as ready to fly as Jim thought. He and Jim crashed but both survived okay." Much to his chagrin, Borge was grounded for almost the rest of the war.[28]

On 11 May, Rogers received orders to return to the United States and William Moore took his place as squadron commander. Moore had scored two Messerschmitt 110 kills flying with the 49th Fighter Squadron over North Africa in 1942, and was a veteran of the Aleutians Campaign. According to Jerry Doughty, he was "a capable and understanding C.O." and "a conscientious officer" who "tried to get the overdue promotions" for his men and "awards for special missions we have flown." Unfortunately, "his pleas fell on deaf ears." Chennault was notorious for his poor administrative abilities and the 14th Air Force was always behind other organizations in decorations and promotions.[29]

The answer to Chennault's intelligence problems finally came when OSS agent Charles Fenn remembered a Vietnamese guerrilla leader who had rescued Lieutenant Rudolph Shaw, a P-51 pilot shot down near Cao Bang, in November 1944, and personally escorted him to Kunming. Despite the Vietnamese's hatred for the French, colonialism under Japan proved even worse. Excessive demands for rice exported to Japan resulted in a devastating famine, especially in the less agriculturally productive north. Many Vietnamese turned to America for help, including the guerrilla leader that rescued Shaw, who introduced himself as Ho Chi Minh. Ho refused payment for the rescue, asking only to see Chennault, "the Westerner we most admire." Chennault was not available at the time, but when Fenn contacted Ho again in March 1945, a meeting was easily arranged. Fenn explained to Chennault that Ho's guerrillas rescued one of his pilots and might prove useful in replacing the defunct French intelligence organization. On 29 March, Chennault met with Ho and thanked him for rescuing Lieutenant Shaw, to which Ho replied he would always be glad to help the Americans. The two worked out an arrangement for intelligence and before he left, Ho requested a photograph of the general to take with him. Chennault produced a folder of eight-by-ten glossies, giving Ho his pick and signing it, "Yours sincerely, Claire L. Chennault." After the meeting, Ho also asked Fenn for six brand-new Colt .45s, which Fenn procured before two L-5s arrived to fly them back to the Indochina border.[30]

Ho Chi Minh was one of the leaders of a Vietnamese nationalist group called the League for the Independence of Vietnam (also known as the Viet Minh). Though the Indochinese Communist Party was the leading faction in the group, Ho was careful to style himself as a nationalist leader rather than a communist for the sake of an alliance with the United States. He solidified his control over the Viet Minh by presenting the signed photo of Chennault and giving each of the factional leaders one of the brand new Colt .45s as evidence of his American backing. OSS agents embedded with the Viet Minh immediately began training the Vietnamese for intelligence work and provided the 14th Air Force with target and weather information, especially along the road and rail corridor between Hanoi and Lang Son.[31]

In the late spring and early summer of 1945, Japanese commanders thought the Allies would make an amphibious assault on either Taiwan or the southern coast of China to facilitate an invasion of Japan. While Admiral Ernest King, Chief of Naval Operations, proposed an invasion of Taiwan as an alternative to the Philippines, General MacArthur argued against it, claiming that he had an obligation to liberate the Filipino people and that they would suffer greatly if the Americans were to blockade rather than conquer the Philippines. General Wedemeyer's drive to Guangzhou (Operation Carbonado) was proceeding ahead of schedule as Japanese troops began withdrawing from southwest China. However, Japanese forces retreating to Guangzhou from Indochina to oppose the imagined landings threatened his plans. The 69th Composite Wing targeted the rail line between Hanoi and Lang Son to prevent this from happening. In addition, they interdicted supplies moving from Haiphong to Hanoi and along the single road and rail corridor connecting Hanoi with Saigon.[32]

Jim Borge standing next to his P-38 Amy Lee. Borge attempted to teach the flight surgeon how to fly a light aircraft in May 1945, but the unsatisfactory results of his efforts left him grounded for almost the rest of the war. Jack Bowman

When the weather finally cleared in late June 1945, the 449th vigorously attacked lines of communication. Road and rail bridges were valuable targets in Indochina because in the Tonkin region there were so many streams and rivers that there was an average of one bridge for every twenty-five miles of railway. The Japanese circumvented destroyed bridges by loading trucks or boats with ammunition and supplies and crossing the river or stream to load trains on the other side. Thus, the 449th also targeted locomotives, trucks, and river transportation on offensive reconnaissance missions ranging from the China border to Vinh.[33] Jack Bowman remembered that on low-altitude missions over the Red River Delta, he could smell "the stench of the swampy, dirty water." They would follow railroads, canals, and roads, or follow the coast looking for shipping. Normally, in attacks on trains the P-38s would fly perpendicular to the tracks, concentrating on the locomotives. Bowman personally claimed eight, and was "noted for my low pullouts," some of which damaged his own airplane when he flew through exploding debris. Jerry Doughty vividly remembered a mission on which he encountered a Japanese truck convoy, describing it as one of the most "distasteful" missions he flew:

> I aimed my P-38 at the truck convoy and pressed the gun trigger. One truck stopped, three people got out and started waving their hands. A slug from my 20 mm cannon hit one of them, dead center. The slug propelled him about

Above: Jerry Doughty next to his P-38L at Mengzi. Jerry Doughty. Right: 449th Fighter Squadron pilots at Mengzi. Standing left to right: Smith, Dougherty, Skipper, Doughty, and Foss; kneeling: Mercer, Richards, Healy, and Savage. Paul D. McCloud

> 10 feet into the air before he disintegrated. It seemed as though I just flew through him.

According to Doughty, "Time has not faded the memory." He often thought back to that mission, wondering what type of person that man was: "Was he like me? Could we have been friends? Did he have a wife, children?"[34] Forrest Green also remembered encountering a convoy on an offensive reconnaissance mission: "We found a truck convoy – I was element leader – and I was the second one in." The first Lightning made a pass and the trucks scattered all over the road. Green dove in and lined up on a truck that had turned over on its side, "but just before I shot I saw some people climbing out of it and instead of Jap soldiers as I expected" they were Vietnamese laborers. Green did not shoot, but "often wondered how close they figured they came to eternity."[35]

By the end of June, the 449th was flying all of its missions from Mengzi. In early July, the remaining personnel and aircraft moved from Chenggong and Mengzi became the squadron's permanent base. Forrest Green was one of the pilots who ferried the P-38s to Mengzi. He recounted that, "There wasn't an airplane available for each pilot in the squadron so the rest of them went by train," and remembered "some of the fellas reporting on it as a pretty primitive trip."[36] Major Moore selected Don McCloud to command the train, much to his dismay. Fortunately, he had the help of the flight surgeon, Captain Hisrt, who had grown up in China.[37]

It did not take long for the squadron to adjust to its new permanent base and missions continued unhindered. Forrest Green remembered one particular mission in which his flight hunted for shipping along the Indochina coast and found two freighters tied up at a dock near Haiphong. The first three

Lightnings missed the ships and Green was the last one in. He "was a little fearful that probably every gun in the area" was trained on him and therefore decided to attack both ships in one pass. "I came in and dropped my bomb on one on the left and switched over – they were pretty close together so you had to do a little maneuvering – and I dropped my bomb on the other one and both of them blew up."[38]

Proud of his bombing prowess, Green employed it on a subsequent mission against a large boat moored in the Red River near Hanoi. He made the perfect setup for a skip-bombing run, dropping his thousand-pounder at just the right moment. It went straight into the side of the boat. He stayed low on the other side of the target. "You stay low, because ... if you get up high there's everybody shooting at you but if you're low they don't get much of a shot." Unfortunately, the ship, though large, was made of wood and the bomb passed through both sides. Green, not realizing this, suddenly felt his plane rise up on the shock wave. It was a close call, but Green's P-38 was not damaged and he managed to return to base without further incident.[39]

In the midst of hunting for locomotives, trucks, and river vessels, encounters with the JAAF were rare. Though most sentais had retreated to Korea, Manchuria, or Cambodia, Lieutenant Dougherty shot down a Ki-27 Nate over Gia Lam Airdrome near Hanoi on 6 July for the unit's last confirmed kill. It was probably Lieutenant Tetsuji Kamiya of the 50th Sentai, who the Japanese reported as shot down and killed.[40] On 10 July 1945, the 449th engaged Japanese aircraft in the air for the last time near Vinh. Joe Fodor and William Jones

Lieutenant Palmer Foss in the cockpit of his P-38. Foss bailed out near Vinh and was rescued by Vietnamese guerillas. Jerry Doughty

were "on the deck looking for railroad engines" when they were ambushed by four Ki-43-IIIs. Sergeant Toshimi Ikezawa was on the ground at Vinh and saw the four Oscars jump the P-38s, though he did not know which unit they were from.[41] According to Fodor, "That was a pain in the butt because we were outnumbered two to one. ... You should never get caught with your pants down – or your flaps down so they say." The Oscars shot out Jones' right engine before Fodor turned into the attack and damaged the leader. "We made it back to base. I just had to escort Jones and ward off the Japanese Oscars. They must have been low on gas or something because they

Dan Church standing with his P-38J-15 (42-104335) My Achin' Ass. Church was Shomaker's wingman when he was shot down by ground fire on 12 July 1945. Jack Bowman

never followed up to try and catch us." Jones had to belly-land his P-38 at Mengzi, but walked away uninjured.[42]

Despite Jones' survival, July was a bad month in terms of pilots lost. Three pilots died in accidents and two were missing in action. Lieutenant Palmer Foss bailed out of his stricken plane on 7 July, as did Lieutenant William Shomaker on the 12th, both near Vinh. Shomaker was an experienced pilot who had shot down one Me 109 and one Fw 190 with the 97th Fighter Squadron over Italy in 1943. He was leading Danny Church on a strafing run when he was hit by ground fire. Church thought that he was too low to bail out, but Don Forsythe, who was flying top cover, searched the area and found a partially-opened parachute on a hillside.[43] Though the Viet Minh rescued Foss and returned him to China in September, Shomaker was not so lucky. Three days after he bailed out, Jerry Doughty was on a mission to bomb the docks at Haiphong. "As I was coming in on the target, I saw the pilot who was shot down. He was stripped naked and tied in a crucifixion position to one of the dock's pillars. His head was down." Doughty figured the Japanese must have received advanced notice of the raid and tied Shomaker to the dock to discourage the Lightnings from bombing it. Doughty "hesitated for a moment, then I realized if he wasn't dead, he was near death. If I broke off the run, the flight would follow my lead and the mission would be aborted." He made "a tough decision for a guy of 23" and "with a prayer for forgiveness, I squeezed the gun trigger and continued the run releasing my bombs on the target."[44]

Also difficult to stomach were the deaths of the three pilots lost in accidents. On 24 July, George Brabec watched as four P-38s took off from Mengzi "carrying their maximum weight limit with bombs and full fuel tanks." After using most of the runway to take off, the P-38s went into a spiral flight pattern to gain altitude. One of the Lightnings was flown by Lieutenant Ray Moore. Moore's left engine cut out soon after takeoff and he crashed into a mountaintop. Brabec and some other men boarded a truck and drove to the crash site. Brabec remembered, "Arriving at the site, there were already some

Lieutenant William Shomaker (right) and his crew chief with their P-38L-5 #302 (44-25280) Chita III. Shomaker had two kills from a previous tour and reportedly died at Haiphong three days after he bailed out near Vinh. Joseph Fodor

Above: P-38L-1 #316 (44-24245) taxiing in preparation for takeoff at Mengzi. Bruce Carnachan. Below: P-38s departing Mengzi on a mission. An ambulance is standing by in the center; the armament truck is on the left. Bruce Carnachan

Lieutenant Walter Savage with P-38J-10 (42-67790) Fini Cas. Savage survived a mid-air collision with his wingman on 27 July 1945, but had to belly land his damaged aircraft. Jerry Doughty

Chinese people – they were appearing to loot whatever could be found. They were promptly removed from the site." The P-38 had penetrated into the mountain and "the ground was still warm to the touch." The Americans began to dig to see what they could recover. Brabec remembered that they dug three or four feet before they found anything. "The body was badly charred and dismembered. What all that was found consisted of, part of his parachute straps, part of his money belt, part of his dog tags and lastly part of his skull with burnt hair." The site was sickening. Brabec commented that, "The site and smell will always stay with me."[45]

That same day, for unknown reasons, Lieutenant Harold Pulliam also crashed and died on takeoff. The third accident happened on 27 July. Forrest Green was on the ground and saw two P-38s peel off for a normal landing approach. "Something went amiss and they had a midair collision. The wingman spun in and was killed." Lieutenant Robert Bentz died in the crash and the flight leader, Lieutenant Walter Savage, could not lower his landing gear. "He had to belly the aircraft in so I think we lost both aircraft on that particular accident."[46] It was tragic that so many men from the 449th died in accidents so near the end of the war.

Major Moore himself almost became a casualty during a mission on 25 July. Don McCloud was flying the Major's wing as he led six P-38s to bomb the railroad yards at Vinh. Each Lightning carried an external fuel tank under one wing and a five-hundred-pound bomb under the other. The targets were the railroad repair shop, the turntable leading into it, and other buildings in the area. McCloud and Moore made the first run while the other fighters remained high to cover them. Moore went in and McCloud waited for his bomb to explode. "No explosion. He broke radio silence and told me to go on in. He admitted he'd forgotten to arm his bomb – so it didn't drop." In the meantime, McCloud had studied the situation: The turntable was on the north side of the repair shop, opposite from him, and he noticed one track going into a big opening on the south side. "I lined up on that track after swinging around to the south a ways – and came in at ground level – putting my bomb in that big doorway." The bomb demolished the building, much to the excitement of the other pilots in the flight. The other Lightnings dropped their bombs and then proceeded to strafe some aircraft revetments to the west of the rail yard. McCloud admitted: "To this day I don't know if they contained real planes or mockups. They looked real to me in the excitement. No fires erupted however."

Reconnaissance photo of the Vinh rail yards. Paul D. McCloud

Up to this point the Lightnings had casually disregarded the sporadic antiaircraft fire. As Moore made another pass, however, a twenty-millimeter explosive shell hit his P-38 and set the right wing on fire. The aileron burned off before the fire finally blew out, and the wing glowed red halfway back to Mengzi. McCloud continued strafing while the other P-38s rallied around Moore and returned to base. "When I finally pulled away from the targets none of my friends were in sight. I had no luck contacting anyone on the radio – so I had to head for home – my head on a swivel." He arrived at Mengzi before the others. "Of course they were sticking with the Major – his plane on single engine – flying about 130 mph." When McCloud landed, he found four bullet holes in his right boom, luckily having just missed the battery. Moore was impressed with his performance and promoted him to flight leader the next day. He received a brand new P-38L, which he named *IGIT* (In God I Trust), in time to fly two final combat missions.[47]

Don McCloud and his brand new P-38L-5 (44-25827) IGIT One of the Boys. Paul D. McCloud

The campaign against Japanese lines of communication in Indochina was very successful. In all, the 449th flew 103 bridge-busting sorties out of the 69th Wing's 643, which left at least fifty-one bridges damaged and thirty-four destroyed. In fact, the 14th Air Force was so successful against bridges in Indochina that the Japanese gave up trying to repair them. Because the Indochinese railways had few alternate routes, the transportation system was in shambles and the Japanese found it impossible to move troops or supplies without great difficulty.[48] By the summer of 1945, however, Indochina was hardly significant in the war against Japan. American troops had invaded Iwo Jima and Okinawa and in August 1945, appeared ready to invade Japan itself. The 14th Air Force's campaign in Indochina did, however, prove significant in its implications for the postwar future of Southeast Asia.

Japanese Surrender

The atomic bombs dropped on Hiroshima and Nagasaki on 6 and 9 August 1945 were a complete surprise to the Americans in China. Jack Bowman related that, "We didn't have any idea what it was. A few days after the second bomb it became reasonably sure that the war was over."[49] The P-38 pilots were eager to go to Hanoi, which appeared to be a beautiful city, but the squadron intelligence officer, Captain James Johnston, beat them to it when he flew there by C-47 to investigate the whereabouts of Lieutenant Foss, still in the hands of the Viet Minh. Johnston returned to Mengzi without any new information.

In mid-August, 14th Air Force headquarters dispatched Major Moore on a scouting mission in preparation for possibly moving the 449th to Gia Lam Airdrome. The 14th Air Force was moving squadrons all across China and Southeast Asia to provide an air presence for occupation troops disarming the Japanese. Transports recently released from flying the Hump moved Nationalist troops to major Chinese cities to occupy them before the Communists and the 311th Fighter Group moved from Xi'an to Shanghai. Moore picked Bowman to accompany him on his scouting mission and the two flew to Hanoi and landed, dodging craters in the runway. The Japanese still had a military presence in the city, but French officials who had evaded the March coup or were recently released from prison met them when they parked and took them to a hotel downtown. According to Bowman, "They killed the fatted calf and rolled out the red carpet. We had a party and then a good dinner. I met a friendly French girl who was grateful that we had won the war." The next morning, Moore and Bowman met with the French officials and decided that it would not be beneficial to move the 449th to Hanoi. The two men returned to their P-38s and returned to Mengzi in the afternoon. Bowman later commented that he was honored that Moore picked him for the mission and proud to be one of the few Americans "who landed military war planes at Hanoi."[50]

On 25 August 1945, the 449th began flying non-offensive reconnaissance missions into Indochina, reporting on local

Jack Bowman's P-38 on the ramp at Hanoi. Bowman was proud to be one of very few Americans to land a U.S. military warplane at the city. Jack Bowman

activity and Japanese troops, ships, aircraft, trucks, and trains. The purpose was not only to monitor the status of the Japanese demobilization, but also to gauge the progress of Ho Chi Minh's takeover of the country. Jerry Doughty flew the first reconnaissance mission to Haiphong after the Japanese capitulation. "I was to fly low and slow. Praying they had gotten the word, I dropped flaps and leveled at 100 feet." He noticed the streets were overflowing with people that waived when they saw him – "or maybe they were giving me the finger." The next day, he delivered film of the flight to Kunming and discovered that the gun emplacements on the approach ends of the runway were pointed at the landing aircraft." It turned out that the night before Vietnamese revolutionaries had battled the Japanese for control of the airfield.[51] In fact, all over Tonkin, Ho Chi Minh's August Revolution used weapons given to them by the OSS to disarm Japanese troops and prevent returning French from asserting control over their former colony. On 19 August, as many as two hundred thousand Vietnamese flooded the streets of Hanoi and took control of the city. Throughout late August and early September, Lightning pilots witnessed crowds carrying red flags with a five-pointed yellow star and signs proclaiming "Independence or Death," deliberately written in English as well as French and Vietnamese.[52]

A banner proclaiming "Long Live Vietnam Independence" in Hanoi. Note the Nationalist Chinese flags. Jerry Ravenscroft

On 2 September, two Lightning pilots observed a large crowd gathered in Hanoi and swooped down low to get a closer view. In fact, the crowd was celebrating the Vietnamese Declaration of Independence, and according to historian David Marr, the flyover by the P-38s was "immediately declared and believed by the people to represent a coordinated U.S. salute to the fledgling Vietnamese government."[53] The pilots were clueless as to the effect of their actions, but Ho Chi Minh capitalized on the supposed show of American support to solidify his government in Vietnam, and in fact attempted to establish relations between his government and the United States despite his communist political ideology. Many OSS agents believed that Ho's desire for an alliance with America was genuine, since the Vietnamese did not trust the Chinese, who historically repressed and conquered Vietnam, and did not want the support of the Soviet Union, which they considered overbearing.[54] As Ho's political ideology came to light, however, the United States distanced itself from his government and eventually supported a French return in 1946. France was never able to regain control of Indochina, and thirty years of war between the Communists and France – and later the United States – eventually left the Communists in control of all of Vietnam. Ironically, one of Japan's goals in invading the Asian mainland was to prevent the expansion of communism. However, by demolishing the Nationalist Chinese Army during Operation Ichi-go, the Japa-

Japanese KI-21 Sally surrender bomber taxing to the parking area after landing at Mengzi. Bruce Carnachan

Japanese Ki-21 Sally surrender bomber on the ramp at Mengzi, 3 September 1945. George Brabec

nese paved the way for the Communist conquest of China in 1949, and by removing the French from Indochina, they created a power vacuum into which stepped Ho Chi Minh and his communist regime.

On 3 September 1945, the day after the Japanese signed the surrender papers on the deck of the USS *Missouri*, the 449th had one more opportunity to make a unique contribution to the war in China when they escorted a Ki-21 Sally carrying Japanese commanders from Hanoi to Mengzi to participate in a surrender ceremony with the Chinese. Four P-38s flown by Lieutenants Callister, Richards, Bowman, and Green flew to Hanoi and met the bomber in the air. Green recalled "how slow that bomber was. It was pretty hard for us in the P-38s to stay in behind it because it was kind of just lumbering along and we had to do 'S's over it and throttle back to minimum RPM." The Japanese knew how to get to Mengzi, and the P-38s followed them in.[55] Armament officer Joe Mapes noted that the bomber made a downwind landing, which was unusual since normally planes land into the wind.[56] After it landed, the Lightning pilots decided to give the field "a super buzz job" since the opportunity was unlikely present itself again. According to Green, "We came down in tight formation at probably five or six hundred miles an hour and we shellacked them."[57]

The Sally was in sorry shape. The Japanese had been instructed to paint the bomber white, with a green cross over the Japanese rising sun, but Green recalled it "was the most primitive paint job you ever saw. It looked like somebody had a broom and just dipped it in white wash and just kind of smeared it on the airplane."[58] Doughty noticed that the "oil lines were wrapped with silk ribbon to stop the oil leaks. We were surprised to see it in such a bad stage of repair."[59] The Japanese officers stepped off the bomber and boarded 19th Liaison Squadron L-5s for transit to a nearby Chinese army base. Armorer Dick Maddox recorded the event with a gun camera taken from a P-38 and mounted on a jeep for auxiliary power and commented that, "It was like celebrating an opening day at a State Fair."[60] The Japanese were not quite as euphoric, and were in fact concerned they would be shot after landing. According to Mapes, "They felt somewhat insulted by the appearance of the motley mob of Americans and others that surrounded the plane. There was no show of dignity or ceremony, and they thought this was planned to humiliate them."[61] Leonard Logar flew a Japanese colonel to the Chinese army base in his L-5 "and waited around and took them back," swooping low over the field at Mengzi, to the obvious delight of the assembled airmen.[62] With the ceremony over, the Japanese were clearly relived to be departing for Hanoi and unloaded cases of alcohol for the crowd of Americans.[63] Joe Chiara led a flight of four P-38s to escort the bomber back to Hanoi. He would "never forget that feeling" of leading his flight at three hundred feet over the Hanoi tarmac "while waiting for that Sally bomber to touch down."[64]

Since the 449th was not moving to Hanoi as part of an occupation force, the pilots delivered their planes to the Chinese Air Force at Chenggong and prepared to leave the country. Forrest Green parked his P-38 in one of the earthen revetments and removed the eight-day clock, which he kept as a souvenir, "mounted in an old wooden propeller that hangs on my wall." Green testified that he "really hated to leave that plane. ... If a man can love an inanimate object, I loved the P-38." He speculated that, "as soon as our troops left, there would be a lot of aluminum cups made out of it."[65] The Chinese, however, put the Lightnings to use in their subsequent war with the Communists, using them along with P-51s in offensives against the Communist Army in 1947.[66] Unfortunately for Chiang, the Communists were skilled in minimizing the effects of airpower through the use of camouflage and terrain. The 1947 offensive appeared at first to be successful, but the Nationalists controlled only the ground they stood on. Once their supply lines were badly overextended, the Communists counterattacked. By 1949, Mao took control of the country and forced Chiang to flee to Taiwan.

Members of the 449th posing with Japanese flight crew at Mengzi. Paul D. McCloud

Japanese surrender bomber at Mengzi. The poor quality of the whitewash paint job is clearly visible. The rising sun emblem is obscured by a green cross. George Brabec

Japanese officer on the surrender delegation at Mengzi. George Brabec

A member of the Japanese surrender delegation stands next to a 19th Liaison Squadron L-5 at Mengzi. Jack Bowman

Maddox recorded these views of P-38s departing Mengzi to escort the Japanese surrender bomber on gun camera film. Richard Maddox

449th armorers (left to right) Dick Maddox, Ivan Odok, Bruce Carnachan, and Gardner Petty (kneeling) at Mengzi. Bruce Carnachan

Dick Maddox, recorder of the day's activities on a gun camera, posing with the squadron's bomb service truck (BST). Richard Maddox

Dick Maddox driving the BST on the flight line. Richard Maddox

Ki-21 Sally bomber arriving at Mengzi. Richard Maddox

P-38 shellacking the field in a low pass. Richard Maddox

L-5 returning to Mengzi with Japanese dignitaries after they participated in surrender ceremonies with Chinese troops at a nearby location. Richard Maddox

The United States, however, disengaged itself from the Chinese Civil War. For American servicemen, the war was over, leaving the 449th Fighter Squadron with much of which to be proud. In two years of combat, the 449th helped establish air superiority over China and Burma, shot down a Japanese general, attacked Taiwan and Hainan, greatly increased Japanese casualties by providing air support and interdiction during the Ichi-go campaign, helped the Chinese to conquer the Salween Front, and neutralized the Japanese in Indochina. Between 24 July 1943 and 9 August 1945, the 449th shot down more than seventy-three enemy aircraft and destroyed many more on the ground; shot up barges and bridges, trucks and trains; and "plane for plane ... contributed to the misery of the Japanese as much as any other squadron in China."[67]

Though Chennault initially had a low opinion of the 449th, the squadron proved itself in combat and he eventually changed his mind. In fact, Bruce Carnachan remembered that when Chennault was removed from command for political reasons in July 1945, he stopped by Mengzi to say goodbye to the 449th.[68] John Charlton, a navigator in the 308th Bomb Group, appreciated the efforts of the P-38 unit in protecting his squadron and others from enemy fighters, stating: "Thank you, pilots of the 449th F.S."[69] B-25 pilot Chapman Hale commented that, "There weren't a lot of P-38s there but the P-38 was awfully good for what they were doing."[70] Matthew Blaszko, from the 19th Liaison Squadron, said he "would like to thank [the] flight of P-38s that came to our rescue over [Baoshan]" in September 1944.[71] Armorer Buck Burris thought the 449th "did a hell of a good job."[72]

In the end, the 14th Air Force turned the war in China into what Ishihara Kanji thought it might become: a quagmire. Without the American air force, it is unlikely the Japanese would have committed half a million troops to Ichi-go that could have been put to better use in the Pacific, and it is certain that the 5th Air Army would have had far less difficulty conducting operations in China. In fact, Lieutenant General Takahashi, commander of the Japanese Army in China, stated after the war:

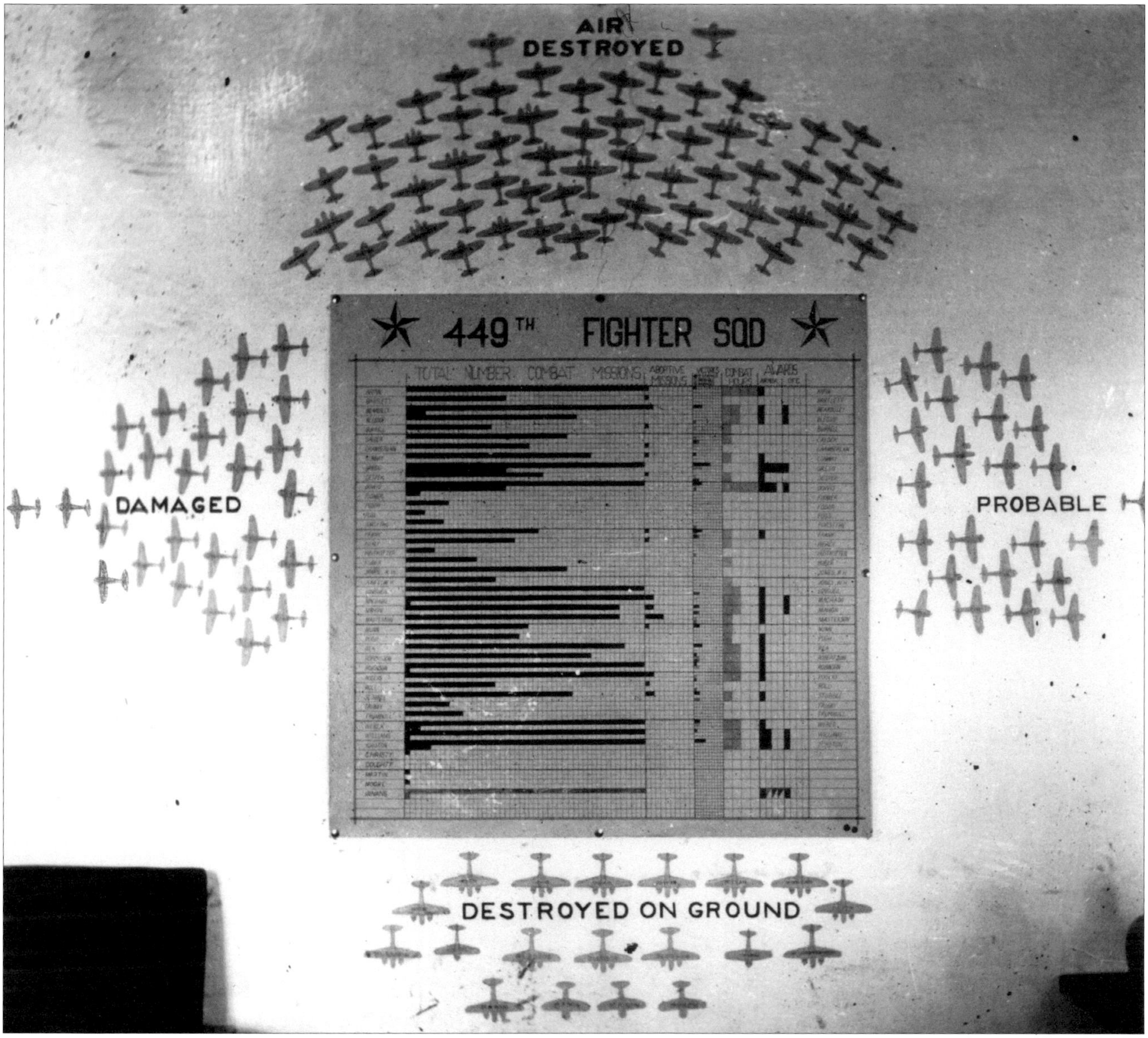

Above: "Kill Board" Showing the victims of the 449th as well as mission statistics for each pilot as of 6 October 1944. James Heitkotter

Right: Statistics compiled by the 21st Photo Reconnaissance Squadron in October 1944 depicting the effect of 14th Air Force operations on the Japanese. National Archives

Considering all the difficulties my armies encountered in China, including guerillas, ground armies, lack of supply, difficult terrain, non-cooperation of the Chinese, I judge the operations of the Fourteenth Air Force to have constituted between 60 per cent and 75 per cent of our effective opposition in China. Without the air force we could have gone anywhere we wished.[73]

Thus with a relatively small force, Chennault drew increasingly large amounts of Japanese troops and war material into a quagmire in China, allowing the Americans to more easily push across the Pacific to Japan. While not the primary theater in the war against Japan, the war in China nonetheless deserves to be remembered, as do the men who fought and died there.

EPILOGUE

As to why the 449th became "The Forgotten Squadron," Dick Conway argued:

> Probably the reason that we were not noticed by a great many of the fellows in the other squadrons was that we were going by them so fast they couldn't get a good look. There should be a few of the boys that flew P-51's later in the war that will have a faint recollection of our outfit.[1]

Though not remembered by others, the members of the 449th remembered each other. Richard Maddox put out a newsletter every month or two keeping the veterans of the 449th up to date with each other and Forrest Green related: "I think we were closer together to begin with – but with Richard's publications we followed each other all the way through and we still communicate with one another now and then."[2] Joe Chiara described Maddox as "the 'glue' that held our organization together for all these years."[3] According to Buck Burris, "We still stay in touch with each other and we have a lot of respect for each other. That says a lot right there."[4]

After World War II, the members of the 449th did not return to the United States as heroes – too many people had served in that epic conflict for each to be treated as such. America wanted to move on with life after the war and few Americans cared about what the 14th Air Force had done in China. Some members of the squadron stayed in the military but many went back to civilian life. When Jim Hyde returned to the United States in May 1945, he learned that the Army had a points system to determine who was eligible for discharge. The minimum number of points was eighty-five; he had 387. He took the discharge and went to see his wife and family – it had been over two years. He thought that would be the end of his military career, but after an eleven month hiatus he returned as a personnel officer. Twenty years and seven months later, he retired as a chief warrant officer and moved to Fresno, California, where he ran into Jim Heitkotter. Hyde became a successful businessman in California, owning a swimming pool construction business, becoming a general building contractor and becoming involved with land development.[5]

Joe Chiara stayed in the Army Air Forces for a year but decided the post-war military was not for him. He spent the next couple of years flight instructing and crop dusting in light aircraft, but the income was too small. He then found a job with a rural electric company as an engineering clerk and, after fourteen years, became the top manager. Twenty-one years later, he retired and relived "the good old China Days" with his wife, son, two grandchildren, and five great-grand children until his death in 2008.[6]

Buck Burris had a rough time after the war. He was discharged as a technical sergeant on the points system, but had no direction or purpose in his life. He bounced around from job to job, got married and had a daughter in 1947 but soon divorced, describing himself not as a bad person, but as a bad husband and a bad father. Burris grew up in the thirty-two months he was overseas, but admitted he did not know how the world worked when he came back. He was not happy with his life, but he did not know what to do to make himself happy. Finally, he realized that he was happy when he was in the AAF and decided to enlist in the United States Air Force. In 1956, Buck Burris reenlisted at the age of thirty-five. Though he had been discharged as a technical sergeant, his records had been lost in China and the Air Force brought him back in with only one stripe. He went to radar school at Lowry Air Force Base in Denver and was assigned to the 324th Fighter Squadron, whose F-86 Sabres were deployed at the time from Massachusetts to Morocco. Burris worked hard and advanced rapidly, working his way up to master sergeant in only eight years. At one point, he was with his squadron on a training deployment to Vincent Air Force Base in Yuma, Arizona, and was sitting around when none other than Warrant Officer Jim Hyde walked in. Hyde was officer of the day and Burris offered to help him with his duties. Though they had been friends during World War II, they lost track of each other afterwards and the chance meeting in Yuma rekindled a friendship that lasts to this day. Though Burris "had

Brabec boarding a transport plane on his way back to India after the war. George Brabec

After the war, most enlisted personnel sailed on troop ships from India to the United States, usually a trip of about thirty days. George Brabec

449th Fighter Squadron veterans at a Chino P-38 meet, 14 May 1987. Back row left to right: Bruce Carnachan, Lovell Callister, Melvin Miller, Kent Copenhaver, Howard Goss, and Joe Fodor. Front row: Thomas Pugh, Joe Chiara, J.F. Green, and Jim Borge. James Heitkotter

Reunion in San Antonio (about 1995) Back row, left to right: Green, Callister, Borge, Goss, Kaiser, Miller, McCloud. Front: Bowman and Maddox. Paul D. McCloud

Members of the 449th and their families at a reunion in Portland Oregon, 13 September 1989. Left to right: David Williams, Howard Goss, Tom Pugh, Pete Pinto, Jack Bowman, Glenna Pugh, Bruce Carnachan, Jim Borge, Amy Borge, Dick Maddox, Charles Richard, Kathryn Maddox, Mr. and Mrs. Bill Wray, June and Jim Heitkotter, Bob Burrell, Pat and Joe Fodor, Jane Burrell, Kent Copenhaver, June Goss, Carroll Huber, Merte Chiara, Joe Chiara and Fred Roll. James Heitkotter

a rough ten years getting my head on straight," his second stint in the military set him on the right path. He remarried, this time for forty years until his wife died in 2000, and became a real-estate appraiser after he retired from the Air Force in 1972.[7]

Jerry Doughty also remained in the military, retiring as a lieutenant colonel after service in Vietnam.[8] Walter Savage became a judge in Glendale, Arizona, after retiring from the Air Force as a colonel.[9] George Brabec wanted to reenlist, but was told his chances for promotion were slim should he decide to stay. He received an honorable discharge and used money from the GI Bill to learn carpentry. He became a contractor in Nebraska and raised a family.[10] Jim Heitkotter received his discharge on 7 December 1945, exactly four years after Pearl Harbor, and immediately went to work with his brother Bob at a muffler shop in Fresno, California. Bob was a former merchant mariner, and after a venture with Jim in limestone mining, returned to sea. Jim served for a time as a draftsman for Fresno County before attending Fresno State College, where he received a degree in industrial education. He then taught 11th and 12th grade auto and aviation mechanics. Heitkotter and his students built a Rutan Vari Eze aircraft which he and his wife June flew for a dozen years, and he spent much time restoring classic automobiles such as the 1914 Cadillac Phantom he acquired in 1946.[11] Bruce Carnachan also took an interest in classic cars, claiming that his 1954 Jaguar XK120 Roadster makes him "feel 30 years younger." Carnachan spent his post-war career teaching wood shop and driver's education for the Los Angeles Unified School District.[12]

Bill Dougherty left active duty for the reserves but was called back into service during the Korean War. He stayed in the Air Force until shortly before his death from liver cancer. His last assignment was flying F-111s at Nellis Air Force Base in Nevada.[13] Jack Bowman also left the Army Air Forces after World War II but joined the USAF in the early 1950s, retiring as a lieutenant colonel in 1969. Both of Bowman's sons graduated from the United States Air Force Academy.[14] J. Forrest Green left active duty for the reserves, where he ultimately achieved the rank of Major. He retired to his dream of ranching in Texas.[15] Tom Harmon married actress Elyse Knox and left the military to become a sportscaster.[16] Harold Franklin retired from the Air Force as a master sergeant and started a family.[17] Don McCloud went back to school and received an associate's degree from Weber College in Ogden, Utah. He worked for the Maytag Corporation as a district manager for five years and then as an appointed commercial distributor for the next twenty-two. He started several businesses of his own, which he eventually sold. Don and his wife, Delores, had four children and eight grandchildren. They retired to St. George, Utah, in 1993.[18] Richard Maddox married his high school sweetheart, Kathryn, and resumed his prewar job at the Federal Reserve Bank of Dallas, Texas.[19] The war left its mark on all the participants. Bruce Schultz was so horrified by the extent of Nazi racism and brutality revealed after the war that he changed his Germanic name to Shoals.[20] He remarked that many of the pilots that returned to the United States in 1944 were "pretty heavy drinkers," and that the "China deal didn't do us any good."[21]

The grateful Chinese passed on stories of the Flying Tigers to their children and grandchildren. Lieutenant Lu Caiwen, the Chinese intelligence officer from Tengchong, stated that prior to the arrival of American airpower, the Japanese "occupied the entire sky. ... After the Flying Tigers came, the sky was our territory. ... We could not have won the war without American support. ... We can never forget their help."[22] Despite suppression of the historic liaison by the Communists after 1949, the stories of the American airmen that came to assist China in her war against the Japanese attained an almost mythical quality until China once again embraced the history in the 1980s and 1990s. According to Jeff Greene, executive director of the Sino-American Aviation Heritage Foundation, "They are the strongest symbol ... of friendship, fidelity, and cooperation that will ever exist between the Chinese and Americans."[23] Though the rest of the world considers the story of the 449th a vague footnote in the history of an epic conflict, it is a real and present memory for those who were there. Jerry Doughty remembered:

> In 1968 I was assigned to operations at Okinawa. I flew one air-refueling mission a week. We would fly along the Gulf of Tonkin, just far enough off the coast to be out of missile range. It was a sad and eerie feeling to see us striking targets we hit in 1945. It brought back memories of days long past of the grand ole 449th. I could almost see the ghosts of those guys flying their P-38s along the beaches.[24]

Service with the 449th was a defining moment in the lives of every man who served with the squadron, no matter what his job or how long his service. The camaraderie and friendships developed during the war lasted a lifetime. According to Jim Heitkotter, "That was a bunch of fun guys."[25]

Appendices

Appendix 1
Chinese Place Names

PINYIN	WADE-GILES	CHINESE CHARACTERS
Anqing	Anking	安庆
Baoshan	Paoshan	保山
Beiping (Beijing)	Peiking	北平（北京）
Changsha	Changsha	长沙
Chengdu	Chengtu	成都
Chenggong	Chengkung	呈贡
Chongqing	Chungking	重庆
Guangzhou	Canton	广州
Guilin	Kweilin	桂林
Hankou	Hankow	汉口
Hengyang	Hengyang	衡阳
Xianggang	Hong Kong	香港
Jiujiang	Kiukiang	九江
Kunming	Kunming	昆明
Lingling	Lingling	零陵
Mengzi	Mengtze	蒙自
Nanchang	Nanchang	南昌
Pingxiang	P'ing-Shang	萍乡
Sanya	Samah	三亚
Suichuan	Suichwan	遂川
Tengchong	Tengchung	腾冲
Xinzhu, Taiwan	Shinchiku, Formosa	新竹，台湾
Yueyang	Yochow	岳阳

Appendix 2
Aircraft Comparison Chart

Aircraft	Max Speed	Climb Rate	Ceiling	Range	Lethality	Bomb load
P-40N	343 mph	2230 fpm	31000 ft	750 miles	39.2	1500 lbs
P-51A	390 mph	2300 fpm	31350 ft	1250 miles	26.1	1000 lbs
P-51C	435 mph	2898 fpm	41900 ft	2440 miles	26.1	2000 lbs
P-38G	404 mph	3342 fpm	39000 ft	1670 miles	41.6	2000 lbs
P-38L	414 mph	3800 fpm	44000 ft	2600 miles	41.6	4000 lbs
Ki-27	275 mph	3010 fpm	32940 ft	389 miles	2.57	220 lbs
Ki-43-IIb	329 mph	2828 fpm	36750 ft	1990 miles	8.25	1102 lbs
Ki-43-IIIa	358 mph	3085 fpm	37400 ft	1990 miles	8.25	1102 lbs
Ki-44-IIa	376 mph	3860 fpm	35500 ft	805 miles	11.2	551 lbs
A6M5	351 mph	2805 fpm	38520 ft	1194 miles	17.1	265 lbs

Gun/Cannon lethality is calculated by the equation: weight of fire (lbs of projectiles fired per second) multiplied by muzzle velocity squared (in feet per second), multiplied by 1 plus the fraction of the projectile's weight composed of high explosive or incendiary material. Lethality is essentially the measure of the energy delivered by the gun/cannon and is a useful way of comparing differing aircraft armament.[1]

Appendix 3
449th Fighter Squadron Timeline

1943

9 June – War Department radiogram orders formation of Squadron X

23 July – First P-38s arrive in Kunming

24 July – Lieutenant Lewden Enslen scores squadron's first victory over Guilin

6 August – Captain Sam Palmer officially made commander

14 August – Squadron moves to Lingling

9 September – Lieutenant Billie Beardsley shoots down General Nakazono near Guangzhou

17 September – Captain Lewden Enslen assumes command

30 October – Mission to Jiujiang; four P-38s shot down and Captain Enslen killed

9 November – Lieutenant Colonel George McMillan assumes command

25 November – Thanksgiving Day Raid on Xinzhu Field, Taiwan; forty-six Japanese planes confirmed destroyed

1944

18 February – Squadron moves to Suichuan

19 April – Japanese begin Ichi-Go Offensive

29 April – Captain Rex Barber shot down near Jiujiang

6 May – 14th Air Force's fifty-four aircraft raid on Hankou

12 May – "Liquidation Day" Japanese send over one hundred aircraft against Suichuan

24 June – Lieutenant Colonel McMillan shot down and killed by ground fire

26 June – Suichuan evacuated

1 July – Captain James Bledsoe takes command

8 July – Squadron moves to Chenggong

25 July – Detachment sent to Yunnanyi

29 July – 449th escort B-24s to Hainan. Seven Japanese fighters claimed destroyed, no B-24s lost

2 August – Chinese troops enter Tengchong

8 August – Japanese take Hengyang

14 September – Tengchong liberated

11 November – Japanese take Guilin

11 November – 449th and 25th Fighter Squadrons attack Lampang Airfield, Thailand

29 December – Captain Ralph Wire assumes command

1945

5 January – 449th and 26th Fighter Squadrons attack Sanya, Hainan Island

21 January – Burma Road opened through Wanding

2 February – Major Wire injured in bailout, Captain Henry Rogers assumes command

February – Yunnanyi detachment shut down

25 February – Mengzi detachment established

9 March – Japanese coup in Indochina

11 May – Major William Moore assumes command

July – Squadron moves to Mengzi

6 July – Lieutenant Dougherty scores squadron's last aerial victory near Gia Lam Airdrome

10 July – Fodor and Jones engage enemy fighters near Vinh in squadron's last aerial engagement

8 August – Major General Chennault leaves China

15 August – Japanese surrender

2 September – Ho Chi Minh declares Vietnamese independence

3 September – Japanese surrender delegation lands at Mengzi

Appendix 4
P-38s of the 449th Fighter Squadron[2]

MODEL	SERIAL NUMBER	NOTES
P-38G-10	42-12948	#320 Flown from North Africa to China
		Converted to two-seater
	42-13031	Flown from North Africa to China
		Lost in action 30 October 1943 (1Lt Tommy J. Taylor killed)
	42-13043	Flown from North Africa to China
	42-13144	Flown from North Africa to China
	42-13194	Flown from North Africa to China
	42-13208	Flown from North Africa to China
	42-13220	Flown from North Africa to China
	42-13221	Flown from North Africa to China
	42-13248	Flown from North Africa to China
		Lost in action 30 October 1943 (2Lt Jordan E. Robins Jr. evader)
	42-13253	Flown from North Africa to China
		Lost in action 30 October 1943 (Capt Lewden M. Enslen died of subsequent illness 11/11/43
	42-13363	Flown from North Africa to China
	42-13368	Flown from North Africa to China
	42-13404	Flown from North Africa to China
		Destroyed in a forced landing 15 December 1943 (2Lt Aloysius J. Calvey killed)
	42-13408	Flown from North Africa to China
		Lost in action 18 June 1944 (2Lt Frederick A. Roll Jr. evader)
	42-13409	Flown from North Africa to China
	42-13415	Flown from North Africa to China
		2Lt Thomas D. Harmon's *Little Butch II*
		Lost in action 30 October 1943 (2Lt Thomas D. Harmon seriously injured, evader)
	42-13418	Flown from North Africa to China
	42-13428	Flown from North Africa to China
		Destroyed in a takeoff accident 14 July 1943 (2Lt Ivan A. Rockwell)
	42-13429	Flown from North Africa to China
	42-13436	Flown from North Africa to China
	42-13437	Flown from North Africa to China
		#310 Capt Bruce Schultz's *Golden Eagle*
		Lt Jim Heitkotter's *Black Lace*
P-38G-15	43-2453	Flown from North Africa to China
		Destroyed in a crash 17 November 1943 (2Lt Keith Mahon)
	43-2469	Flown from North Africa to China
	43-2549	Flown from North Africa to China
P-38H-1	42-66715	Received 1 December 1943
	42-66716	Received 31 December 1943
P-38H-5	42-66978	Received 31 December 1943
	42-66985	Received 1 December 1943
		Lost in action 29 April 1944 (2Lt Robert W. Campbell evader)
	42-66987	Received 31 December 1943
	42-66991	Received 31 December 1943
		Lost in action 18 June 1944 (2Lt James W. Bartlett Jr. evader)

	42-66993	Received 31 December 1943
	42-66999	Received 1 December 1943
	42-67000	Received 31 December 1943
	42-67006	Received 1 December 1943
	42-67007	Received 1 December 1943
		Lost in action 29 April 1944 (Capt Rex T. Barber seriously injured, evader)
	42-67010	Received 1 December 1943
		Lost in action 6 May 1944 (2Lt William P. Jones killed)
P-38J-5	42-67287	#322 Damaged on the ground 26 November 1944
	42-67289	Destroyed in flying accident 18 April 1945 (2Lt Gilbert R. Schowengerdt killed)
	42-67295	Lost in action 6 May 1944 (1Lt John T. Opsvig killed)
P-38J-10	42-67630	#314
	42-67633	#305 Lost in action 24 June 1944 (Lt Col George B. McMillan killed)
	42-67790	Lt James Nunn's *Fini Cas*
	42-67837	Lost in action 6 May 1944 (1Lt Lee O. Gregg evader)
	42-67846	2Lt Donald R. Forsythe's *Sonnova Beast*
P-38J-15	42-104152	Lost in action 5 January 1945 (1Lt Robert W. Christy evader)
	42-104153	Damaged 11 November 1944 (1Lt Leonard W. Flomer)
	42-104335	#312 2Lt Grover W. Stubbee's *Queen of the Sky*
		Lt Dan Church's *My Achin' Ass*
		Destroyed in a takeoff accident 17 June 1945 (2Lt Jack L. Bowman)
	42-104339	Lost in action 5 January 1945 (1Lt James Heitkotter seriously injured, evader)
	42-104378	#320 Lost in action 8 May 1945 (Capt Peter A. Bunce killed)
	42-104382	Damaged 26 December 1944
	43-28562	#307 Damaged 3, 6, and 17 November 1944
	43-28564	#326 Damaged 18 December 1944
	43-28566	Lost in action 9 November 1944 (1Lt James E. Nunn killed)
	44-23145	#328
P-38J-20	44-23309	1Lt David E. Tribby's *Ruthie*
P-38L-1	44-23791	#304
	44-24245	#316
P-38L-5	44-25048	Destroyed in flying accident 27 July 1945 (1Lt Walter Savage)
	44-25084	Capt Keith Mahon's *Eula D II*
	44-25113	#321
	44-25114	#326 Destroyed in flying accident 27 July 1945 (Lt Robert M. Bentz killed)
	44-25132	2Lt John Forrest Green's *Ranger*
	44-25141	#305 (#13 on white nose cap) 1Lt Walter Savage's *Sweet Anne Robbins*
	44-25280	#302 1Lt William E. Shomaker's *Chita III*
	44-25434	#308
	44-25827	#309 1Lt Paul D. McCloud's *IGIT One of the Boys*
	44-25852	Lost in action 7 July 1945 (1Lt Palmer T. Foss evader)
	44-25853	#322
	44-25918	#311
	44-26099	Lt Jerry Doughty's *Nina Gal*
	44-26518	Lost in action 12 July 1945 (1Lt William E. Shomaker reportedly died as a POW)
	44-26564	#333
	44-26571	#317 Capt. Francis H. Skipper's *Martha Lee*
	44-26579	#313 Flown by 1Lt Walter Savage

Appendix 5

449th Fighter Squadron Personnel Killed in Service[3]

NAME (Last, First, M.I.)	RANK	DATE	NOTES
Barrett, Robert J.	2Lt	8 August 1943	Crashed in foul weather crossing Himalayas from Chabua to Kunming
Enssler, George J. Jr.	2Lt	31 August 1943	Aircraft hit by ground fire
Rockwell, Ivan A.	2Lt	12 September 1943	Aircraft hit by ground fire
Taylor, Tommy J.	1Lt	30 October 1943	Shot down by enemy fighters near Jiujiang
Enslen, Lewden M.	Capt	11 November 1943	Shot down by enemy fighters near Jiujiang on 30 October 1943, died later from injuries
Calvey, Aloysius J.	2Lt	15 December 1943	Forced landing at Kunming
Jordan, William D.	TSgt	1 January 1944	Stabbed by Japanese agent in Kunming
Jones, William P.	2Lt	6 May 1944	Shot down by enemy fighters over Dongting Lake
Opsvig, John T.	1Lt	6 May 1944	Shot down by enemy fighters over Dongting Lake
Rose, Walter L.	1Lt	29 May 1944	Injured in landing accident near Suichuan, died before reaching hospital
Scudday, Fred R. Jr.	Capt	14 June 1944	Barracks shooting accident
McMillan, George B.	Lt Col	24 June 1944	Forced landing after aircraft hit by ground fire near Pingxiang
Nunn, James E.	1Lt	9 November 1944	Crashed on mission in Indochina
Schowengerdt, Gilbert R.	2Lt	18 April 1945	Drowned in Lake Dianchi after bailing out because of engine fire
Bunce, Peter A.	Capt	8 May 1945	Reported bailing out after engines quit near Phong Saly, Indochina
Shomaker, William E.	1Lt	15 July 1945	Reportedly died as a P.O.W. after bailing out near Vinh on 12 July 1945
Moore, Ray E.	1Lt	24 July 1945	Takeoff accident at Mengzi
Pulliam, Harold W	2Lt	24 July 1945	Takeoff accident at Mengzi
Bentz, Robert M.	Lt	27 July 1945	Crashed after midair collision with flight leader at Mengzi

Appendix 6
Aerial Victory Claims of the 449th Fighter Squadron[4]

Name (Last, First, M.I.)	Rank	Claim	Date	Time	Location
Enslen, Lewden M.	1Lt	Zero	24 July 1943	0950-1105	Guilin
Enslen, Lewden M.	1Lt	Zero	26 July 1943	0500-0815	Hengyang
Enslen, Lewden M.	1Lt	Zero probable	26 July 1943	0500-0815	Hengyang
Enslen, Lewden M.	1Lt	Zero probable	26 July 1943	0500-0815	Hengyang
Helms, Earl E.	2Lt	Zero	29 July 1943	1045-1500	Hong Kong
Burbank, Edward W.	1Lt	Zero probable	21 August 1943	0835-1305	Hengyang
Bolton, Willard L.	1Lt	Zero	21 August 1943	0835-1305	Hengyang
Goss, Edmund R.	Maj	Zero probable	21 August 1943	0835-1305	Hengyang
Schultz, Robert B.	1Lt	Zero probable	21 August 1943	0835-1305	Hengyang
Palmer, Sam L.	Capt	Zero	26 August 1943	1030-1645	Guangzhou
Beardsley, Billie, M.	2Lt	TE Transport	9 September 1943	1530	Southeast of Huangpu
Gregg, Lee O.	2Lt	Zeke	10 September 1943	1500-1800	Guangzhou
Weber, Wallace Z.	2Lt	Tojo probable	10 September 1943	1500-1800	Guangzhou
Opsvig, John T.	1Lt	Zero	1 October 1943	1520	Haiphong
Palmer, Sam L.	Capt	2 Zeros damaged	4 October 1943	Unknown	Guilin
Harmon, Thomas D.	2Lt	2 Zeros	30 October 1943	0735-unknown	Jiujiang
Rea, Stuart A.	2Lt	Tojo	30 October 1943	0735-unknown	Jiujiang
Robins, Jordan B.	2Lt	Tojo	30 October 1943	0735-unknown	Jiujiang
Schultz, Robert B.	1Lt	2 Tojos	30 October 1943	0735-unknown	Jiujiang
Dowis, Kendal B.	1Lt	Sally	25 November 1943	1700	Xinzhu, Formosa
Moon, Ryan M.	Capt	2 Sallys	25 November 1943	1700	Xinzhu, Formosa
Palmer, Sam L.	Capt	Zeke	25 November 1943	1700	Xinzhu, Formosa
Palmer, Sam L.	Capt	2 unidentified type aircraft	25 November 1943	1700	Xinzhu, Formosa
Rose, Walter L.	2Lt	Val	25 November 1943	1700	Xinzhu, Formosa
Rose, Walter L.	2Lt	Nell	25 November 1943	1700	Xinzhu, Formosa
Rose, Walter L.	2Lt	Zero damaged	25 November 1943	1700	Xinzhu, Formosa
Schultz, Robert B.	1Lt	Mary	25 November 1943	1700	Xinzhu, Formosa
Schultz, Robert B.	1Lt	Transport	25 November 1943	1700	Xinzhu, Formosa
Yorston, Alfred Jr.	1 Lt	2 Sallys	25 November 1943	1700	Xinzhu, Formosa
Hammond, Gerry H.	1Lt	Tojo	6 December 1943	1410	Changde
McMillan, George B.	Lt Col	Nick	10 December 1943	0940-1115	Hengyang
Gregg, Lee O.	1Lt	Tojo	12 December 1943	1020	Hengyang
Gregg, Lee O.	1Lt	Tojo probable	12 December 1943	1020	Hengyang
McMillan, George B.	Lt Col	Tojo	12 December 1943	1020	Hengyang
McMillan, George B.	Lt Col	Zero damaged	12 December 1943	1020	Hengyang
Robinson, Charles J.	1Lt	Zero probable	12 December 1943	1020	Hengyang
Mahon, Keith	2Lt	Nick	10 February 1944	1345-1550	35 miles east of Kanchang
McMillan, George B.	Lt Col	Nick	10 February 19444	1345-1500	35 miles east of Kanchang
Barber, Rex T.	Capt	Nick damaged	10 February 1944	1345-1500	35 miles east of Kanchang
Arpin, Arthur N.	1Lt	Oscar	12 February 1944	0700-0820	18 miles north of Ganzhou
Conway, Richard D.	2Lt	Oscar	12 February 1944	0700-0820	18 miles north of Ganzhou
Gregg, Lee O.	1Lt	Tojo	12 February 1944	0700-0820	18 miles north of Ganzhou
Gregg, Lee O.	1Lt	Oscar probable	12 February 1944	0700-0820	18 miles north of Ganzhou
Helms, Earl E.	1Lt	2 Tojos	12 February 1944	0700-0820	18 miles north of Ganzhou

Helms, Earl E.	1Lt	Oscar probable	12 February 1944	0700-0820	18 miles north of Ganzhou
Yorston, Alfred Jr.	1Lt	Tojo	12 February 1944	0700-0820	18 miles north of Ganzhou
Barber, Rex T.	Capt	2 Oscars probable	12 February 1944	0700-0820	18 miles north of Ganzhou
Campbell, Robert W.	2Lt	Oscar probable	12 February 1944	0700-0820	18 miles north of Ganzhou
Rose, Walter L.	2Lt	Tojo probable	12 February 1944	0700-0820	18 miles north of Ganzhou
Robertson, Russell	2Lt	Oscar damaged	29 February 1944	1215	Anqing
Gregg, Lee O.	1Lt	Oscar	4 March 1944	1305	Shihuiyao, Yangzi River
Gregg, Lee O.	1Lt	Oscar damaged	4 March 1944	1305	Shihuiyao, Yangzi River
Desper, Dale D.	1Lt	Oscar damaged	4 March 1944	1305	Shihuiyao, Yangzi River
Nunn, James E.	2Lt	Hap	4 March 1944	1305	Shihuiyao, Yangzi River
Schultz, Robert B.	Capt	Oscar	4 March 1944	1305	Shihuiyao, Yangzi River
Schultz, Robert B.	Capt	Hap damaged	4 March 1944	1305	Shihuiyao, Yangzi River
Desper, Dale D.	1Lt	Zero probable	10 March 1944	1340	15 miles east of Anqing
Weber, Wallace Z.	1Lt	I-45 photo plane	18 March 1944	0900-1100	30 miles NW of Suichuan
Beardsley, Billie M.	1Lt	Oscar	29 April 1944	1030	6 miles west of Jiujiang
Campbell, Robert W.	2Lt	Oscar	29 April 1944	1030	6 miles west of Jiujiang
Weber, Wallace Z.	1Lt	Oscar	29 April 1944	1030	6 miles west of Jiujiang
Dowis, Kendal B.	1Lt	Oscar damaged	29 April 1944	1030	6 miles west of Jiujiang
Gregg, Lee O.	1Lt	2 Oscars	6 May 1944	1210	40 miles southeast of Hankou
Longueil, Charles L.	1Lt	Oscar probable	6 May 1944	1210	Hankou
Longueil, Charles L.	1Lt	Oscar damaged	6 May 1944	1210	Hankou
Burrell	2Lt	Oscar probable	6 May 1944	1210	Hankou
Scudday, Fred Jr.	1Lt	Oscar probable	6 May 1944	1210	Hankou
Roll, Frederick A. Jr.	2Lt	Oscar probable	6 May 1944	1210	Hankou
Scudday, Fred Jr.	1Lt	Oscar	12 May 1944	0630-0830	10 miles northeast of Suichuan
Mahon, Keith	2Lt	Oscar damaged	12 May 1944	1400	10 miles north of YK9, Suichuan area
Frank, Jack V.	2Lt	Tojo	11 June 1944	0940-0955	Near Anqing
Nunn, James E.	2Lt	Tojo	11 June 1944	0940-0955	Near Anqing
Mahon, Keith	2Lt	Tojo damaged	11 June 1944	0940-0955	Near Anqing
McMillan, George B.	Lt Col	Oscar	13 June 1944	0745-unknown	15 miles southest of Puchi
Newnom, Keith G.	1Lt	Oscar	13 June 1944	0745-unknown	15 miles southeast of Puchi
Rogers, Henry H.	2Lt	Oscar damaged	13 June 1944	0745-unknown	15 m SE of Puchi
Stubbee, Grover W.	2Lt	Oscar damaged	13 June 1944	0745-unknown	15 m SE of Puchi
Desper, Dale D.	1Lt	Oscar damaged	13 June 1944	0745-unknown	15 m SE of Puchi
Williams, David A.	1Lt	Oscar	18 June 1944	1050-1125	Anqing
Masterson, Arthur W.	2Lt	Oscar probable	18 June 1944	1050-1125	Anqing
Masterson, Arthur W.	2Lt	Tojo damaged	18 June 1944	1050-1125	Anqing
Stubbee, Grover W.	2Lt	Tojo damaged	18 June 1944	1050-1125	Anqing
Beardsley, Billie M.	1Lt	Val	19 June 1944	0630-0650	28-55N, 113-15E, Changlokai area
Frank, Jack V.	2Lt	Oscar damaged	19 June 1944	1140-1210	North of Changsha
Dowis, Kendal B.	Capt	2 Oscars	29 July 1944	1435-1445	Sanya Bay, Hainan
Dowis, Kendal B.	Capt	Oscar probable	29 July 1944	1435-1445	Sanya Bay, Hainan
Frank, Jack V.	2Lt	Oscar	29 July 1944	1435-1445	Sanya Bay, Hainan
Frank, Jack V.	2Lt	Oscar damaged	29 July 1944	1435-1445	Sanya Bay, Hainan
Calder, Thomas	1Lt	Oscar damaged	29 July 1944	1435-1445	Sanya Bay, Hainan
Bledsoe, James L.	Capt	Oscar damaged	29 July 1944	1435-1445	Sanya Bay, Hainan
Mahon, Keith	2Lt	Oscar	29 July 1944	1435-1445	Sanya Bay, Hainan
Stubbee, Grover W.	2Lt	2 Oscars	29 July 1944	1435-1445	Sanya Bay, Hainan
Robertson, Russell	1Lt	Oscar probable	29 July 1944	1435-1445	Sanya Bay, Hainan

Robertson, Russell	1Lt	Nate damaged	29 July 1944	1435-1445	Sanya Bay, Hainan
Robinson, Charles J.	1Lt	Oscar probable	29 July 1944	1435-1445	Sanya Bay, Hainan
Rogers, Henry H.	1Lt	Oscar probable	29 July 1944	1435-1445	Sanya Bay, Hainan
Weber, Wallace Z.	1Lt	Oscar probable	29 July 1944	1435-1445	Sanya Bay, Hainan
Yorston, Alfred Jr.	1Lt	Oscar	29 July 1944	1435-1445	Sanya Bay, Hainan
Rea, Stuart A.	1Lt	2 Oscars	8 September 1944	1505	Baoshan
Calder, Thomas	1Lt	Oscar probable	8 September 1944	1505	Baoshan
Calder, Thomas	1Lt	Oscar damaged	8 September 1944	1505	Baoshan
Heitkotter, James	2Lt	Oscar damaged	8 September 1944	1505	Baoshan
Forsythe, Donald R.	2Lt	Oscar damaged	8 September 1944	1505	Baoshan
Robertson, Russell	2Lt	Oscar	10 September 1944	1110-1435	South of Tengchong
Robertson, Russell	2Lt	Oscar probable	10 September 1944	1110-1435	South of Tengchong
Desper, Dale D.	1Lt	.25 Nate	11 November 1944	0920-1445	Lampang
Flomer, Leonard W.	1Lt	.25 Nate	11 November 1944	0920-1445	Lampang
Roll, Frederick A. Jr.	1Lt	.33 Nate	11 November 1944	0920-1445	Lampang
Jones, Robert H.	1Lt	Nate	11 November 1944	0920-1445	Lampang
Jones, Robert H.	1Lt	Nate probable	11 November 1944	0920-1445	Lampang
Conway, Richard D.	1Lt	Nate probable	11 November 1944	0920-1445	Lampang
Stubbee, Grover W.	2Lt	Nate	11 November 1944	0920-1445	Lampang
Fodor, Joseph N.	2Lt	Nate probable	11 November 1944	0920-1445	Lampang
Wire, Ralph L.	Capt	2 Oscars	5 January 1945	1450-1520	Sanya Bay, Hainan
Orlando Green Flight		4 Oscars damaged	5 January 1945	1450-1520	Sanya Bay, Hainan
Mahon, Keith	1Lt	3 Oscars	5 January 1945	1450-1520	Sanya Bay, Hainan
Tribby, David E.	1Lt	Oscar	5 January 1945	1450-1520	Sanya Bay, Hainan
Tribby, David E.	1Lt	Oscar damaged	5 January 1945	1450-1520	Sanya Bay, Hainan
Dougherty, William E.	1Lt	Nate	6 July 1945	1005-1325	20 miles south of Gia Lam Airdrome
Fodor, Joseph N.	1Lt	Oscar damaged	10 July 1945	0650-1130	Linh Cam (18-30N, 105-33E)

449th Fighter Squadron Pilot Claims for Enemy Aircraft[5]

Pilot	**With 449th** *(confirmed/probable/damaged)*	**Other credits**
Capt Lee O. Gregg	6/2/1	1/0/0 with 71st FS, 1st FG, North Africa
Capt Keith Mahon	5/0/2	
Capt Robert B. Schultz	5/1/1	
Lt Col George B. McMillan	4/0/1	4.5/0/0 with 3rd PS, AVG, China
Maj Sam L. Palmer	4/0/2	0/1/0 with 37th FS, 14th FG, North Africa
Capt Alfred Yorston Jr.	4/0/0	
1Lt Billie M. Beardsley	3/0/0	
Capt Kendal B. Dowis	3/1/1	
1Lt Stuart A. Rea	3/0/0	
Capt Earl E. Helms	3/1/0	
1Lt Grover W. Stubbee	3/0/2	
Capt Lewden M. Enslen	2/2/0	
1Lt Jack V. Frank	2/0/2	1/1/0 with 26th FS, 51st FG, China
2Lt Thomas D. Harmon	2/0/0	
Capt Ryan M. Moon	2/0/0	

1Lt James E. Nunn	2/0/0	
1Lt Walter L. Rose	2/1/1	
Capt Wallace Z. Weber	2/2/0	
Maj Ralph L. Wire	2/0/0	3/3/0 with 9th FS, 49th FG, New Guinea
1Lt Arthur N. Arpin	1/0/0	
1Lt Willard L. Bolton	1/0/0	2/0/0 with 71st FS, 1st FG, North Africa
2Lt Robert W. Campbell	1/1/0	
1Lt Richard D. Conway	1/1/0	
1Lt William E. Dougherty	1/0/0	
Capt Gerry H. Hammond	1/0/0	
1Lt Robert H. Jones	1/1/0	
Capt Keith G. Newnom	1/0/0	
1Lt John T. Opsvig	1/0/0	
1Lt Russell Robertson	1/2/2	
2Lt Jordan B. Robins	1/0/0	
Capt Fred R. Scudday Jr.	1/1/0	2/0/1 with 4 SAAF Sqn, North Africa
1Lt David E. Tribby	1/0/1	
Capt David A. Williams	1/0/0	
1Lt Frederick A. Roll Jr.	.33/1/0	
Capt Dale D. Desper	.25/1/2	
1Lt Leonard W. Flomer	.25/0/0	
1Lt Charles J. Robinson	0/2/0	
Maj Rex T. Barber	0/2/1	5/0/0 with 70th FS and 339th FS, Guadalcanal
1Lt Edward W. Burbank	0/1/0	
1Lt Robert L. Burrell	0/1/0	
1Lt Thomas Calder	0/1/2	
1Lt Joseph N. Fodor	0/1/1	
Maj Edmund R. Goss	0/1/0	6/1/0 with 16th FS and 75th FS, China
Capt Charles L. Longueil	0/1/1	
Capt Arthur W. Masterson	0/1/1	
Capt Henry H. Rogers	0/1/1	
Maj James L. Bledsoe	0/0/1	
1Lt Donald R. Forsythe	0/0/1	
1Lt James Heitkotter	0/0/1	
Maj William P. Moore	0/0/0	3/0/1 with 49th FS, 14th FG, North Africa
1Lt Robert J. Barrett	0/0/0	2/0/0 with 95th FS, 82nd FG, North Africa
1Lt William E. Shomaker	0/0/0	2/0/0 with 97th FS, 82nd FG, North Africa
unnamed pilots	0/0/4	
Total:	**73.83/30/32**	

Notes

Chapter 1

[1]Conway, 1980, 22.
[2]Doughty, 2007.
[3]Conway, 1980, 22.
[4]Burris, 2007.
[5]Cosgrove, n.d., 56.
[6]Maddox, 2000, 5.
[7]Conway, 1980, 22.
[8]Maddox, 2000, 5.
[9]Conway, 1980, 22.
[10]Murray and Millett, 2000, 151-153.
[11]Xi, 2001, 49.
[12]De-min, 2001, 34.
[13]Shinkichi, 2001, 46.
[14]Murray and Millett, 2000, 162.
[15]Ibid., 158.
[16]Chennault, *Way of a Fighter*, 1949, 59.
[17]Tregear, 1965, 234.
[18]Molesworth, *Sharks Over China,* 1994, 11.
[19]Xi, 2001, 147.
[20]Tsou, 1963, 25.
[21]Murray and Millett, 2000, 168.
[22]Xi, 2001, 127; Kelley, 1993, 10.
[23]Chennault, *Way of a Fighter,* 1949, 57.
[24]Ibid., 112.
[25]Weinberg, 2005, 620.
[26]Tsou, 1963, 46.
[27]Weinberg, 2005, 639.
[28]By 1938 Japan controlled sixty-percent of China's wheat growing regions and twenty-percent of its rice growing regions. Moreover, during the entire year of 1943 the airlift over the Hump did not even deliver enough supplies to maintain one infantry division. Pusen, 2001, 158; Ch'i, 1982, 63-64.
[29]Tsou, 1963, 44.
[30]Weinberg, 2005, 639.
[31]Xi, 2001, 181.
[32]Arnold, 1989, 417-422.
[33]Craven and Cate, *The Pacific: Guadalcanal to Saipan August 1942 to July 1944,* 1950, 440.
[34]Glines, 1995, 43.
[35]Stilwell, 1948, 119.
[36]Hyde, 2007.
[37]Patterson, 1944.
[38]Harmon, *Missing*, 22.
[39]Blake, 1992, 19-20.
[40]Harmon, *Pilots Also Pray*, 104.
[41]Harmon, *Pilots Also Pray,* 106-108.
[42]Enslen, 26 October 1943.
[43]*Springfield News and Leader*, September 1943.
[44]Scultz, 15 May 1945.
[45]Harmon, *Pilots Also Pray*, 105-106.
[46]Ibid., 110.
[47]Hyde, 2007.
[48]Ravenscroft, 2008.
[49]Tregear, 1965, 265.
[50]Bowman, 2008.
[51]Arnold, 1989, 410.
[52]Harmon, *Pilots Also Pray,* 120-121.
[53]Blake, 1992, 55-56.
[54]Molesworth, *Sharks Over China,* 1994, 124-125.

Chapter 2

[1]*The Japanese Air Forces in World War II*, 1979, 23.
[2]Shiba, 1956, 117, 131.
[3]Chennault, *Way of a Fighter,* 1949, 247.
[4]Craven and Cate, *The Pacific: Guadalcanal to Saipan August 1942 to July 1944,* 1950, 441, 528.
[5]Chennault, *Way of a Fighter,* 1949, 15, 21.
[6]Chennault, *The Role of Defensive Pursuit,* 1935, 18-19.
[7]Chennault, *Way of a Fighter*, 1949, 48.
[8]Kelley, 1993, 23.
[9]Chennault, *The Role of Defensive Pursuit*, 1935, 14.
[10]*Jing Bao Journal*, October-December 2003, 7.
[11]Chennault, *Way of a Fighter*, 1949, 58.
[12]Alison, 2007.
[13]Chennault, *Way of a Fighter,* 1949, 173.
[14]D'Olier, 1947, 95.
[15]Doughty, 2007.
[16]*CBI Roundup*, 24 August 1944.
[17]Stilwell, 1948, 120.
[18]Green, 2007.
[19]Beardsley, n.d.
[20]Soong, 1943.
[21]Arnold, 1989, 429.
[22]*Army Air Forces Statistical Digest World War II.*
[23]Arnold, 1943.
[24]Hyde, 2007.
[25]Chennault was actually referring to the Nakajima Ki-44 Tojo. All Japanese fighters were referred to as "Zeros" whether they were Oscars, Tojos, or actual Zeros.
[26]*CBI Roundup,* 16 September 1943.
[27]Green, 2003.
[28]Army Air Forces Proving Ground Command, *Final Report on Tactical Suitability of the P-38F Type Airplane.*
[29]Ibid.
[30]Green, 2007.
[31]Harmon, 1944, 123.
[32]Kissick, 1983, 49-50.
[33]Harmon, 1944, 123-124.
[34]Molesworth, *Sharks Over China,* 1994, 133.
[35]Ibid., 125, 157.
[36]*The Japanese Air Forces in World War II*, 1979, 8.
[37]Ichimura, 12 August 2008.
[38]Molesworth, *Sharks Over China,* 1994, 128.
[39]Hata, Izawa, and Shores, 2002, 296.
[40]Beardsley, n.d.
[41]Enslen's claim was filed for 26 July, but this does not match numerous other records showing the action as taking place on the 25th.
[42]Ichimura, 12 August 2008.
[43]Molesworth, *Sharks Over China,* 1994, 131.
[44]Craven and Cate, *The Pacific: Guadalcanal to Saipan August 1942 to July 1944,* 1950, 523.
[45]Hyde, 2007.
[46]Schultz, May 1945.
[47]Bergerud, 2000, 267-268.
[48]Harmon, *Pilots Also Pray*, 1944, 130.
[49]Hata, Izawa, and Shores, 2002, 296; Ichimura, 19 August 2008.
[50]Miller, 1956, 10.
[51]Brawner, 2005, 69.
[52]Long, *Oscar Tactics in Burma,* www.j-aircraft.com.
[53]Harmon, *Pilots Also Pray,* 1944, 130.
[54]Millman, 19 December 2007.
[55]Penick, 2007.

[56]Patterson, 1943.
[57]Harmon, *Pilots Also Pray,* 1944, 131.
[58]Long, *Oscar Against the P-38*, 2 November 2007, www.j-aircraft.com.
[59]Chennault, *Way of a Fighter,* 1949, 251.
[60]Harmon, *Pilots Also Pray,* 1944, 140.
[61]Conway, 1980, 22.
[62]Channault, *Way of a Fighter,* 1949, 252.
[63]Shiba, 1956, 117, 131.
[64]Glines, 1995, 72.
[65]Chennault, *Way of a Fighter,* 1949, 252.
[66]Millman, 2007; Ichimura, 19 August 2008.
[66]Glines, 1995, 84.
[67]McClure, 1975, 119.
[68]Ichimura, 19 August 2008.
[69]Craven and Cate, *The Pacific: Guadalcanal to Saipan August 1942 to July 1944,* 1950, 527; Glines, 1995, 87.
[70]Brown, December 1996-January 1997, 38-39.
[71]Craven and Cate, *The Pacific: Guadalcanal to Saipan August 1942 to July 1944,* 1950, 527.
[72]*Army Air Forces Statistical Digest World War II.*
[73]Disharoon, 7 February 2008; Jung, 6 October 2008.
[74]Harmon, *Pilots Also Pray,* 1944, 134.
[75]Hyde, 2007.
[76]Shiba, 1956, 134; Miller, August-September 1984, 16.
[77]Ichimura, 19 August 2008.
[78]Miller, August-September 1984, 16.
[79]Maddox, 2007.
[80]Ibid.
[81]Glines, 1995, 89; Shiba, 1956, 76, 134; D'Olier, 1947, 69.
[82]Ichimura, 19 August 2008.
[83]Harmon, *Missing,* 22.
[84]*Springfield News and Leader,* 13 September 1943.
[85]Hyde, 2007.
[86]Chennault, *Way of a Fighter,* 1949, 252.

Chapter 3

[1]Taylor, 1956, 1, 2, 4.
[2]Craven and Cate, *The Pacific: Guadalcanal to Saipan August 1942 to July 1944,* 1950, 528.
[3]Taylor, 1956, 14; Tregear, 1965, 248-249.
[4]Craven and Cate, *The Pacific: Guadalcanal to Saipan August 1942 to July 1944,* 1950, 528.
[5]Harmon, 1944, 151.
[6]Harmon,19 May 1945.
[7]Craven and Cate, *The Pacific: Guadalcanal to Saipan August 1942 to July 1944,* 1950, 466.
[8]*Missing Air Crew Report 759,* National Archives.
[9]Glines, 1995, 90.
[10]Burris, 2009.
[11]Cosgrove, n.d., 28.
[12]Enslen, 20 October1943.
[13]Atkinson, 28 October 1943.
[14]Enslen, 20 October 1943.
[15]Enslen, 26 October 1943.
[16]Atkinson, 28 October 1943
[17]Blake, July 2007; *CBI Roundup*, 8 October 1943.
[18]Taylor, 1956, 20.
[19]Blake, 2007.
[20]Harmon,19 May 1945.
[21]Harmon, *Pilots Also Pray*, 1944, 161-162; *Escape and Evasion Report 149*, Air Force Historical Research Agency.
[22]Harmon, *Missing*, 40.
[23]Taylor, 1956, 16, 19.
[24]Harmon, *Pilots Also Pray*, 1944, 63.
[25]Millman, 2007.
[26]*Missing Air Crew Report 1053*, National Archives.
[27]Harmon, *Pilots Also Pray*, 1944, 163; *Escape and Evasion Report 149,* Air Force Historical Research Agency.
[28]Harmon, *Pilots Also Pray,* 1944, 164.
[29]*Missing Air Crew Report 1052*, National Archives.
[30]Harmon, *Pilots Also Pray,* 1944, 163.
[31]Thorpe, 1968, 153.
[32]New York Times, 25 January 1944.
[33]Harmon, *Missing,* 40.
[34]Holmes, 2004, 22, 28, 42.
[35]Harmon, *Pilots Also Pray,* 1944, 164.
[36]*Missint Air Crew Report 1054*, National Archives.
[37]Harmon, *Pilots Also Pray,* 1944, 165.
[38]*Missing Air Crew Report 1054*, National Archives.
[39]Hata, Izawa, and Shores, 2002, 298; Ichimura, 19 August 2008.
[40]Alison, 2007.
[41]*The Fourteenth Air Force to 1 October 1943*, Air Force Historical Research, 95.
[42]Alison, 2007.
[43]*Escape and Evasion Report 149,* Air Force Historical Research Agency.
[44]Ibid.
[45]Cosgrove, n.d., 48-49.
[46]Harmon, *Missing,* 40.
[47]Schultz, 15 May 1945.
[48]Ulio, 3 February 1945.
[49]Enslen, 26 August 1943.
[50]Schultz, 21 December 1943.
[51]Enslen, 26 August 1943.
[52]*Springfield News and Leader*, September 1943.
[53]Chennault, 21 January 1944.
[54]Chow, 29 December 1943.
[55]Chennault, 21 January 1944.
[56]Disharoon, 31 March 2008.
[57]Cosgrove, 24 November 1943.
[58]Schultz, 15 May 1945.
[59]Hill, 2003, 225-226.
[60]Blake, 27 October 2007.
[61]Murray and Millett, 2000, 191.
[62]Cosgrove, n.d., 50.
[63]Taylor, 1956, 23.
[64]*CBI Roundup*, 15 October 1943.
[65]Patterson, 1943.
[66]Burris, 2007.
[67]Chennault, *Way of a Fighter,* 1949, 232; Hyde, 2007.
[68]Brawner, 2005, 13.
[69]McClure, 1975, 123, 129-130.
[70]Alison, 2007.
[71]Chennault, *Way of a Fighter*, 1949, 255.
[72]Brawner, 2005, 82. Cross-controlling is when a pilot inputs rudder and opposite aileron to put the aircraft into uncoordinated flight, making it very difficult to shoot.
[73]Hill, 2003, 227-228.
[74]Blake, 2007.
[75]Molesworth, *Sharks Over China,* 1994, 163.
[76]Hill, 2003, 229.
[77]Coox, June 1980, 75.
[78]Patterson, 1943.
[79]Hill, 2003, 229-230.
[80]Ichimura, 19 August 2008.
[81]McClure, 1975, 126.
[82]Brawner, 2005, 81.
[83]*CBI Roundup*, 3 December 1943.
[84]Hill, 2003, 230.
[85]Kelley, 1993, 27, 34.
[86]McClure, 1975, 132.
[87]Cochran, 1988, 380-381.
[88]Taylor, 1956, 25.
[89]Craven and Cate, *The Pacific: Guadalcanal to Saipan August 1942 to July 1944,* 1950, 535.
[90]Chennault, *Way of a Fighter,* 1949, 264.
[91]Shiba, 1956, 117, 140.
[92]*The Japanese Air Forces in World War II*, 1979, 10; Chennault, *Way of a Fighter,* 1949, 126.
[93]Molesworth, *Sharks Over China,* 1994, 172, 174.
[94]Ibid., 172.
[95]Blake, 25 February 2009.
[96]Calder, 26 December 1943.
[97]Harmon, *Pilots Also Pray,* 1944, 145-146.
[98]Maddox, 2007.
[99]Burris, 2007.
[100]Harmon, *Pilots Also Pray,* 1944, 152.
[101]Hyde, 2007.
[102]Burris, 2009; Cosgrove, n.d., 54.
[103]Harmon, *Pilots Also Pray,* 1944, 153.
[104]Ibid., 148.
[105]Hyde, 2007.
[106]Glines, 1995, 117.

Chapter 4

[1]Ch'i, 1982, 71-72.
[2]van der Ven, 2003, 50.
[3]Ch'i, 1982, 74; Shiba, 1956, 143.
[4]Millman, 2007; Shiba, 1956, 146.
[5]Chennault, *Way of a Fighter,* 1949, 270.
[6]Perry, 1955, 6.
[7]Ichimura, 19 August 2008.
[8]Molesworth, *Sharks Over China,* 1994, 188; Ichimura, 19 August 2008.
[9]Ichimura, 19 August 2008.
[10]Millman, 2007; Ichimura, 19 August 2008.
[11]Hata, Izawa, and Shores, 2002, 256, 286.
[12]Shiba, 1956, 161.
[13]Brawner, 2005, 60-61.
[14]Molesworth, *Sharks Over China,* 1994, 189.
[15]Blake, July 2007.
[16]McClure, 1975, 153.
[17]Tunner, 1964, 59.
[18]Hyde, 2007; Heitkotter, 2007.
[19]Taylor, 1956, 27.
[20]Blake, 2007.
[21]Ichimura, 4 September 2008.
[22]Stanaway, 1997, 78.
[23]Schultz, 14 May 1945.
[24]Shoals, n.d.
[25]Taylor, 1956, 17-18.
[26]Pugh, 1986, 31.
[27]Hata, Izawa, and Shores, 2002, 211.
[28]Pugh, 1986, 31.
[29]Ichimura, 4 September 2008.
[30]Green, 2007.
[31]Cosgrove, n.d., 103.
[32]*Missing Air Crew Report 4510*, National Archives.

[33]Kissick, n.d., www.flyingtiger.org.
[34]Chennault, *Way of a Fighter,* 1949, 243.
[35]Cosgrove, n.d., 94.
[36]Ch'I, 1982, 74-76.
[37]McClure, 1975, 160.
[38]Beneda, 2008.
[39]McClure, 1975, 148.
[40]Beneda, 2008.
[41]Kinzev, 1998, 10-11.
[42]Ichimura, 17 September 2008.
[43]Hill, 2003, 239.
[44]*Escape and Evasion Report 491,* Air Force Historical Research Agency; *Missing Air Crew Report 4730,* National Archives; *Missing Air Crew Report 4731,* National Archives; *Missing Air Crew Report 4732,* National Archives.
[45]Roll, 19 October 1999.
[46]Ichimura, 17 September 2008.
[47]Hill, 2003, 240.
[48]*Missing Air Crew Report 11971,* National Archives; Beneda, 2008.
[49]Cosgrove, n.d., 84-85.
[50]McClure, 1975, 160-161.
[51]Ichimura, 17 September 2008.
[52]Shiba, 1956, 20.
[53]Brawner, 2003, 84-85.
[54]Ichimura, 17 September 2008.
[55]Molesworth, *Wing to Wing,* 1990, 64.
[56]Patterson, 1944.
[57]Molesworth, *Sharks Over China,* 202.
[58]Burris, 2009.
[59]Hyde, 2007.
[60]Ibid.
[61]*Final Report on Tactical Suitability of the P-38F Type Airplane,* www.wwiiaircraftperformance.org.
[62]Hyde, 2007.
[63]Burris, 2009.
[64]Heitkotter, 2007.
[65]Doughty, 2007.
[66]Ch'I, 1982, 77.
[67]Burris, 2007.
[68]Perry, March 1958, 10.
[69]Cosgrove, n.d., 93-94.
[70]Taylor, 1956, 28, 41.
[71]Chennault, *Way of a Fighter,* 1949, 291.
[72]Taylor, 1956, 37, 82.
[73]Slessor, 1936, 94-95.
[74]Shoals, n.d.
[75]Taylor, 1956, 29, 41.
[76]Shiba, 1956, 159.
[77]Ichimura, 17 September 2008.
[78]*Missing Air Crew Report 6147,* National Archives.
[79]Ichimura, 17 September 2008.
[80]Burris, 2009; Cosgrove, n.d., 99.
[81]Chennault, *Way of a Fighter,* 1949, 296.
[82]Doughty, 2007.
[83]Pearsall, 2008.
[84]Burris, 2009.
[85]Hyde, 2007.
[86]*Missing Air Crew Report 6145,* National Archives.
[87]Cosgrove, n.d., 102.
[88]Burris, 2007.
[89]Chennault, *Way of a Fighter,* 1949, 292.
[90]Hyde, 2007.
[91]Molesworth, *Sharks Over China,* 1994, 240.
[92]Kissick, 2008.
[93]Kissick, 1983, 95; Kissick, 2008.
[94]Molesworth, *Sharks Over China,* 1994, 251.
[95]Conn, 2008.
[96]Ch'i, 1982, 80; Murray and Millett, 2000, 349, 359.
[97]Millman, 2007.

Chapter 5

[1]At airspeeds between 460 and five hundred miles per hour, the air accelerating over the top of the wing exceeds the speed of sound and creates a local shockwave, blanketing the controls.
[2]*Escape and Evasion Report 431*, Air Force Historical Research Agency.
[3]Beneda, 2008.
[4]Beneda returned to Luojia in 2005, where he witnessed the partial excavation of his airplane and renewed friendships with many of his rescuers.
[5]*Escape and Evasion Report on Glenn Beneda,* Air Force Historical Research Agency.
[6]Zhang, 2005, 5.
[7]Xi, 2001, 35.
[8]Elleman, 2001, 205.
[9]*Escape and Evasion Report 431*, Air Force Historical Research Agency.
[10]Mao, 2000, 107.
[11]Asprey, 2002, 260.
[12]Tsou, 1963, 51.
[13]*Escape and Evasion Report 431,* Air Force Historical Research Agency.
[14]Mao, 2000, 22-23, 104.
[15]Beneda, 2008.
[16]Zhang, 2005, 7.
[17]Gregg, 1944.
[18]Ibid.; *Escape and Evasion Report 431*, Air Force Historical Research Agency.
[19]Gregg, 1944.
[20]Beneda, 2008.
[21]Gregg, 1944.
[22]Mao, 2000, 93.
[23]Zhang, 2005, 38-41.
[24]Gregg, 1944.
[25]Jayapalan, 1999, 15.
[26]Asprey, 260.
[27]Glen Jackson, n.d., 107.
[28]*Escape and Evasion Report 431,* Air Force Historical Research Agency.
[29]Molesworth, *Sharks Over China,* 1994, 208.
[30]Chennault, *Way of a Fighter,* 1949, 278.
[31]Craven and Cate, *the Pacific: Matterhorn to Nagasaki June 1944 to August 1945*, 1953, xv.
[32]Gregg, 1944.
[33]Beneda, 2008.
[34]Zhang, 2005, 8.
[35]Bowman, n.d., 134-135.
[36]Simpson, 2003, 87.
[37]Chiara, 2007.
[38]Kelley, 1993, 30.
[39]Green, 2007.
[40]Bowman, n.d., 176.
[41]Fodor, 2007.
[42]Chennault, *Way of a Fighter,* 1949, 74.
[43]Doughty, 2007.
[44]Heitkotter, n.d.
[45]Glines, 1995, 130.
[46]Feuer, 2006, 117, 124.
[47]Jones, April-May 1990, 10-11.
[48]Patterson, 1944.
[49]Charlton, December 1992-January 1993, 20-21.
[50]Glines, 1995, 144-145.
[51]Ichimura, 4 November 2008.
[52]*CBI Roundup*, 3 August 1944.
[53]Patterson, 1944.
[54]Glines, 1995, 145.

Chapter 6

[1]Stilwell, 1948, 106.
[2]van der Ven, 2003, 39, 54; Romanus and Sunderland, *Stilwell's Command Problems*, 1956, 331.
[3]van der Ven, 2003, 50; Romanus and Sunderland, *Stilwell's Command Problems*, 1956, 355.
[4]Romanus and Sunderland, *Stilwell's Command Problems,* 1956, 336-340; Craven and Cate, *the Pacific: Matterhorn to Nagasaki June 1944 to August 1945*, 1953, 214; Binzer, 16 January 2008; Binzer, 31 December 2007.
[5]Fodor, 2007.
[6]Mitchell, 2007.
[7]Mark, 2008.
[8]Romanus and Sunderland, *Stilwell's Command Problems*, 1956, 390; *CBI Roundup*, 24 August 1944.
[9]Tuan, 2008, 103-104.
[10]Lu, 2009.
[11]*CBI Roundup*, 13 July 1944; D'Olier, 1947, 87.
[12]Long, 2008.
[13]Romanus and Sunderland, *Stilwell's Command Problems*, 1956, 392.
[14]*25th Fighter Squadron History*, Air Force Historical Research Agency.
[15]Hale, 2007.
[16]Long, 2008.
[17]Doughty, 2007.
[18]Mark, 2008.
[19]Mitchell, 2007.
[20]Romanus and Sunderland, *Stilwell's Command Problems*, 1956, 394; *CBI Roundup*, 17 August 1944; *CBI Roundup*, 24 August 1944; D'Olier, 1947, 87.
[21]Ichimura, 4 November 2008.
[22]Shores, 2005, 245.
[23]Ichimura, 4 November 2008.
[24]Lees, 2008.
[25]Waymire, 2008.
[26]Jones, 2008.
[27]Disharoon, 2008.
[28]Ibid.
[29]Long, 2008.
[30]Shores, 2005, 256.
[31]Jones, 2007; Ichimura, 4 November 2008.
[32]Long, 2008.
[33]Ichimura, 4 November 2008; Binzer 2008.
[34]Disharoon, 2008.
[35]Binzer, 2008
[36]Ichimura, 4 November 2008.
[37]Binzer, 2008; Shores, 2005, 260.
[38]Long, 2008.
[39]Heitkotter, n.d.
[40]Shores, 2005, 260.
[41]Binzer, 2007.
[42]Heitkotter, n.d.
[43]Binzer, 2008.
[44]Shores, 2005, 261.
[45]*27th Troop Carrier Squadron History*, Air Force Historical Research Agency.
[46]Binzer, 2007.
[47]—, 2005, 201.
[48]Shores, 2005, 261.
[49]*27th Troop Carrier Squadron History*, Air Force Historical Research Agency.

[50]*25th Fighter Squadron History*, Air Force Historical Research Agency.
[51]—, 2005, 201.
[52]Shores, 2005, 261.
[53]—, 2005, 202; Bi, 2009.
[54]*CBI Roundup*, 14 September 1944; *CBI Roundup*, 21 September 1944.
[55]Craven and Cate, *the Pacific: Matterhorn to Nagasaki June 1944 to August 1945*, 1953, 236.
[56]Heitkotter, n.d.
[57]Fodor, 2007.
[58]Hale, 2007.
[59]Doughty, 2007.
[60]Fodor, 2007.
[61]Forsgren, www.j-aircraft.com; Maddox, 2000, 3.
[62]Fodor, 2007.
[63]Doughty, 2007.
[64]Heitkotter, n.d.
[65]Pike, *Napalm*, www.globalsecurity.org.
[66]Barrow, 2007.
[67]Heitkotter, n.d.
[68]Pearsall, 2008.
[69]Conway, 1980, 22.
[70]*CBI Roundup*, 25 January 1945; *CBI Roundup*, 1 February 1945; Chennault, *Way of a Fighter*, 1949, 273; Wedemeyer, 1958, 334-5.
[71]Romanus and Sunderland, *Time Runs Out in CBI*, 1959, 135.
[72]Tsou, 1963, 82-84; Arnold, 1989, 524.

Chapter 7

[1]Mahon, 2006, 6.
[2]United States Strategic Bombing Survey, *Interrogation of Rear Admiral Horiuchi Shigetada.*
[3]Heitkotter, n.d.
[4]Tribby, 1984.
[5]Heitkotter, 2007.
[6]Ravenscroft, 2008
[7]Ibid.
[8]Ichimura, 6 January 2009.
[9]United States Strategic Bombing Survey, *Interrogation of Rear Admiral Horiuchi Shigetada.*
[10]There is some contention as to what exactly happened to Wilson. The 26th's mission report stated that Wilson left Hainan Island and perhaps bailed out over friendly territory in China. Ravenscroft remembered hearing that he bailed out over Laos and was tortured and killed by natives. Heitkotter's brother, Don, serving with the occupation forces in Tokyo after the war, had a Japanese cook who had been a fighter pilot and told him of a battle over Hainan Island with P-51s and P-38s in which a Mustang was shot down over the airfield. P-51 pilot Grant Forsythe also remembered a P-51 crashing on Hainan. Regardless, the fact was that Wilson never returned from the mission. Ravenscroft, 2008; Heitkotter, n.d.
[11]Tribby, 1984.
[12]Heitkotter, n.d.
[13]Heitkotter, 2007.
[14]Ravenscroft, 2008.
[15]Tribby, 1984.
[16]Heitkotter, n.d.
[17]Tribby, 1984.
[18]Heitkotter, n.d.
[19]Disharoon, 2008.
[20]Heitkotter, n.d.
[21]Mosier, 1999, 7-8.
[22]Heitkotter, n.d.
[23]Ibid.; Heitkotter, 2007.
[24]Feuer, 2006, 173.
[25]Molesworth, *P-40 vs Ki-43 Oscar,* 2008, 38, 42.
[26]Hyde, 2007.
[27]McCloud, 2007, 6-7; McCloud interview, 2007; Green, 2003.
[28]Bowman, n.d., 168-169.
[29]Carnachan, 2007.
[30]Bowman, n.d., 169.
[31]Heitkotter, n.d.
[32]Franklin, 2007.
[33]Hyde, 2007.
[34]Doughty, 2007.
[35]Fodor, 2007.
[36]Doughty, 2007.
[37]Bowman, n.d., 187-88.
[38]Ibid., 182.
[39]Doughty, 2007

Chapter 8

[1]Chennault, *Way of a Fighter,* 1949, 326.
[2]Craven and Cate, *the Pacific: Matterhorn to Nagasaki June 1944 to August 1945*, 1953, 259.
[3]Asprey, 2002, 396.
[4]Fall, *Street Without Joy,* 1961, 23-24; Bartholomew-Feis, 2006, 121-126.
[5]Doughty, 2007.
[6]Brabec, 2007.
[7]Green, 2007.
[8]Bowman, n.d., 177.
[9]Carnachan, 2007; Miller, 1984, 98-102.
[10]Bartholomew-Feis, 2006, 122-125.
[11]Ibid., 125-128.
[12]Chennault, *Way of a Fighter,* 1949, 342.
[13]Rittenhouse, 2008.
[14]Fodor, 2007; Fodor, 2008.
[15]Chennault, *Way of a Fighter,* 1949, 342.
[16]Logar, 2008.
[17]Fall, *Hell in a Very Small Place,* 1966, 9.
[18]Bowman, n.d., 186.
[19]Brabec, 2007.
[20]*Missing Air Crew Report 14304,* National Archives.
[21]*Missing Air Crew Report 14396,* National Archives.
[22]Barrett, 2007.
[23]Brabec, 2007.
[24]Asprey, 2002, 400.
[25]Bartholomew-Feis, 2006, 128.
[26]Ibid., 143.
[27]*449th Fighter Squadron History,* Air Force Historical Research Agency.
[28]Bowman, n.d., 186.
[29]Doughty, 2007.
[30]Bartholomew-Feis, 2006, 111-112, 140, 143, 156-157.
[31]Ibid., 169.
[32]Chennault, *Way of a Fighter,* 1949, 344; Wedemeyer, 1958, 337; Shiba, 1956, 216.
[33]Taylor, 1956, 50.
[34]Doughty, 2007.
[35]Green, 2007.
[36]Ibid
[37]McCloud, July 2007, 6-7.
[38]Green, 2003.
[39]Ibid
[40]Shores, 2005, 373.
[41]Ichimura, 22 August 2008.
[42]Fodor, 2007.
[43]*Missing Air Crew Report 14754*, National Archives.
[44]Doughty, 2007.
[45]Brabec, 2007.
[46]Green, 2007.
[47]McCloud, 2007.
[48]Taylor, 1956, 50-51.
[49]Bowman, n.d., 190.
[50]Ibid., 190.
[51]Doughty, 2007.
[52]Bartholomew-Feis, 2006, 234.
[53]Marr, 1995, 537.
[54]Bartholomew-Feis, 2006, 5-6, 247-248.
[55]Green, 2007.
[56]Hyde, 2007.
[57]Green, 2007.
[58]Ibid.
[59]Doughty, 2007.
[60]Maddox, 2007.
[61]Hyde, 2007.
[62]Logar, 2008.
[63]Hyde, 2007.
[64]Chiara, February 2001, 1.
[65]Green, 2008.
[66]Xi, 2001, 209.
[67]Conway, 1980, 22.
[68]Carnachan, 2007.
[69]Charlton, 1993.
[70]Hale, 2007.
[71]Binzer, 2007.
[72]Burris, 2007.
[73]Chennault, *Way of a Fighter,* 1949, 355.

Epilogue

[1]Conway, 1955, 4.
[2]Green, 2007.
[3]Chiara, 2007.
[4]Burris, 2007.
[5]Hyde, 2007.
[6]Chiara, 2008.
[7]Burris, 2007.
[8]Doughty, 2007.
[9]Carnachan, 2007.
[10]Brabec, 2007.
[11]Heitkotter, 2007.
[12]Carnachan, 2007.
[13]Tribby, 1984.
[14]Bowman, n.d., 340.
[15]Green, 2003.
[16]bentley.umich.edu
[17]Franklin, 2008.
[18]McCloud, 2007.
[19]Maddox, 2007.
[20]Stanaway, 1997, 72.
[21]Schultz, 14 May 1945.
[22]Lu, 2009.
[23]Greene, 2008.
[24]Doughty, 2007.
[25]Heitkotter, 2007.

Appendices

[1]www.xs4all.nl/~fbonne/warbirds.html; www.geocities.com/capecanaveral/hanger/8217/fgun/fgun-in.html; www.quarry.nildram.co.uk/ww2guneffect.htm; Shaw, 1985, 6.
[2]Because there is no comprehensive list of the specific P-38s operated by the 449th, only the serial numbers for planes originally assigned to the squadron, as well as those lost in combat, accidents, or identified in photographs are known. Blake, 2008; Molesworth, 2008.
[3]Maddox, 2007; Blake, 2008.
[4]Maddox, 2007.
[5]Blake, 2008.

BIBLIOGRAPHY

Primary Sources

Interviews and Correspondence

Barrow, Sterling Sr. September 2007.
Bi Shixian. March 2009.
Binzer, Robert. December 2007-January 2008.
Bowman, Jack. July-December 2007.
Brabec, Robert. August 2007.
Burris, Robert. July 2007-August 2009
Carnachan, Bruce. June-December 2007.
Chiara, Joseph. August 2007-February 2008.
Cosgrove, Joseph. Unpublished memoirs.
Disharoon, Jerry. February 2007.
Doughty, Jerry. May 2007-February 2008.
Fodor, Joseph. August 2007-February 2008.
Franklin, Harold. July 2007-January 2008.
Green, J. Forrest. May-December 2007.
Hale, Chapman. December 2007.
Heitkotter, James. August-December 2007.
Hyde, James. May2007-January 2008.
Ichimura, Hiroshi. August 2008-January 2009.
Jones, Robert. December 2007.
Lees, Leonard. January 2008.
Logar, Leonard. March 2008.
Long, Clifford. February 2008.
Lu Caiwen. March 2009.
Maddox, Richard. June-December 2007.
Mark, Edward. January 2008.
McCloud, Paul D. October-December 2007.
Mitchell, William. December 2007.
Osborn, Lewden. January-February 2009.
Penick, Edward. September-October 2007.
Ravenscroft, G.W. January-April 2008.
Rittenhouse, Paul. January 2008.
Waymire, Melvin. January 2008.

Government Documents

Army Air Forces. *Memo to Henry H. Arnold, 11 June 1943*, by Tse-Ven Soong. AAF Central Decimal Files, Record Group 18, Entry 300, Box 918.

Army Air Forces, *Memo to Franklin D. Roosevelt, 18 October 1943*, by Henry H. Arnold. AAF Central Decimal Files, Record Group 18, Entry 300-A, Box 914.

Army Air Forces Proving Ground Command. "Final Report on Tactical Suitability of the P-38F Type Airplane." World War II Aircraft Performance. http://www.wwiiaircraftperformance.org/p-38/p-38f-tactical-trials.html (accessed on 31 March 2008).

Department of the Army, Office of the Chief of Military History. *Air Operations in the China Area: July 1937 to August 1945,* by Major Takejiro Shiba. Japanese Monograph No. 76. Tokyo, 1956.

Department of the Army, Office of the Chief of Military History. *Army Operations in China, January 1944 to August 1945.* Japanese Monograph No. 72. Tokyo, 1956.

Fourteenth Air Force, 25th Fighter Squadron. *Squadron History: September 1944,* by 25th Fighter Squadron Intelligence Department. Online. Air Force Historical Research Agency.

Fourteenth Air Force, 27th Troop Carrier Squadron. *Squadron History: September 1944,* by 27th Troop Carrier Squadron Intelligence Department. Online. Air Force Historical Research Agency.

Fourteenth Air Force, 449th Fighter Squadron. *End of the Line: A History of the 449th Fighter Squadron From 9 June 1943 to 31 December 1944,* by Robert Patterson. Online. Air Force Historical Research Agency.

Office of Statistical Control. "Army Air Forces Statistical Digest World War II." Air Force Historical Research Agency. http://afhra.maxwell.af.mil/aafsd/aafsd_pdf/t084.pdf (accessed on 31 March 2008).

United States Strategic Bombing Survey. "Interrogation of Rear Admiral Horiuchi Shigetada." Hyper War: A Hypertext History of the Second World War. http://www.ibilio.org/hyperwar/AAF/USSBS/IJO/IJO-47.html (accessed on 7 April 2008).

U.S. Strategic Bombing Survey: Air Operations. China, Burma, India. WW II. By Franklin D'Olier, chairman. Washington, D.C.: Government Printing Office, 1947.

Published Sources

Arnold, H. H. *Global Mission.* Blue Ridge Summit, PA: Tab Books Inc., 1989.

Brawner, Steve. *As Time Goes By: The War Years.* Bryant, AR: Brawner Enterprises, 2005.

Brown, Roy . "Friendly Fire." *Jing Bao Journal* (December 1996-January 1997): 38-39.

Charlton, John. "Mission to Samah Bay." *Jing Bao Journal* (December 1992-January 1993).

Chennault, Claire Lee. *Way of a Fighter: The Memoirs of Claire Lee* Chennault. Edited by Robert Hotz. New York: G.P. Putnam's Sons, 1949.

Conway, Dick. *14th Air Force Bulletin* (February 1955): 4

Conway, Dick. "The Forgotten Squadron." *Jing Bao Journal* (October-November 1980): 22.

Harmon, Thomas. *Pilots Also Pray*. New York: Thomas Y. Crowell Company, 1944.

Hill, David Lee and Reagan Schaupp. *"Tex" Hill: Flying Tiger*. 2003. Reprint. San Antonio: Universal Bookbindery, 2004.

Jones, Bob. "Three Hours Over The Gulf Of Tonkin." *Jing Bao Journal* (April-May 1990): 10-11.

Kissick, Luther C. Jr. *Guerrilla One*. Manhattan, KS: Sunflower University Press, 1983.

Mahon, Keith. "A Hairy Christmas." *Lightning Strikes: P-38 National Association* (July 2006): 6-7.

McCloud, Paul D. "I'm Glad I was a Fighter Pilot." *Lightning Strikes: P-38 National Association* (July 2007): 6-7.

McClure, Glenn E. *Fire and Fall Back: Casey Vincent's Story*. Universal City, TX: Barnes Press San Antonio, 1975.

Miller, Milton. "B-24's Join the Fight." *14th Air Force Bulletin* (May 1956): 7-12.

Miller, Milton. "Still More on General Moritaka Nakazone." *Jing Bao Journal* (August-September 1984): 16.

Miller, Milton. *Tiger Tales*. Manhattan, KS: Sunflower University Press, 1984.

Mosier, Dewey. "One Hour to Touchdown." *Jing Bao Journal* (October-November 1999): 7-8.

Perry, Curtis. *14th Air Force Bulletin* (March 1955): 6.

Perry, Curtis. *14th Air Force Bulletin* (March 1958): 10.

Pugh, Tom. "Coolant Burning." *Annual Pictorial Magazine of the Flying Tigers of the 14th Air Force Association* (1986): 31.

Stilwell, Joseph W. *The Stilwell Papers*. Edited by Theodore H. White. 1948. Reprint. Cambridge, MA: Da Capo Press, 1975.

腾越文化研究会，东方诺曼底之战：滇西缅北战役 . Beijing: 燕山出版社，2005.

Wedemeyer, Albert C. *Wedemeyer Reports*. New York: Holt, 1958.

Secondary Sources

Bartholomew-Feis, Dixee R. *The OSS and Ho Chi Minh: Unexpected Allies in the War Against Japan*. Lawrence, KS: University Press of Kansas, 2006.

Ch'i, His-sheng. *Nationalist China at War*. Ann Arbor, MI: University of Michigan Press, 1982.

Coox, Alvin D. "The Rise and Fall of the Imperial Japanese Air Force." *Aerospace Historian* 27 (June 1980).

Craven, Wesley Frank and James Lea Cate. *The Pacific: Guadalcanal to Saipan August 1942 to July* 1944. Volume 4 of *The Army Air Forces in World War II*. 1950. Reprint. Washington, D.C.: U.S. Government Printing Office, 1983.

Craven, Wesley Frank and James Lea Cate, *The Pacific: Matterhorn to Nagasaki June 1944 to August* 1945. Volume 5 of *The Army Air Force in World War II*. 1953. Reprint. Washington, D.C.: U.S. Government Printing Office, 1983.

Elleman, Bruce A. *Modern Chinese Warfare, 1795-1989*. New York: Routledge, 2001.

Fall, Bernard B. *Street Without Joy: The French Debacle in Indochina*. 1961. Reprint. Mechanicsburg, PA: Stackpole Books, 2005.

Forsgren, Jan. "Japanese Aircraft in Royal Thai Air Force and Royal Thai Navy Service During World War II." Japanese Aircraft, Ships, & Historical Research. http://www.j-aircraft.com (accessed October 25, 2007).

Glines, Carroll V. *Chennault's Forgotten Warriors: The Saga of the 308th Bomb Group in China*. Atglen, PA: Schiffer Publishing Ltd, 1995.

Hata, Ikuhiko, Yasuho Izawa and Christopher Shores. *Japanese Army Air Force Fighter Units and Their Aces: 1931-1945*. London: Grub Street, 2002.

Janowicz, Krzysztof. *64 Sentai*. Lublin: Petit s.c., 2002.

Long, Jim. "Oscar Against the P-38." Japanese Aircraft, Ships and Historical Research. http://www.j-aircraft.com (accessed 23 December 2007).

Long, Jim. "Oscar Tactics in Burma." Japanese Aircraft, Ships and Historical Research. http://www.j-aircraft.com (accessed 31 March 2008).

Molesworth, Carl. *P-40 Warhawk vs Ki-43 Oscar: China 1944-45*. Oxford: Osprey Publishing, 2008.

Molesworth, Carl. *Sharks Over China: The 23rd Fighter Group in World War II*. 1994. Reprint. Edison: Castle Books, 2001.

Murray, Williamson and Allan Millett. *A War to be Won: Fighting the Second World War*. Cambridge, MA: Belknap Press of Harvard University Press, 2000.

Pike, John. "Napalm." Incendiary Weapons. http://www.globalsecurity.org (accessed 5 April 2008).

Pusen, Jin. "To Feed a Country at War: China's Supply and Consumption of Grain During the War of Resistance." Translated and edited by Larry N. Shyu. In *China in the Anti-Japanese War, 1937-1945: Politics, Culture, and Society*, edited by David P. Barrett and Larry N. Shyu, 157-69. New York: Peter Lang Publishing Inc., 2001.

Romanus, Charles F. and Riley Sunderland. *United States Army in World War II, China-Burma-India Theater: Stilwell's Command Problems*. Washington, D.C.: Government Printing Office, 1956.

Romanus, Charles F. and Riley Sunderland. *United States Army in World War II, China-Burma-India Theater: Time Runs Out in CBI*. Washington, D.C.: Government Printing Office, 1959.

Shinkichi, Eto. "Japanese Maneuvers for Peace with China, 1937-1940." In *China in the Anti-Japanese War, 1937-1945: Politics, Culture, and Society*, edited by David P. Barrett and Larry N. Shyu, 45 61. New York: Peter Lang Publishing Inc., 2001.

Shores, Christopher. *Air War for Burma*. London: Grub Street, 2005.

Stanaway, John. *P-38 Lightning Aces of the Pacific and CBI*. Oxford: Osprey Publishing, 1997.

Tao, De-min. "Japan's War in China: Perspectives of Leading Japanese Sinologists." In *China in the Anti-Japanese War, 1937-1945: Politics, Culture, and Society*, edited by David P. Barrett and Larry N. Shyu, 31-43. New York: Peter Lang Publishing Inc., 2001.

Thorpe, Donald W. *Japanese Army Air Force Camouflage and Markings: World War II*. Fallbrook, CA: Aero Publishers Inc., 1968.

Tsou, Tang. *America's Failure in China: 1941-50*. Chicago: University of Chicago Press, 1963.

U.S. Department of the Air Force, USAF Historical Division. *Air Interdiction in China in World War II*. By Joseph Taylor. Maxwell Air Force Base, AL: Air University, 1956.

van de Ven, Hans J. *War and Nationalism in China: 1925-1945*. New York: RoutledgeCurzon, 2003.

Weinberg, Gerhard. *A World at Arms: A Global History of World War II*. 2nd ed. New York: Cambridge University Press, 2005.

INDEX

Photos indicated in boldface.